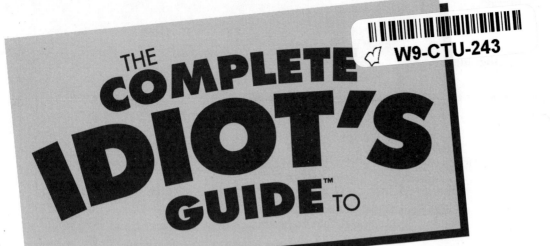

THE COMPLETE IDIOT'S GUIDE™ TO

Managing Your Money in Canada

♦ **Simple steps** for getting your personal finances on track

♦ **Secrets** for earning top dollar on your investments and cutting your debt in half

♦ **Down-to-earth answers** to the toughest money questions

An Alpha Books/Prentice Hall Canada Copublication

Robert K. Heady, Christy Heady, & Bruce McDougall

Prentice Hall Canada Inc., Scarborough, Ontario

Canadian Cataloguing in Publication Data

Heady, Robert

    The complete idiot's guide to managing your money in Canada

Includes index.

ISBN 0-13-080935-7

1. Finance, Personal – Canada.
I. Heady, Christy. II. McDougall, Bruce, 1950-   . III. Title.

HG179.H42 1998   32.024'00971   C98-932025-1

Prentice-Hall, Inc., Upper Saddle River, New Jersey
Prentice-Hall International (UK) Limited, London
Prentice-Hall of Australia, Pty. Limited, Sydney
Prentice-Hall Hispanoamericana, S.A., Mexico City
Prentice-Hall of India Private Limited, New Delhi
Prentice-Hall of Japan, Inc., Tokyo
Simon & Schuster Southeast Asia Private Limited, Singapore
Editora Prentice-Hall do Brasil, Ltda., Rio de Janeiro

ISBN 0-13-080935-7

Director, Trade Group: Robert Harris   Art Direction: Mary Opper
Copy Editor: Allyson Latta   Cover Design: Kyle Gell
Assistant Editor: Joan Whitman   Cover Photograph: Image Bank
Production Editor: Lu Cormier   Page Layout: Gail Ferreira Ng-A-Kien
Production Coordinator: Shannon Potts

1 2 3 4 5   RRD   02 01 00 99 98

Printed and bound in the United States of America

This publication contains the opinions and ideas of its authors and is designed to provide useful advice
in regard to the subject matter covered. The authors and publisher are not engaged in rendering legal,
accounting, or other professional services in this publication. This publication is not intended to provide a basis for action in particular circumstances without consideration by a competent professional.
The authors and publisher expressly disclaim any responsibility for any liability, loss, or risk, personal
or otherwise, which is incurred as a consequence, directly or indirectly, of the use and application of
any of the contents of this book.

Visit the Prentice Hall Canada Web site! Send us your comments, browse our catalogues, and more.
www.phcanada.com

Contents

13 Better Homes and Mortgages II: Making Decisions about Financing   121

Part 4: Simple Investment Strategies — 135

14 Taking Stock — 137

15 Everything you Ever Wanted to Know About Bonds 154

16 Everything You Need to Know About Mutual Funds   166

Part 1
You and Your Money

Money affects everything we do. It gives us freedom to travel, shop and live extravagantly. It also determines whether or not we can do these things at all. And when we plan wisely, money gives us a sense of accomplishment, like that feeling you get when you pay all the bills and have some money left over!

The most important reason to manage your money is to get control. It goes beyond you and your wallet. Acquiring control over your personal finances can change your future. But to get control, you must make the first big decision—to get started.

Once you make the decision to manage your money, this section will teach you how to get ahead in the world of personal finance. This section tells you how to cut costs on everything you buy, what to read, what to watch, and who to believe. Knowing these secrets will help you and your pocketbook.

Chapter 1

Grab Good Financial Planning by the Tail

In This Chapter

➤ Financial planning won't bite you

➤ How scare tactics trick you into not planning for your future

➤ How the five biggest secrets of financial planning have nothing to do with money

Do you know what the hardest thing about managing your money is? *Making the decision to do it.*

You wouldn't think it would be difficult. We make decisions every day of our lives: what to wear to work, what to eat for lunch, which video to rent for the children. Those decisions are easy. It's when the word "money" is brought up that your palms start to sweat and your brain turns to oatmeal.

It shouldn't be that way. We have access to more information about managing our finances than ever before. Just go to your local bookstore and browse through the business section for proof. Titles that promise "No More Money Problems—GUARANTEED!" grace the shelves. So if we have all of these resources, *why* do we still have problems managing our money?

Two reasons. First, no one has taught us how to make the *decision* to manage our money—a crucial first step in financial planning. Second, none of the books, magazines, newspapers, TV or radio programs have offered a secret decoder ring to help us decipher all the financial gobbledygook they report. Yet you can't pick up a newspaper without reading about the rise and fall of mortgage rates, the increase in fees at your local bank, or the topsy-turvy action on Bay Street. What does all this have to do with you? Plenty.

The decisions you make about you and your money are affected by all these factors and more. Think about it. If you're in the market to buy a home and mortgage rates go up, you may not be able to afford the home of your dreams. End result? Your decision about which home to buy changes. Perhaps your bank charges you a buck every time you use an ATM machine. You need to decide if you still want to bank with Nova Royal Dominion Canadian of Montreal.

You don't need a superhero to help you begin. This chapter will help you learn how to make the decision to manage your money and teach you simple steps to create financial security.

Don't Let the Scare Tactics Trick You

The next time you're in a bookstore, look at the first chapter of five other financial planning books. You'll find a common theme: scare tactics from scary statistics—

Here's a list of some freebies that can help you manage your money and reduce the hassle of reaching your financial goals.

➤ Free information is available if you call the Credit Counseling Service in your particular city. In Toronto, for example, you can reach the service at (416) 593-7434. You can locate the credit counseling service in your area through your provincial ministry of consumer affairs.

➤ The Canadian Association of Financial Planners (www.cafp.org) publishes a free consumer's guide to financial planning, including a detailed list of member planners. CAFP's head office in Toronto can be reached at (416) 593-6592.

➤ The Investor Learning Centre at the Canada Trust Web site is a good place to find information on investing and related issues (www.ctsecurities.com/ilc/).

➤ The Canadian Bankers Association publishes a series of booklets on managing your money and related topics. You can reach the CBA at (416) 692-6093.

➤ The Canadian Association of Retired Persons provides information and publications on retirement issues such as pensions, insurance, etc. CARP can be reached at (416) 363-8748.

➤ All of Canada's major banks publish well-written and useful guides to financial planning, including booklets on mortgage planning, investing, budgeting, buying a car and planning for retirement. You can obtain this material at any bank branch or through each bank's head office.

except the authors call it "motivational information." Who do they think they're kidding?

Although the information they report is accurate, it's far from motivating. Sure, it's true that by the year 2010 it will cost nearly $50 000 to get a four-year education at a public university. It's also a fact that if you make a $2000 purchase on your VISA with 19.8-percent interest and only meet the minimum payments, it will take you more than 30 years to pay off that purchase. And we've all seen the projections: if you currently make $26 000 a year, you should expect to receive about $980 a month in Canada Pension and Old Age Security benefits when you retire—that is, if the programs are still around.

While all of that information is correct, are these scare tactics working? Do they make you get off your duff and start managing your finances? After hearing from thousands of Canadians who still have money problems, we didn't think so.

No Matter How Much You Make, You CAN Do It

A friend of ours (let's call her Melba) makes $24 000 a year. She is 32 years old and supports herself and her daughter on her salary as a receptionist for a law firm in Vancouver. She works hard to make ends meet, often skimping on luxuries to afford day-to-day necessities.

Melba doesn't live beyond her means but rather *within* her means. She carries only one major credit card with no annual fee and the lowest interest rate in the country. (She demanded her interest rate be reduced; the credit card company obliged.) She keeps a daily record of her pocket money and contributes the maximum amount to her company's retirement program. In fact, she has accumulated more than $7500 in her company's group RRSP program—and still pays the bills. What's Melba's secret? Motivation.

We all make excuses to get out of managing our money (no time, not enough extra cash, or retirement is far, far away). One big reason we avoid planning is fear. Many people think that if they take a bare-bones look at their finances,

REALLY?

The statistics on how we relate to managing our money to save for our futures are not encouraging. One study concludes that if Canadians continue to save at the rate they do now, they may end up with only 36 percent of the money they'll need to maintain their current standard of living. Meaning: they will have only 36 percent of what they need *if they continue to save at their current rate*, independent of Canada Pension and Old Age Security.

they'll have to accept that they're in debt or don't have enough money to pay for their child's college or university education. Then they may think that they'll wind up old and impoverished. Goodness, why worry about that now? Others simply think managing their money is B-O-R-I-N-G. Save for the future? D-U-L-L. No instant gratification. Why put that extra $100 bucks in a savings account to earn 23 cents?

Why have we developed such a nonchalant attitude toward the future, anyway? During our childhood, many of our parents gave us a piggy bank and a few pennies and taught us to "save for a rainy day." But few explained *why* we were supposed to do it.

Planning for your future doesn't mean you're expecting something terrible to happen. Buying a life insurance policy doesn't mean you're going to die, does it? Much of your fear will quickly disappear once you realize how easy it is to make your savings grow for retirement. It's never too early to learn—or to start. The whole idea of managing your money is to save a dollar here and there and then take that dollar and build it into two. Believe it or not, it's a concept that you can practise—and you don't need to be a money whiz to do it, either.

Begin Without Even Thinking About Money

No matter how much money you make, there are investment products available to you—even $25 a month can get you started. And even if your expenses seem out-of-sight, you can learn how to cut back on some expenses to help save and to meet your financial goals. It's easy once you learn how—and you will when you read this book!

Are you ready? Put away your wallets and your pocketbooks because getting started in financial planning has nothing to do with money. Zip. *Nada.* It has to do with you and how you make decisions.

Achieving success is really the result of making good decisions, and achieving your success is based on a long-term focus. That's all. A bad decision results in a learned experience, but it's still a decision. What happens when you don't make any decisions? Someone else makes them for you. Do you want someone else making the decisions about building your financial security? Think of this as something you've been putting off; ask yourself the following:

➤ Why have I been putting it off?

➤ What do I have to fear from not doing it?

➤ What type of pleasure do I derive from indulging in procrastination?

➤ What will it cost me if I don't do it now?

Take this information and apply it to the following simple steps toward getting started in financial planning:

➤ **Make the decision to *make a decision*** Sound silly? Making a decision is often the hardest step. But if you break it up into simple little steps, you'll find decision-making easy and far from intimidating. Just say "okay," and you've done it.

➤ **Make decisions often** Let's use an analogy. Every year without fail, during the first week of January, memberships and the line for the Stairmaster at your local health club increase. The New Year's diet is in full swing, and every gym rat in the nation has made the decision to do something about his health, his image and his weight. But this doesn't last very long, because these people only make a decision once; they don't decide on a daily basis "I'm going to go to the gym today." If these people made decisions often, perhaps they would reach their fitness goals. If you make the decision to create a personal financial plan, are you going to stick with it just once?

➤ **Be flexible** You don't live in a black-and-white environment. You need to allow for some grey areas—which often disguise themselves as mistakes. Remember, although mistakes come from making the wrong decision, they create experiences you learn from, which might help you make the *right* decision next time!

➤ **Enjoy making decisions** Making decisions can be a blast! For example, if your mistakes help you learn to make better decisions, and the next time you make a decision it turns out to be a great opportunity, wouldn't you have enjoyed making that decision? You'll enjoy it more when you create more great opportunities!

➤ **Create short-term and long-term goals** Many people plan for their financial futures by working so hard today that by the time they reach their long-term goals, they're exhausted and have forgotten why they worked so hard to get there. Long-term goals are important, but so are short-term goals. If you create and meet short-term goals, you won't have to wait 30 years to feel a sense of accomplishment or satisfaction.

➤ **Do your homework** It'll be more fun than studying for that geometry test you prepared so hard for in high school! Doing your homework in the money world will allow you to make your money work as hard for you as you do for it.

When you work through these secrets, you are shaping your financial destiny, and it all starts with a simple decision!

And Now for the Money Part

It's time to take step two in the lessons of financial planning: setting some goals.

If your goal is to win Saturday night's lottery, forget it. Winning the lottery is a great way to create instant wealth, but playing it is not. And if you do win the lottery, you'll have enough financial planning burdens to make you go berserk. So let's talk about setting some more practical goals.

Setting goals isn't difficult. It's figuring out how to reach them that gives you a run for your money (no pun intended). You know that you need short-term and long-term goals, so take out two pieces of paper and let's get started. On the first piece of paper, write down any short-term goals you want to accomplish. These may include, but are not limited to, creating an emergency fund and paying off your credit cards and student loans.

Divide the next piece of paper into four time frames: five years, 10 years, 20 years and 30 years. Write down what you want to accomplish in each. For example, in five years you may want to buy a house. Ten years from now you may want to take a vacation in Europe. Twenty years from now you'll have to send the kids to college or university. And 30 years from now, you plan to retire.

On both pieces of paper, write down how much money each goal is going to require. Be honest with yourself; the amount of money you'll need to meet each goal may surprise you. You may have already allocated some of the money that you'll need. If so, good for you. Whether you have or not, most of you are going to have to learn how to manage your money to be able to achieve your goals.

Now total up how much money you're going to need to meet all of your goals. The numbers are astounding, aren't they? But that doesn't mean you have to change your goals. In fact, you can keep those goals and accomplish many of them by following the concepts in this book! This book is designed specifically to help you meet the short-term and long-term goals that you have set for yourself and for your family—and save money in the process.

All it takes is a little knowledge and some self-discipline. Most folks say that knowledge is power. But we disagree. Knowledge is power if—and only if—you put it to use!

The Least You Need to Know

➤ The first step toward managing your money is making the decision to start planning for your financial future.

➤ Don't let mistakes keep you from making more decisions. Think of a mistake as something that will help you make a better decision the next time.

➤ Write down your short-term and long-term financial goals and how much money you need to achieve them. Then read the rest of this book for information on how to reach those goals.

➤ Good financial planning requires you to do your homework, and you've already started your research: you are studying this book!

➤ When you're looking for free pamphlets, don't rule out mutual fund companies. Often they offer a number of investment and personal financial planning kits.

Chapter 2

Managing the Debt Monster

In This Chapter

➤ Top secrets to help break those bad money habits

➤ Learn how to be a debt-buster

➤ Tips on getting—and remaining—out of debt

➤ Filing for bankruptcy: the last resort

It's Sunday afternoon and you're perusing the classified ads. You come across an ad that reads, "For only $159.95, the Bills 'n Thrills Company can reveal the secret to reducing your debt! No more ugly credit card bills!" In fact, it guarantees to get rid of any bad marks on your credit report.

Only $159.95! You mull it over. "Gee, I'm tired of paying those finance charges on my VISA," you say. "And I don't want to talk to my creditors anymore."

"Don't worry—we'll call your creditors and arrange a payment schedule," says this promising advertisement. Sound like a deal? No way.

Unfortunately, many Canadians have fallen prey to swindlers who promise to get rid of their ugly bills or pledge a squeaky-clean credit report. These scam artists cause more harm than good. If you're trying to tackle the debt monster, a swindler won't help you—but this chapter will. You'll learn ways to reduce your debt, measure your financial health and reduce your expenses.

Are You in Debt Trouble?

To determine whether you're having problems managing your debts, indicate whether the following statements are true or false:

_____ You use credit cards where you used to pay cash, such as at grocery stores and restaurants.

_____ You've depleted your savings—or worse, use cash advances from credit cards—to pay past-due bills.

_____ You've lost track of how much you owe.

_____ You put off paying your telephone and utility bills to pay high credit card bills and other debts.

_____ You regularly receive letters from collection agencies.

If most of these statements apply to you, you have a debt problem. Read on to find out what you can do about it.

Measuring Your Financial Health

Checking in with a financial doctor rates right up there with having your teeth cleaned. Painful—and the taste of rubber gloves is not pleasant—but if you want pearly whites, you've got to go through the torture.

In managing your money, your goal is to get out of debt, right? Once you meet that goal, what do you want to accomplish financially? Do you want to

➤ Buy a car? (See Chapter 11)

➤ Buy a house? (See Chapters 12 and 13)

➤ Send the kids to college or university? (See Chapter 22)

➤ Retire comfortably? (See Chapter 23)

Before you reach those goals, you must figure out how bad the problem is. To do that, you must do three things to measure your financial health. First, compare your assets to your liabilities. Second, determine what your expenses are. Third, create a budget and trim the financial fat. The best way to begin is to…

Add Up the Pluses and Minuses

There's no greater mess to clean up than unorganized, mismanaged financial affairs—which is why so many people stick to organizing their financial records about as long as they stick to a New Year's diet. Determining your *assets* (what you own) and *liabilities* (what you owe) gives you a clear picture of what you're worth.

Begin with organized records. These may include, but are not limited to, chequebook registers, recent bank and brokerage statements, copies of your income tax returns (keep these for at least six years) and paycheque stubs. Forget the shoe-box theory—keep your financial records in a well-organized file cabinet.

Once you have all your information, you can list all the money in your bank accounts, brokerage accounts, and other investments. These are your financial assets.

Next, you can estimate the value of your personal property, which is also an asset. For example, your home is probably the largest physical and financial asset you own. You can also figure out how much your car is worth, along with other big-ticket items such as a stereo, appliances, jewellery, even clothing.

Finally, calculate your liabilities—all the things you owe. Car loans, student loans, and your mortgage will probably be the largest liabilities on your list, but remember to put down ALL your outstanding credit card balances. Your liabilities show how much debt you carry.

There are three kinds of debt: good debt, bad debt, and you-just-have-to-pay-it-to-live debt. This last type of debt would include electric bills, gas bills and telephone bills. More often, they're referred to as expenses, although they are "owed" debts.

The single largest component of good debt would be your mortgage loan, because your mortgage is for your house, which is an asset. But you must include your mortgage loan as a liability.

Bad debt makes up the bulk of your liabilities and depletes most consumers' paycheques. Bad debt is what you still owe on your car, your credit cards, your unsecured personal loans, and even your student loans. Obviously, the name of the game is to have as few "bad-debt" liabilities as possible and to increase your wealth substantially.

Bad debt works *against* you, although many Canadians are too happy living moment to moment to realize this. They relish the ability to "buy now and pay later." Credit cards, the biggest enticers, have lured many consumers into vulnerability—almost one in two Canadian credit card holders don't pay off their monthly bills in full.

Chapter 8 is chock-full of credit card tips and tricks. It's a must-read for anyone who wants (or needs) to know how to get the best deal on a credit card and how to avoid nasty fees and finance charges.

As an example, suppose you buy a leather couch for $1500 and put it on your MasterCard. You can't pay the entire bill this month, but that's no problem! You only have to make a minimum payment to remain in the issuer's good graces. However, as other debts start adding up, you meet the minimum payment only for the next year or so, or at least until you get out of the hole with your other bills. Then, one year later, a friend drops her cigarette on the couch. Now it's torched, and you need a new couch. You get rid of the couch, but you're still paying for it on your credit card. "Surely I've paid it off by now," you think. Well, think again.

How long does it take to pay off such a debt? If you *only* meet the minimum monthly payments, and your credit card has an average annual percentage rate (APR) of, let's say, 19.8-percent interest, it will take you more than 22 years to pay off that $1500 couch. This is a classic example of how bad debt can work against you. The more debt you're burdened with, the longer it will take to dig yourself out of a hole. Therefore, your first priority should be to eliminate nonproductive debt.

Motivate Your Mind to Kick the Habit

There aren't any self-hypnotic tapes to help cure overspending. (Maybe there should be.) However, your personal motivation and goal-setting can surely help. Picture this: You have no debt and an investment account worth $75 000. How does it feel? Many psychology experts urge consumers to use their imaginations instead of their wallets to help with their finances.

Once you have the proper motivation, try the strategies discussed in the following sections to reduce your debt.

REALLY?

Here's a motivating statistic that might light a fire under your seat. If you're making 12-percent interest on your investments but are paying off a credit card balance of 19.8 percent on your $1500 purchase, the money you make on your investments turns into a negative 7.8 percent. Wait—there's more! If your money is in a taxable account, you have to pay taxes on any income or capital gains; you can't even write off the credit card interest on your taxes.

Use Your Savings

Before you use your savings to pay off the budgetary fat, determine your debt-to-equity ratio. Oooh, all those numbers sound intimidating, don't they? It's simple! All you have to do is answer one question: How much of your paycheque goes to pay your debts? The smaller the percentage of your monthly pay allocated to credit cards (as well as other loans and debt), the better.

You know you're in bad shape—completely overextended—if you're flirting with a debt-to-equity ratio of 75-percent debt to 25-percent equity. Even 50/50 isn't good. The rule of thumb is this: *Current assets should be approximately two times greater than current liabilities.*

So lump together all your assets (what you own) and your liabilities (what you owe). If you've socked away a ton of cash in your bank account and you have revolving debt on your credit cards, it's time to pay them off. Why not use your savings? It'll be in your best interest, since you won't be paying any

more than you have to, and you'll save more by
reducing your debt than you'd earn by leaving
your savings intact.

Go on a Money Diet

Is that extra $10 burning a hole in your
pocket? Do you feel compelled to spend it?
Even if you're deluged with preapproved credit
card offers in the mail, it doesn't mean you
should take them. It is not wise to buy now
and pay later.

Since there aren't any nutrition labels that warn
consumers that they're not getting a good deal,
it's up to you to spend your money wisely. You
can look at where your money goes to see where you can trim the fat.

Here are 10 ways not to spend money—starting today:

➤ Never buy extended warranties or service contracts. Buy products that come with
good warranties from retailers who stand behind what they sell. Since many
service contracts generate high profits for businesses, some experts agree they're
generally not a good deal for consumers.

➤ Are speed dialing and three-way calling really necessary? The services cost approximately $2 to $3 extra per month, but that adds up to hundreds of dollars
over a few years. Stick with basic telephone coverage.

➤ If you're in the market for a new car, make
sure you carefully read the tips and tricks
offered in Chapter 11. Many consumers
see a flashy new car as an investment, but
it's not! When you drive a new car off the
lot, it immediately loses a certain percentage of its value—typically 20 percent! If
you do your homework, you can buy a
used car that's next to new for a fraction
of the original sticker price.

➤ One of the most superfluous items that
Canadians buy—and don't use—is new
exercise equipment. If you sell the tread-
mill and exercise bike that are collecting
dust, you probably could pay off one of
your credit card bills.

If you're still swimming in debt and
can't make ends meet by reducing
your expenses, consider boosting
your income—either through a
part-time job or odd jobs you can
do on weekends. Every little bit
helps.

If you're knee-deep in debt, you
could liquidate some—but not all—
of your assets to help pay the bills.
Which ones you liquidate will be
up to you. If one of them is an
investment that will give you a
huge capital gain to pay a lot of
taxes on, however, consider other
alternatives—for example, selling
old items at a garage sale (really!).

➤ Never go shopping when you're bored, down in the dumps, or hungry. That's recreational shopping, and it can cost you plenty! You'll probably buy things you don't need, and probably can't afford, just to make yourself feel better. Think of an alternative: exercise, play with the dog, or make your spouse a romantic dinner.

➤ Most consumers don't realize that everything goes on sale eventually. Wait for the sale. (You'll learn more about shopping tricks in the next chapter.)

➤ The biggest mistake consumers make is carrying more than one credit card. The more plastic you own, the more chance you'll lose track of your spending. One major credit card is enough.

➤ Here's a great way to cut costs on expensive water-heating bills: Reduce your water-heater temperature from 145° F to 120° F, and you'll save 10 to 15 percent on your next bill.

➤ Go to matinees instead of evening movies. They're often discounted. In some cities, matinee prices are as much as 50 percent less than regular evening prices. You can also buy movie theatre "fun-pack" tickets at reduced prices.

➤ Better yet (for all you movie buffs out there), save the $8.50-per-movie charge and wait for the flick to come out on video. They always do, don't they?

These are specific examples of how you can immediately start saving on some of your expenses, which ultimately reduces your debt.

Get Outside Help

If you're having trouble implementing these strategies to resolve your debt crisis, it may be time to seek outside help. Contact your local credit counseling office. You can locate the nearest one through your provincial ministry of consumer affairs.

It's a Budget to Your Rescue!

Unless we light a firecracker and place it under your chair, the only way we can motivate you to keep track of where your money goes is to scare you. So here goes. If you don't track where all your money goes, over time the following things will happen: You'll wind up in the cold month of January wondering how the heck you spent $2769 on Christmas presents for the family; you'll know your banker better than you'd like because you'll probably bounce cheques all over town as a result of mismanaging your finances; and someday you'll live on a monthly pension check of $700 or $800 (that's all!) because you frittered all your money away when you were young. Does that scare you? It should!

"Budget" is a scary word; it's too restrictive for some folks. What you need to understand, however, is that everybody needs to keep a daily record of where all their money goes. Accept it and motivate yourself toward the feeling of accomplishment. The true reward of having a budget is something all Canadians want: control. Imagine having control over *all* your finances. Once you do, you can reach your dreams and financial goals even faster!

What Do You Spend Money On?

First, you need to figure out where your money goes. Create your expense categories and fill in the amount you spend on a monthly basis for each category. To get a more accurate picture, you may want to check all your receipts from the past several months. Your categories can include but are not limited to

Stay away from anyone who promises to help you with your debt trouble "for a small fee." These people work for places known as recovery houses, and they're preying on everybody—especially the elderly.

➤ **Auto expenses**   Car payments, auto insurance, maintenance, gas (save your receipts!)

➤ **Clothing expenses**   Overgarments, undergarments (all your garments), shoes, socks

➤ **Dental expenses**   Periodic cleaning, dental work, oral surgery, and so on (not covered by insurance)

➤ **Dining expenses**   Restaurant expenses, even if it's for fast food

➤ **Entertainment**   Movies, plays, concerts, the zoo, whatever

➤ **Education**   School supplies, tuition bills, and so on

➤ **Gifts**   Birthdays, holidays, weddings, Bar Mitzvahs

➤ **Groceries**   Separate into two categories—food and drugstore items—if possible

➤ **Home-based business**   This should be broken down into smaller categories, including equipment, supplies, taxes, and so on

➤ **Household items**   Plants, furniture, and so on

➤ **Household expenses**   Items necessary for the upkeep of the house: paint, lawn maintenance, and so on

➤ **Insurance**   Separate your policies into categories, such as life, health and homeowners

➤ **Rent/Mortgage**   Your biggest expense (probably); important for tax return purposes

➤ **Taxes**   Property and income taxes (Don't forget income tax refunds as a source of income.)

➤ **Utilities**   Phone, electricity, gas, water

➤ **Vacations**   Hotel stays, airplane tickets, new luggage, meals, sightseeing tours, souvenirs

There's probably more, but this list gets you started off on the right foot.

Trim the Fat!

From the expense categories you create, pick a few expenses you can live without—for good. If the children are stuck on seeing a movie every Friday night, rent a video instead of going to the show.

As another example, set yourself a limit—such as to eat out only twice a month. The second largest component of "where your money goes" is dining out. That nasty habit costs the average Canadian almost $4200 a year. You could pay for Junior's tuition at university with that dough. Keep the following tips in mind to help reduce some of your expenses and save money in the long run:

➤ Establish an emergency fund that equals about three months' worth of basic expenses. Then you won't have to turn to plastic for every unexpected bill.

➤ Lower your tax withheld at source by your employer. Why give Revenue Canada a free loan while you're paying an average 10-percent interest on your debts?

➤ Increase the deductibles on your auto insurance. Even bumping up a $100 deductible to a $500 deductible could lower your premiums on comprehensive insurance by 25 or 30 percent a year.

Battling Debt's Biggest Culprit

Canadians have been able to *buy now and pay later* since the evolution of the plastic credit card. But this plastic has caused millions of Canadians a problem: with enticing credit card offers promising generous credit lines, it has become impossible to climb out of debt.

That's why you should treat your credit card as a tool, not a cure-all. The rule of thumb: If you don't have the cash, don't use the card! A credit card should be used as a convenience for emergencies; it is nothing more than a tool. Having a credit card or two is a necessity, but becoming laden with $20 000 in credit card debt is a burden—and a very common one. Typical clients of credit counseling centres are dual-income families with high incomes. However, they have fallen into the habit of overspending; they have no savings—and up to $20 000 in credit card debt.

To save a few hundred dollars a year on finance charges (and work at maintaining a squeaky-clean credit report), follow the tips listed in Chapter 8 on how to cut your credit card costs in half.

Be a Debt-Buster!

If there's one rule you remember from this chapter, let it be this one: *Pay your bills on time.* Almost all lenders will look at whether you're current or late with your bills. Most lenders are lenient, and will tolerate a maximum of 30 days late. If you're currently behind on your accounts, catch up before you apply. This is how you can make the grade to get credit. You have to fit the profile of a person who pay bills on time.

Filing for Bankruptcy

Financial troubles have led thousands of Canadians to file for bankruptcy, often using the process as an "alternative." Wrong. Filing for bankruptcy is the *last resort* to your financial woes, not a choice. If you're in debt and *need* to file, however, there are pitfalls you can avoid.

Most often, you don't have to file unless it's necessary—declaring yourself bankrupt is not an alternative, it's a necessary solution.

However, if you're having difficulty meeting your rent or mortgage payments, you're completely extended beyond your credit limit, the collection agencies are uncooperative, and you need more than a credit counselor, you may need to consider bankruptcy or the preliminary step, called filing a proposal.

In filing a proposal, usually through a trustee, you are alerting your creditors to the fact that you may not be able to repay your debts in full under the terms established in your original agreement. Creditors do not have to accept your proposal. If they don't, you may have no other option than to file for bankruptcy.

Bankruptcy does not relieve you of paying certain debts such as your mortgage, alimony or child support. One year after you declare bankruptcy, you can apply to have the bankruptcy discharged. But your bankruptcy remains on your credit record for at least seven years.

Before choosing such a drastic step, however, make sure you contact Consumer and Corporate Affairs Canada, listed in the *Blue Pages* of your phone book.

The Least You Need to Know

➤ To measure your financial health, add up the worth of everything you own (assets) and compare it to the cost of everything you owe (liabilities). A financially healthy person should have twice as much in assets as she has in liabilities.

➤ To reduce debt, use some of your assets (such as your savings) and reduce expenses so that you can pay more towards the debt.

➤ If you need extra help dealing with your debt problems, contact your local credit counseling office.

➤ To keep your spending on track, you need to establish a budget. Budgeting basically involves recording how you currently spend your money and then figuring out how you can change your spending habits in order to achieve your financial goals.

➤ Filing for bankruptcy is not an "alternative" or a "choice." It should be looked upon as a last resort.

Chapter 3

Shop 'Til You Drop—It Really Pays Off!

> **In This Chapter**
>
> ➤ Money-saving tips your folks never gave you
>
> ➤ Warehouse clubs: Are they for you?
>
> ➤ How to choose a long-distance carrier
>
> ➤ Shopping from the easy chair: Does it really pay off?

There's a four-letter word that sends chills down the spines of millions of consumers:

SALE.

Canadians have developed a voracious appetite for anything that's a bargain. People like to shop at discount stores, scan newspaper ads for bargains and look for savings tips in newsletters. Frugality is in.

This focus on frugality has forced consumers to become better informed and make better choices. And it doesn't mean that you're a penny-pincher or a tightwad. You're just smart about your money. (After all, you work very hard for that paycheque). This chapter will alert you to some pretty interesting money-saving strategies to help you save some dough.

What Supermarkets Don't Tell You

Next time you're at the grocery store, look at all the items on the shelf from top to bottom. Notice anything? Grocery stores usually place the most expensive items at eye

19

It's a dog-eat-dog world in the manufacturer's coupon business. The real reason companies offer cents off here and there on products is to get consumers to switch to their brand—and once they switch, to keep them there by offering more coupons. In fact, a trend has formed in the coupon industry: no need to clip coupons anymore. Now they're dispensed in machines right in the store. It's a point-of-purchase marketing ploy that has allowed companies to rake in the bucks.

level, where they're more likely to be selected on impulse. If you want to be a smart shopper, look at the entire group of products before you decide which to purchase.

Don't fall prey to all those "on sale" items at the front of the store, either. The company that distributes those products actually pays for the space to place the merchandise. You won't really find any bargains until you dig deep inside store aisles.

Finally, make sure you comparison shop. Although the generic brands usually save you money, some house and national brands can actually be cheaper than generic brands.

Well, if you're going shopping, get on out there. But don't forget your coupons!

Smart Shopping 101

Did you know that a pack of razor blades costs $6.80 in Tokyo but only $3.75 in Los Angeles? Lipstick that averages $5 a tube in Canada costs five times that much in Brazil. And in Tahiti, a can of ginger ale runs $4 and a bag of Doritos goes for $5. If you think domestic prices are high, you should know that most goods and services cost less in Canada than anywhere overseas. However, that doesn't mean we shouldn't practise smart shopping!

If you make a concentrated effort to be a smart shopper, you can develop better spending habits and save money. Whenever you hit the mall or grocery store, keep these tips in mind:

Did you know that every time you use a "preferred-shopper" card to pay for groceries or drugstore items, your grocer compiles personal information about you? Sure, you may be using the card for the three or four bucks it saves you right then, but it's actually saving you more than that. What you buy with that card is added to a computer file corresponding with your number. When you receive coupons in the mail, you'll find some for similar products that you buy frequently. If you don't mind having someone monitor your shopping habits, those coupons can help save you money on your groceries in the long run!

➤ **Just because an item is on sale doesn't mean the price has hit rock-bottom**   Shopaholics love a sale, but often merchandise (especially clothing) isn't a bargain until it's at least 40 percent off the regular price. When a store takes 10 percent off an item, it's barely paying for your GST and provincial sales tax.

➤ **Buy only what you can afford**   If you don't have the cash to buy something, don't use a credit card to make the purchase, no matter how inexpensive the item. Carrying a balance on a credit card only requires you to carry debt for months and months.

➤ **Bargain with the merchant**   You can't do this at a grocery store (unless the merchandise is damaged), but try it at privately owned stores. How? Above all, be discreet. A store owner will not reduce a price if she thinks your deal will become public information. Likewise, don't strong-arm the owner; instead, be tactful with your approach. Come across as a serious shopper who intends to spend some cash (you'll lose your edge if you use plastic). Select a couple of the items you want to purchase, have the owner add up the entire bill, and then act uncertain. Ask the owner if this is the best price she can give you. It may not always work, but it's worth a shot.

➤ **Don't buy for convenience**   If you want to save money on groceries, don't shop for the convenient items, such as carrots that are already cut up or pancake batter that's premixed. Even if you have coupons for these items, you'll save more money in the long run if you cut your own carrots and mix your own pancake batter. If you do buy for the sake of convenience—for example, at that local 24-hour, all-night corner place with the gas pumps out front—understand that you'll pay extra for those chocolate-covered doughnuts and a gallon of milk. Sometimes you may have to pay "convenience store" prices for diapers, cough medicine or toilet paper—but don't make a habit of it.

➤ **Keep your receipts**   Then watch for ads featuring the merchandise you already bought. Some stores will honor your receipts and returns if you buy the item at full price one week and it goes on sale the next.

Buying in Bulk

You can save 30, 40, even 50 percent on your next grocery bill if you buy in bulk—and borrow a friend's station wagon to haul the goods home. But it doesn't always work to your advantage.

The common misconception about buying your groceries in bulk (at a warehouse food club, for example) is that you have to buy the 10-gallon jar of peanut butter to get a deal. Not true, unless you like a lot of peanut butter. You may

It pays to comparison shop. Items such as sugar, flour, milk, eggs, laundry soap and coffee filters tend to be less expensive at a warehouse supermarket, while other items such as meat tend to cost less at the grocery store.

have to buy more of a certain item, but if you're going to buy that amount in smaller quantities over an extended period anyway, you're better off. If you do the math, you can see how much you save on some items.

For example, a three-gallon tub of laundry soap is $9 at your favourite warehouse supermarket goes for $5 a gallon in your regular supermarket. If you bought three gallons, you'd pay $15. So you save $6 by shopping at a warehouse supermarket. But that's for an item like laundry soap, which won't perish. A 10-pound bag of bananas is a different story.

One thing to consider is that it costs money to join a warehouse supermarket—the membership fee can be as high as $35 a year. Most of these warehouse clubs also require that you be a member of an organization or have an employee membership through your company. If you want to join a warehouse club, see if your church, employer, or another organization with which you have a connection, participates.

Once you shop at one of these places, you'll find that warehouse clubs are fun. Where else can you buy a rack of lamb, a VCR and a sweat suit all under one roof? But be careful. You don't have to buy one of everything. And remember to take your coupons to these warehouse supermarkets to see if they honor them; you could save even more!

Fiber-Optic Wars

Feeling bombarded by all of the telephone advertising ammunition? Not sure if you need flat-rate long-distance service or big discounts with selected calls? Telephone companies have armed themselves for combat. And it could sabotage your pocketbook if you're not careful.

What many consumers don't know is that since the deregulation of the telephone industry, dozens of companies have begun to provide long-distance service.

The bottom line is that there's very little difference in the standard rates charged by the big phone carriers. Mind-boggling? Well, it doesn't have to be if you follow these important steps:

➤ **Choose a plan based on YOU**   Even if all your friends and your family have one type of plan, that doesn't guarantee that you'll save more money. You need to evaluate your calling patterns. Do you make most of your calls during the day? Are you a chatterbox only from 7:00 p.m. to 9:00 p.m. on weekends? Whatever the case, once you log your calling patterns, you can choose a program that suits your needs—and is easy on the wallet!

➤ **Make sure you *choose* some type of plan**   If you don't specifically request a certain plan, some companies will pick one for you. And, as you learned in Chapter 1, you can't grab good financial planning by the tail if you let someone else make your financial decisions. It's the plan—not the company—that's most important.

➤ **Even if you've picked a plan, reevaluate your telephone patterns six**

months from now Yes, this gives you more homework, but you want to save money, don't you? If your calling pattern has changed dramatically, you'll need to analyse your bills to make sure you're still saving as much as possible.

➤ **Rates shouldn't be the sole factor in your decision** If one major carrier charges only 22 cents a minute for a long-distance call, and another carrier charges 24 cents per minute but offers you more perks (such as prepaid calling cards), choose the latter. Although you want the best price, you also want the best components.

If your schedule allows you to, take a bump if it's offered. Typically an airline will offer free tickets to volunteers who give up their seats if the airline has overbooked the flight. Unless the airline can get you on another flight for the same destination within an hour, you'll get a free flight. However, if you are willing to take a bump, bring a good book.

Flying the Friendly Skies on the Cheap

If you want to be a shrewd traveler, you're going to have to do more to save money than travel to vacation spots during the off-peak season. One way to save on traveling is to never ever accept the first fare quoted. Research indicates that about half the time, some other airline has a flight around the same time you want to leave, but has a special, less-expensive fare.

One of the best money-saving strategies for travelers is to change eating habits. Eating every meal in restaurants can eat up (forgive the pun) all your money. To control your food budget, try to eat only twice a day and, if possible, buy your food at a nearby supermarket and eat it in your hotel room. You can save hundreds of dollars by doing this. In fact, some smart travelers opt for a room with a kitchenette so they can cook their own meals—a wise decision.

Finally, check the Internet for discount fares. Air Canada, for example, distributes a last-minute list every Wednesday of weekend fares to destinations throughout North America. If you absolutely have to get to Cleveland on Friday, this won't help you much. But if you just want to spend a weekend in another city, you may find the destination you want—and the fare you want to pay—through this source (www.aircanada.ca/schedules/edirect).

Lazy Shopping

Suppose it's late at night, and you're flipping channels. All of a sudden you see it—the bargain of a lifetime. A genuine 14k-gold bracelet with cubic zirconia diamonds interlaced with faux emeralds for only $79.95. "Only seven left!" screams the

Notice the easy payment schedule shopping channels offer. Instead of paying $79.95 right off the bat for your bracelet, you can make three easy payments of $29.95. Do the math: $29.95 multiplied by three is almost $90—a lot more than you'd pay if you were to pay in full. It's their way of financing. And here's another catch: Because these three easy payments are billed to your credit card, you can end up paying interest twice: once for their financing, and again for your credit card's financing if you don't pay the balance off each month.

shopping channel host. Panic ensues as you pick up the phone and dial the number so you can buy your dream present. But alas, you're too late. All gone.

Tragedy? No. It's probably the best thing that could happen to you.

Shopping channels entice millions of Canadians to buy more unneeded merchandise than ever. How? Because they're very visual, provoking the "see-it-buy-it" habit. Ted Rogers owns the Canadian Home Shopping Network, and he didn't buy it because he likes fake diamonds. Is this merchandise a bargain? No, not when you consider the mistakes people can make when they shop via TV.

For example, you can't send cash or write a cheque when you purchase an item from a shopping channel. Each time you make a purchase, you must use a credit card, which is a habit you're trying to cut back on. Plus, you have to pay shipping charges, which often add $10 to $20 depending on where you live.

And what happens if you receive defective merchandise? Sure, you can send it back, but it's often a troublesome process. Otherwise you're stuck with a gadget that looks like it belongs in a *Star Trek* mausoleum.

The Least You Need to Know

➤ It may be worth the price of joining a warehouse supermarket if you usually buy lots of nonperishable items (and have room to store them).

➤ Getting the best deal on long-distance is easy: Match your calling habits to a phone company's plan. And remember, you don't have to stick with one of the big phone companies.

➤ Buying stuff you see on TV is usually not a good idea. You have to buy it with a credit card, and it's difficult to return if something is wrong with it.

Chapter 4

The Quickest Route Through the Money Jungle

In This Chapter

➤ Why you can't believe interest rate experts

➤ How to map your money game plan

➤ Which investments are safe and which ones aren't

➤ How asking the right questions pays off

If one fact comes crashing through today's money-management jungle, it's that millions of average people are just as baffled, confused and frustrated by investments as you are.

The guy with $20 000 in cash to stash somewhere doesn't have a guaranteed clue of where to put it, or for how long, or at what interest rate. He wonders whom he should trust, whether his broker is telling it to him straight, and how much his bank is really charging him.

Expert advice is hard to come by. Even top economic gurus goof when they try to call the shots on interest rates. This chapter is the first step toward carving your way through the jungle.

Watch Those Conflicting Reports!

Sure you scan the newspaper, watch TV, subscribe to a financial newsletter or two, or chat with your banker, broker or financial planner to try to keep up. You even perk up when your neighbour tells you she has a friend who has a friend who knows somebody named Mabel who's been living comfy off her investments. You have to sponge up every tip you can. But then you have to sort through the maze of information. Your gut says you still don't have the right information, and so much is happening so fast that the knowledge you went to bed with last night is outdated by the time you wake up.

For example, the stock market is super-sensitive to interest rates. When rates have gone down in recent years, stock prices have gone up; when rates rise, stocks prices drop. In early 1994, when everyone was positive that the Federal Reserve was going to boost rates, stockbrokers were dancing on Bay Street. New economic data showed the U.S. inflation rate was only 2.7 percent, the same as the year before, because consumer prices weren't moving up as fast as expected. As a result, stock prices jumped because experts believed that maybe the Fed wouldn't have to raise rates to head off inflation after all. Because our own markets depend so heavily on trends in the U.S., Canadian stocks followed.

A few days later more data came out, painting a whole different picture. Industrial prices on things like paper and steel had taken a big jump. *Wham!* The stock market tumbled, the experts said, because if manufacturers began charging more for their products, those higher prices would be passed on to consumers in a few months. Analysts did a quick flip-flop. Inflation was still a threat, they said, and interest rates would definitely rise.

The so-called economic experts who track the financial world have an unimpressive batting average when it comes to predicting anything. One big problem is that news reporters often pick up the wrong predictions from the experts. For example, a TV financial reporter may warn that higher rates are around the corner and that they'll affect consumer mortgage-and-loan prices. You're better off comparing many different news sources—especially the business pages of leading newspapers—because these will give you a more balanced view of what's happening.

Where You Can Go for All the Good Stuff

You've already learned that many jungle guides (the economic and financial experts) don't carry a compass. Some—but not all—people in the media don't really know their way, either. Even if some of them did, you couldn't learn everything you need to know from a 20-second sound bite.

So where can you go? Here's a rundown of the different sources of information and what you should look for from each.

Newsworthy Newsletters

There are hundreds and hundreds of newsletters around, eagerly gobbled up by millions of novices and professional investors. All those little journals can't be right, can they?

No, not all of them. Many simply give their opinions and theories without backing them up with good, solid data. Others make a killing by preaching gloom and doom, scaring the pants off readers in hopes they'll want to be better prepared before the world ends. All too often, the publishers who create these newsletters are churning 'em out in the front room and taking in money through the back door to manage investment portfolios.

Don't waste your time or money on every single newsletter out there. Your subscription bill alone would reach thousands of dollars before you invested one red cent! Instead, zero in on respected sources who know what they're talking about and who have the best track record for picking good investments, giving good advice, and providing the facts and figures to back it all up.

For the names of good newsletters, check in the local library for back issues of the *Financial Post* or the *Globe and Mail*. Ask the librarian to help you locate articles on financial newsletters. You can also get information on a number of Web sites, including Gordon Pape's (www.gordonpape.com) and IE:Money (www.iemoney.com).

What's on the Boob Tube?

A few financial programs on television, such as *Venture* on CBC, report on financial market news and business industry changes. By learning the information provided in this book, you'll be able to determine how the stories and reports on these TV programs affect your wallet. But you get more detailed information from newspapers and periodicals.

Reading All the Fine Print

The *Financial Post* and the *Globe and Mail's Report on Business* cover the most urgent stories of the day about financial markets, and also give information about the nation's top business happenings along with personal finance stories that affect you. The weekly *Investment Executive* is also a good source of information about funds, managers and investment-related information.

For U.S. information, the *Wall Street Journal* is the most authoritative daily business newspaper available. It covers virtually every type of financial market—nationwide and worldwide—and reports world events that have an impact on your money.

Understanding the Mumbo-Jumbo

What's the difference between rate and yield? Once you get the answer, which we provide below, you can tell your banker a thing or two about compound interest. How about that!

A **rate** is what you earn on a GIC or savings account before compounding (don't worry—that's defined here too), or the interest you're charged on a loan.

A **yield** is the interest you earn after the rate has been compounded.

Compounding simply means more interest being added to the interest you've already earned, then being added to the entire amount, which is multiplied by the rate to determine the yield. Get it?

APY stands for Annual Percentage Yield. It's the total amount of interest you earn on an account in one year.

APR stands for Annual Percentage Rate. Usually associated with loans, the APR is a complex mathematical formula that basically includes other charges on the loan, in addition to the interest rate.

An **index** is a well-known benchmark, such as the prime rate used by a financial institution to set its interest rates. The rate you earn or pay will move up or down according to changes in the index.

We've been tracking interest rates and bank, stock, bond and mutual fund accounts for years and answering thousands of questions from troubled average Joes and Janes. From these experiences, we've learned that you need to know the basic concepts outlined in the next sections to make your way successfully through the jungle.

What Kind of Investor Are You?

You do have a personal financial game plan, don't you? You should have a fairly good idea of your cash position and costs in the near and distant future. (If you need a good review, go back to Chapter 2.)

So ask yourself: What will that picture look like today, next month or next year? Get a pencil and jot it down. How much have you set aside for investing? What are your short-term and long-term debts? What is your likely income over the next couple of years? Your job position? Your age? Your health?

It doesn't stop there. Are you living off a comfortable inheritance left to you by a rich uncle, or are you scraping along with monthly cheques from investments that are, indeed, your lifeline? Are you saving for a little cottage by the sea? Will Junior need *beaucoup de* bucks if he decides to go for his Master's degree? How much will you need to retire, excluding your Old Age Security and Canada Pension? What about unforeseen medical bills and other emergencies?

Before you set foot in the money jungle, estimate how much extra money you have to invest, how much more you're shooting for, and when you'll need it. This rule applies whether you're out to make just a few hundred bucks, or are wheeling and dealing in the seven figures. The number of investment choices can be mind-boggling. So before you set out on your financial safari with machete in hand, find a quiet corner and have an honest little chat with yourself to determine what kind of investor you are.

How Willing Are You to Take a Risk?

Are you the super-conservative type who can't—or doesn't want to—risk a penny? For example, do you need an extra-safe, regular fixed income to make ends meet? If so, your game plan should zero in on federally insured banks, trust companies, credit unions, Treasury bills and guaranteed investment certificates.

If you're not extremely conservative, and you have some money you'd like to speculate with (in case some tipster told you the stock of New Electronic Widget Company would go through the roof), and you won't miss the money if you lose, you might want to try a slightly more risky investment. If you're feeling a little adventurous, you can dabble in the stock and bond markets or stash your cash in mutual funds.

However, if you're not at all conservative, and you like to fly by the seat of your pants, no holds barred, tinker in the commodities or futures markets.

Whichever approach you take, keep in mind that your goal should be to obtain the greatest reward with the least amount of risk. Once you establish your risk tolerance, you can find your way through the money jungle more easily. Part 4 reviews the different types of investments available to you (no matter what your threshold of pain is), and provides smart money moves you should make based on your level of risk. For a complete review of how to invest successfully on Bay Street, pick up a copy of *The Complete Idiot's Guide to Making Money on the Canadian Stock Market*.

Ottawa Offers the Best Safety Net

Keeping your money in Canadian banks and trust companies is very safe. Any institution that displays the Canada Deposit Insurance Corporation (CDIC) sticker provides guaranteed protection of all funds deposited up to $60 000. If you don't see any sticker displayed, make sure to request proof of CDIC coverage.

How Does CDIC Insurance Work?

CDIC insures your deposits in case a member institution becomes insolvent. The maximum basic protection you can have with one member institution is $60 000, including principal and interest. The $60 000 maximum includes all the insurable deposits you have with the same CDIC member. Deposits at different branches of the same member institution are not insured separately.

However, in addition to the basic coverage, CDIC insures certain classifications of deposits separately, including joint deposits, deposits in trust, RRSPs and RRIFs. CDIC insures joint deposits, for example, separately from any deposits held by the individual owners in their own right, to a maximum of $60 000, including principal and interest.

What About Credit Unions?

CDIC coverage does not extend to credit unions. However, provincial deposit insurance programs can provide them with insurance coverage of customer accounts up to $60 000 apiece. Ask about this coverage. Many credit unions also allow clients to keep as many RRSPs as they want, guaranteeing the funds in each of them up to $60 000.

Each account you open is insured up to $60 000. So if you open more than one account, you can put $60 000 in each without risk.

How Much Money Can You Afford to Lose?

This question applies only to uninsured investments. If, say, a federally insured bank offers you a yield of 8 percent on a one-year, $10 000 GIC, you're guaranteed to earn $800 in a year. You'll get back $10 800 on your $10 000 investment. You can't say that about speculative investments such as stocks and bonds, although the gamble may pay off with earnings higher than what you'll earn from a bank.

For example, if in 1924 you had invested $1000 in the top 300 stocks in Canada and let it ride through the ups and downs of the stock market, you'd have nearly $400 000 today! Does that mean the stock market isn't risky? No, because the stock market could average a negative 10-percent return one year and a positive 10-percent return the next. It just means that the longer your money is invested and the more diversified your investments are, the more you reduce your risk.

Here's another example:

In the 40 years between 1956 and 1996, there were 13 bull markets and 12 bear markets.

➤ The bull markets lasted seven to 44 months.

➤ Each was followed by a bear market lasting between two and 36 months.

➤ The gains during the bull markets ranged from 22 percent to 150 percent.

➤ The losses during bear markets ranged from 16 percent to 45 percent.

Conclusion: Over time, the market gains more than it loses.

As we'll see later, you should diversify the types of investment groups you hold, as well as the types of stocks or bonds within each group.

How Long Can You Be Without the Money?

If you need your cash six months or a year down the road for an emergency, what are you going to do? What if the investment rate picture and other financial factors change and you want to move your money to a higher-earning instrument? What do you do then? If you withdraw your funds early, you'll probably be charged a stiff penalty.

Answering these questions helps you figure out what type of liquidity you are looking for in an investment. The following table, Liquidity in the Money Jungle, shows how each investment product is ranked not only by risk but also by liquidity—and whether there are any penalties for cashing in!

Table 4.1 Liquidity in the Money Jungle

	Investment Type	How Quickly Can I Get My Money?	Penalties?
LEAST RISKY:	Federally insured:		
	Savings accounts	Immediately	No
	Chequing accounts	Immediately	No
	Guaranteed Investment Certificates	At maturity	Yes, if you cash them early
	Treasury bills	Five days after selling or wait until maturity	No
SMALL TO MODERATE RISK:	Savings bonds	Six months	Loss of interest
	Money market mutual funds	Next day	No
MODERATE TO SLIGHTLY HIGHER RISK:	Mutual funds	Next day	No
RISKY:	Blue-chip stocks	Five days after selling	No
	Closed-end mutual funds	Five days after selling	No
	Small cap stock mutual funds	Next day	No
	Small cap stocks	Five days after selling	No
	Corporate bonds	Five days after selling or wait until maturity	No
	Convertible bond funds	Next day	No
VERY RISKY:	Futures/commodities	Depends on contract	Varies
	Options	Next day	Varies
	Gold	Varies	N/A
	Sector funds	Next day	No
	Junk bonds	Five days after selling	No

Which Type of Investment Will Probably Earn Top Dollar?

We don't have a crystal ball, but we can explain how and where the laws of the jungle come into play.

The disadvantage of bank investments is that they usually pay less than you could earn with stocks, bonds or mutual funds. How much you'll earn at the bank depends on current interest rates and where they'll be months or years from now. The advantage is that you won't lose your shirt.

Sometimes GICs earn more than do other investments. This is unusual, though, and happens most often during periods of high inflation.

Interest rates, especially bank rates, go up and down like a roller coaster. You must not only time your investment just right, you must also know for how long (or short) a period you should invest, such as how long to lock up a GIC rate. All these tricks are explained in Chapter 18.

Ask the Right Questions—Get the Right Answers!

Failing to ask the right questions is a mistake that goes to the top of the pile. It often separates the winners from the losers in investing. The time to pin down your banker or broker, or even your financial planner, is before you sign on the dotted line, not afterward. That sounds simple enough, right? Of course. Except very few people know which questions to ask! It's an art in itself, but you can do it.

For bank accounts, study the key questions in Chapter 5. These cover buying GICs and basic savings accounts, opening a chequing account, and figuring out which fees to avoid.

Never—I repeat, never—take the word of the average teller at a bank. They're honest and well-meaning folks, but often they haven't been clued in on the bank's latest interest rates or other changes in bank policies. Always ask to speak to an account representative.

If you're still confused by all the rates, yields and gibberish, ask the bank one simple question: If I give you my money today, how much will I have in my account at the end of one year—in dollars and cents, not percent—after subtracting all fees and charges? It works like a charm, and you'll probably see the bank rep's face turn 12 shades of purple. But don't stop there. Ask the same type of question when you borrow: How much will the total cost of the loan be in dollars?

If you're dealing with a full-service broker, tell him that you want discounts on your commissions. Ask him if he'll meet with you every three months to review your account. Most brokers do business only by phone, rarely face-to-face.

Ask the broker the same question: How many dollars will I have at the end of the year?

It may be difficult to pinpoint an answer since the financial markets fluctuate quite a bit, but if you can nail down the track record and performance history of this broker, you're ahead of the game.

Last, make sure you watch those hidden fees. At first glance, it looks as if there are only two big patches of trees in the jungle:

➤ The money you put in

➤ The money you take out

Not so. There's something else lurking out there. Hidden among the jungle's branches and vines are a million fees and charges that can whittle down your cash without you even noticing it! (See Chapter 5.)

The best way to protect yourself is to compare fees at several outfits. Before you sign any document, ask for a copy of the bank's or broker's complete fee schedule. Take it home and study it. When you go back, ask for an explanation of every conceivable charge you could get hit with in the type of account you're opening. Just by following those tips alone, you'll probably get back many times your small investment in this book!

The Least You Need to Know

➤ Take any investment advice you get—whether it's from a neighbour, the newspaper, or a TV financial expert—with a grain of salt. Check out the sources and the facts for yourself before you put your money down.

➤ Before you invest a dime, know what your financial goals are, how much money you can play around with, and how much risk you can handle.

➤ Federally insured GICs and Treasury bills are the safest investments, but you can make more money over the long haul in stocks, bonds, and mutual funds. Check out chapters 14, 15 and 16 for more information.

➤ Don't be afraid to ask your banker or broker questions, especially if you don't understand something. Make sure you're aware of all the fees that could be involved when you do business with these people.

Part 2
Banking Fundamentals

Name one person you know who doesn't have a bank account. It's pretty difficult, isn't it?

When you learn about the mechanics of banking fundamentals, it goes beyond avoiding having your ATM machine swallow your ATM card. Many financial institutions are nickel-and-diming you to the poorhouse. Banks are making tons of money from all those bank accounts—whether you have $100 or $100 000 in them, the banks are raking it in. How do they do it? Fees, fees, fees.

By doing your homework in this section, you'll learn how to get the best deals on chequing and how to beat those low-paying savings accounts by kicking the 2-percent habit that millions of people fall into. But we don't stop at chequing and savings accounts. We reveal who pays the top rates on GICs, how to check the real bottom-line value in a "relationship package," and how to spot the warning signals that it's time to kiss your banker good-bye.

I KNOW HE TAKES IT A LITTLE SERIOUSLY, BUT HE'S THE BEST INVESTMENT BANKER AT THE COMPANY...

WINICK

Chapter 5

Banking Basics: Chequing and Savings Accounts

In This Chapter

➤ How banks make a bundle by nickel-and-diming you with fees and charges

➤ Which type of chequing account will fit you like a glove

➤ Deciding when to put your money in a GIC instead

The average person knows zilch when it comes to understanding how and why banks operate the way they do. It's all a person can do to balance a chequebook and hunt for high savings rates and low borrowing rates. But banks have a strategy when they raise rates or lower them. There's a method to their madness when they lure you to automatic tellers and when they charge outrageous interest on credit cards and loans. And they know you probably won't complain when they pay you measly interest on your savings and chequing accounts.

Banks have to make money to stay alive. And because individuals and corporations can borrow money from so many different sources, banks can no longer rely on lending for their profits. So they have to charge a fee for things that used to cost the individual customer nothing.

You can keep more of that money in your pocket if you learn some of the banker's innermost secrets. This chapter explains some of the key ones.

How Banks Stay in the Black

Banks come out ahead when they rent your money from you (savings accounts and GICs) at one price, then peddle the same cash to someone else in the form of loans (credit cards, auto loans and mortgages). Look at the bank as though it were a little one-room building with two doors—one in front, the other in back. You deposit your savings at the front door, the bank marks it up, then lends the money to borrowers lined up at the back door.

Fees and Charges: The Other Money-Makers

Borrowers can now borrow money from more sources than ever before. Want a car loan? Ask a car manufacturer such as Ford or GM. Want a mortgage? Ask a real estate company such as Royal LePage or Canada Trust. Want to buy a computer? The computer manufacturer will lease it to you instead, at very attractive rates.

Banks no longer control the lending market, but they still have to make money. So they've begun charging for things they used to do for nothing, like processing cheques and maintaining your savings account. They also charge a fee for using an ATM or conducting a telephone banking transaction, although this fee hardly covers the cost of the technology used in the process, which has to be upgraded constantly.

Bank-beater secret: Most banks provide accounts and other services for senior citizens at a fraction of the usual fee or for no fee at all.

Nevertheless, from the consumer's point of view, these fees and charges have been growing like weeds. One year it costs you 50 cents to use an automatic teller machine; the next year the fee has crept up to 75 cents. That might not sound like much, but multiply it by millions of customers using their ATMs three or four times a month, and you get an idea of how much money is involved.

Banks have set up different packages for different types of customers, with different fee schedules. If you seldom write a cheque, but use an ATM almost every day, there's probably a package geared to your needs. You won't avoid fees altogether, but at least you'll pay only for the services you use.

Keep Track of Your Money

Bank-beater secret: You don't really need more than three months' worth of living expenses in a readily accessible account. Anything more should go into a GIC.

Banks pay you little or no interest on chequing, money market, and savings accounts. But for some strange reason, Canadians keep stashing billions of dollars in low-paying savings accounts and even lower-earning chequing accounts. Banks are happy to accommodate such idiotic consumer behaviour. But consumers could make a bundle more by shifting to GICs.

Chequing Account Basics

Banks want to get their hands on your chequing account more than any other type of account. They refer to chequing customers as their "core accounts," because they figure if they've got your chequing, they also have the best shot at landing your GIC, personal loan and mortgage business. And if you're a high-balance chequing customer (instead of somebody whose balance consistently runs below $1000), all the better for institutions. They have more money to lend at a profit while they're paying you no interest.

For most of us, carrying a chequebook is as natural as getting up in the morning and brushing your teeth. But the fees creep in so quietly that you probably don't even notice them—50 cents here, $1 there. It's not until your monthly statement arrives that you discover strange, new little costs popping up like measles.

Mistakes You Should Avoid—Beginning on Day One

Chances are that when you walked into a bank and told them you wanted to open a chequing account, an account representative sat you down, filled out your application, then asked, "Would you like our Miserbuck Special where you only have to keep a $100 balance and pay a $10-a-month 'maintenance' fee? Or our Jumbo Megabuck account where we waive the fee provided you keep a balance of $5000?" Then came the emotional closer: "Do you prefer the blue cheques with the whale art in the background or the green ones with the daffodils and philodendrons?"

He then gave you a set of starter cheques and a fee disclosure document on the bank's fees and charges (required by law). You probably didn't bother to read all that fine print. That was mistake number one.

The account rep may not have reviewed with you your month-by-month chequing behaviour so that you could match it against the different kinds of fees on the types of accounts the bank has available. That was mistake number two. It would have helped you trim your chequing costs.

The fact is, many people could put an extra $100 to $200 in their pockets every year if they only knew what their chequing was really costing them. Problem is, few people bother to add up the almost-invisible costs of using their chequebooks. Even fewer bother to shop for the best deal.

Most chequing accounts fall into one of three broad categories:

➤ An account that charges lower fees but pays you no interest.

➤ An account that pays you a small interest rate but charges higher fees.

➤ A basic chequing account for people with low income. These accounts don't pay any interest, but they have low minimum balance requirements and low fees.

Those Frightening Fees

Banks hand out fee disclosure documents to new customers. We've seen one that listed 64 separate fees of various types! That's enough to throw even an accounting major for a loop, much less the average Joe or Jane. To help you focus on fees, here's a list of the most common services for which banks will charge you:

Monthly maintenance

Per-cheque fee

Exceeding number of monthly transactions

Dropping below the minimum balance

Using your bank's ATM

Using another bank's ATM

Higher fees if account pays interest

Bouncing a cheque (NSF)

Depositing someone else's bad cheque

Stopping payment on a cheque

Copies of stored cheques

Certified cheque

Money order

Overdraft protection

Wire transfer

Travellers' cheques

Fees often vary with the amount of money you usually keep in your account. When banks look at your chequing account, they classify you as to whether you are a low-balance, medium-balance or high-balance customer, and their fees favour the high-balance crowd. After all, the bank gets to use the money in a chequing account at little or no cost; the more you give them, the less they'll charge you in fees. For example:

➤ Mrs. Gottrocks is high-balance. Because she keeps $5000 or $10 000 in her account, she is given a better break, such as having many of her fees—including her monthly balance charge—waived.

➤ Susie Smith, with $1000, is considered a medium-balance customer. She doesn't go below her required balance during the month, so she's charged normal fees, such as monthly maintenance.

➤ Joe Doaks, with a $400 balance, is a low-balance guy, so the bank discourages him from making too many transactions that cost the bank money. They hit him with charges on a slew of services—for example, a monthly maintenance charge that may be $2 higher than what Susie Smith pays.

Balancing Act

Finding out how banks calculate your balance sounds like an exercise for Einstein, but it's not. You simply need to know which method a bank uses, because it will tell you when a fee will kick in on your account. The method the institution uses typically is based upon one of the following:

➤ Your *low minimum balance*, which activates a fee if the balance falls below a certain level at any time during the month.

➤ Your *average daily balance*, where the fee kicks in if the monthly average of each day's balance drops below a certain amount.

The average-daily-balance method is better, because it protects you if your balance takes a sudden, temporary dive during the month. By contrast, if you choose an account using the low-minimum method, and your balance sinks to $10 one day but is $1000 on all the other days of the month, you'll still get hit with a penalty. The dollar difference between the two kinds of accounts can be substantial, as shown in the following example.

Mary and Thelma, who have chequing accounts at two different banks, usually keep about $600 each in their accounts, give or take a few hundred dollars. Mary's bank uses the low-minimum-balance method, and charges her a $10 fee if her balance falls below $300 any day of the month. Mary deposited her paycheque the first week of the month and her account balance went up to $950. Ten days later, after she paid her rent and other bills, Mary's balance sank to $285 for one day. But the next day she deposited another paycheque that pushed the balance up to $700. Mary's average balance for the whole month was $600, but the bank still whacked her with the $10 charge because it uses the low-minimum-balance method. Multiply that situation times 12 months a year, and you'll begin to understand why it pays to ask the right questions.

Thelma's numbers were the same as Mary's—same pay, same rent, same bills, same everything. Thelma's balance dropped to $285 for just one day, just like Mary's. Even her average monthly balance was the same, $600. But she wasn't charged any fee because her bank uses the average-daily-balance method. The $600 figure was all that mattered.

What Kind of Chequing Creature Are You?

When people need to write a cheque, they write one, period, and once a month they balance their statement and pray they have enough in the account to get through next week.

When you dashed over to the ATM last Sunday to get some emergency cash, you may not have thought about how many similar trips you made in the past month. Or about whose automatic teller you were using—your bank's, or a different outfit's machine across the street. But those individual actions form a pattern of behaviour. The account that's just right for you probably won't be the one that's right for your child in college or university, or for your neighbor. They're going to need one that fits their own financial lifestyles.

Take stock of how you do things. Ask yourself the following:

➤ How do you usually buy merchandise and pay your bills? By cheque, credit card, debit card, or a combination of all three?

➤ What's the average amount of money you keep in chequing every month?

➤ How likely are you to let your balance slip below that level?

➤ By how much does the amount in your chequing account vary throughout the month?

➤ How many cheques per month do you write?

➤ Which bank's ATM do you use? Your own bank's? Another bank's machine in the same town? An out-of-town ATM?

➤ Do you ever bounce cheques or issue stop-payment orders?

➤ Do you ever ask the bank for back copies of your statement or copies of old cheques?

Next, haul out your last three or four monthly chequing statements and add up all the various fees, including ATM deposits and withdrawals, cheque reorders—the works. Then estimate the cost of your chequing activities per month and per year, because those are the bottom-line costs you want to cut to ribbons. Tape that information on your refrigerator door (or put it on your desk), then get ready to play hardball with the bank. Believe it or not, you're on your way to putting extra money in your pocket.

Finally, don't make the same mistake that many other consumers make and foolishly trap yourself into a high-fee account because you don't want the headache of closing out an account or haven't bothered to balance your chequebook. Get ready to switch banks by keeping a record of how many cheques are outstanding and how much money you'll need to cover them. Then you won't sweat the transition.

If you don't prepare, you can wind up costing yourself some money. For example, a fellow we know wrote his ex-wife a cheque that she didn't cash for two months. After he closed out his account—forgetting about the check—the ex deposited the cheque and it came back marked NSF (non-sufficient funds), whereupon she nailed him for issuing a bounced cheque.

Using Your Chequing Account Wisely

The biggest mistake consumers make, over and over again, is not understanding that there's a cost almost every time they engage in chequing activity. For example, Joe

Doaks thinks he's exercising discipline by taking out only $10 whenever he withdraws chequing funds from an ATM. Say he takes out $10 a day for five days in a row. He forgets that each time he does this, the bank charges him $1. That's $5 in fees based on a $1 charge per transaction. Had he withdrawn the $50 all at once, he would have been nicked only $1. This section tells you how to avoid such costly mistakes, and provides some additional money-saving tips.

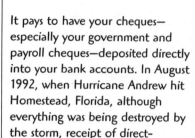

It pays to have your cheques—especially your government and payroll cheques—deposited directly into your bank accounts. In August 1992, when Hurricane Andrew hit Homestead, Florida, although everything was being destroyed by the storm, receipt of direct-deposit payments was not interrupted.

Using ATMs

You can reduce your ATM charges if you do the following:

➤ Keep your chequing account at a bank that doesn't charge you for using its machines.

➤ Don't use an ATM belonging to an institution where you don't bank.

➤ Withdraw all the cash you'll need for the next few weeks instead of making several small transactions that run up your total ATM fees.

You should also follow these rules to use an ATM safely:

➤ Memorize your Personal Identification Number (PIN) and keep it to yourself. Don't keep it in your wallet.

➤ Keep your ATM card in a safe place. It's as valuable to you as your credit card. If the ATM card is lost or stolen, immediately report it to your bank.

➤ Keep extra deposit envelopes in your car, so you can fill them out before approaching the ATM.

➤ Have your paperwork and your ATM card ready when you reach the ATM so you won't have to reach into your purse or wallet.

➤ Stand between the ATM and people waiting in line so no one can see your PIN number or your transaction.

➤ Don't accept help from strangers while you're using the ATM. If you have a problem, contact the bank.

➤ Take your ATM receipt. Put away your cash, ATM card and receipt before you leave the ATM.

➤ Immediately report all crimes to the ATM owner and local law enforcement officers.

You can reduce your account fees by not getting your cancelled cheques back every month. The banks call this "truncation" or "cheques storage." It works like this: You receive only your statement, and they keep your cheques in their warehouse. That will shave a few bucks off your chequing fees, but if you suddenly need a copy of one of the cheques—*zing!*—you may be charged about $3 to $5 per copy. And the process will take a few days.

Cost-Cutting Tips

As high as chequing fees are getting, you can still get around them. For example, many banks will waive certain chequing fees if you do the following:

➤ Keep a high balance in your account.

➤ Agree to forgo getting your cancelled cheques back with your monthly statement.

➤ Are older than 50 or 55 years, depending on the bank's "seniors' chequing" requirements.

➤ Open a package account that combines several of your accounts, such as GICs and passbooks, under one statement.

➤ Limit the number of cheques you write per month to the maximum allowed without a fee.

➤ Don't exceed a certain number of ATM transactions per month.

The Ugliest Fee of All

The one fee you should definitely try to avoid is the bounced-cheque charge—the banks call such cheques "NSFs" (non-sufficient funds). Though industry studies show it costs a bank less than $2 to handle a bounced cheque, the average NSF today costs a customer $19.92.

Stop Payments

You just issued a cheque to Big Bubba's garage for a new transmission for old Betsy. On your way home the transmission sounds likes a blender full of rocks, and you don't want Bubba to pocket the money until he makes good on the deal. What do you do? Immediately inform the bank to stop payment on the cheque. Tell them your account number, the cheque number, the exact amount (in dollars and cents), date of the cheque, and the name of the person or company you wrote it to.

The problem with stop payments is that they don't come cheap. They'll cost you $20 or thereabouts, and fees have been going up. You'll have to decide whether the action is worth it, by considering who you're doing business with, and how important it is that that party not cash the cheque.

Savings Account Basics

The major advantage of savings accounts is that they're liquid, which means you can add to your savings or withdraw funds at any time—without getting socked with a penalty. Savings accounts provide a temporary financial garage where you can park your funds while you're scouting around for higher paying investments.

Fees

Nothing in life is free, especially not savings accounts. The following types of fees are common:

➤ A monthly or quarterly "maintenance fee," just for keeping your money in the bank. It will probably be about $3 to $12.

➤ A special fee if your account balance falls below a certain minimum in the month. Figure about $10.

➤ An ATM fee every time you use an automatic teller.

Shopping for Savings Accounts

Banks covet your basic savings and chequing business, because those are their bread-and-butter core accounts. Once you become a customer, you're also a prospect for buying GICs, mutual funds, personal loans and mortgages.

From your point of view, you want the highest interest rate you can find at a bank that won't slap you silly with ridiculous fees and charges.

Key Questions to Ask about Bank Accounts

You need a guidebook to figure out which account is which, but you can cut through the jungle by asking the following key questions:

➤ What are the rate (before compounding) and yield (after compounding) on the account?

➤ Is the account tiered? That is, does it pay higher yields on larger balances?

➤ What is the monthly maintenance fee?

➤ Is there an additional fee if I don't keep a certain minimum balance?

➤ Is there a per-cheque fee? Is there an additional charge if I exceed the limit?

Consider an Alternative: The GIC

If you continually carry a substantial balance in your savings account, you could be costing yourself some serious cash. Even if your bank offers as much as 3 percent on a savings account, you can earn more with a GIC. And if you're not using the money anyway, why not make as much as you can when you lend it to the bank?

How much are Canadian savers losing by keeping so much money in low-paying savings accounts? Plenty. Suppose that 1000 people each keep $1000 in a savings account paying 2-percent interest. That comes to a grand total of $200 000 in interest per year. Now let's assume those same 1000 customers move their accounts into GICs paying 5 percent. The interest jumps to $500 000.

Look Before You Leap

Keeping a lot of money in a savings account might be the better strategy if any of the following apply:

➤ You think you might need the money suddenly for some reason, such as putting a new roof on the house or getting Junior a set of braces. There's no penalty for withdrawing funds from a savings account, as there is with a GIC.

➤ The high-tier rate on a savings account is paying more than GICs are paying. One-year GICs (or longer) usually pay higher interest than even savings accounts with high balances.

Connecting Your PC to the Information Superhighway

In today's electronic world, it makes a lot of sense to stay connected, and technology has provided the world with a number of choices. The onslaught of online services has allowed many Canadians the opportunity to ride the information superhighway.

In fact, there are so many sources of online financial information that we could fill another book with their addresses and a brief description. But here are a few useful ones:

www.pointcast.ca   The *Globe and Mail*'s free news service, with articles from the *Globe* and other publications.

www.newswire.ca   Canada Newswire's site of current business-related information

www.bloomberg.com   Detailed information about companies and markets

www.exchange2000.com   Silicon Investor, a chat line for investors (charges US$75 for a password)

www.fapages.com   Financial Advisor Pages for information on investing and financial planning

Home Banking Basics

Move over ATM. The PC is gaining on you. Thousands of Canadians have access to the banking industry's latest advertising gimmick to keep your deposits: home banking online. It goes beyond the concept of an automatic teller machine handling transactions. You can pay bills and balance your chequing account all with the help of your personal computer and a modem.

Banks in the U.S. and Canada spent more than $23 billion on technology last year, much of it related to consumer services. Bank of Montreal and Royal Bank together spent $1.4 billion, and the meter is still ticking. Computer giants are also raking in the online financial bucks. Intuit markets the hot financial software program Quicken, which is the critically acclaimed number one personal finance software.

Home banking (or online banking) is easy to use. You need a computer, the financial software (depending on the bank, when appropriate), and a modem to do it. That's it. Each home banking software differs slightly. Typically, you can pay utility bills, make a mortgage payment, and even pay your insurance premiums. Costs for each source varies, so check with your financial institution to see if it offers a home banking feature.

The advantage to home banking is obvious: you can easily do your banking—from balancing your chequebook to paying your mortgage—from home. No need to jump in the car and fight traffic to get to the bank before it closes. Plus, you can do your banking whenever you want. You are not limited to lobby hours. On the other hand, it can be time-consuming to enter all your financial information. And in many cases, telephone banking is just as easy, if not as thorough.

The result of all of this home banking activity? The percentage of transactions made at bank branches, such as depositing your paycheque with a live teller, is falling. Fast. Last year, consumers conducted fewer than 50 percent of their transactions at a bank branch. The rest was done by ATM, telephone and PC.

The positive side of online banking is also a negative. Since people are likely to see electronic banking as being more like a debit card than a credit card, they may change their "buy-now-pay-later" attitude. But because a debit card deducts money from your account immediately, online users may feel vulnerable and fear giving up control of their money to a computer. If your bank offers an online banking program, make sure you understand all the features, and whether or not additional charges are assessed.

The Least You Need to Know

➤ Banks earn much of their money by renting your money in savings, chequing and GICs at lower rates than they charge to lend it out.

➤ Another way banks make money is to charge customers fees (which are increasing all the time) to use their services.

➤ Knowing your personal chequing habits will help you figure out what bank and which kind of chequing account will cost you the least money.

➤ Basic savings accounts almost always pay less than GICs.

➤ You can can earn 2 to 3 percent more with a GIC than a savings account. But make sure you don't need quick access to the money.

Chapter 6

GICs and Other Vehicles

In This Chapter

➤ Is your bank safe?

➤ What's a term deposit? A GIC? A Canada Savings Bond? A mortgage-backed security?

➤ What's an index-linked GIC?

Canadians are notorious for being "C" investors. We love CSBs (Canada Savings Bonds). We love GICs (guaranteed investment certificates). And we love the fact that our money is insured by the CDIC (Canada Deposit Insurance Corporation).

For most of us, the description Cautious and Conservative sums up our entire investment philosophy. And that's fine. But many of us don't know how to use even these fundamental saving guidelines to our best advantage.

The Canadian Way

Although Canadians have discovered the higher returns available from mutual funds, most of us still pack our money away in more conservative places. By 1997, Canadians had invested $273 billion in mutual funds. But we still had $600 billion stashed in GICs, term deposits, chequing accounts and other guaranteed investments.

Where Do Most Canadians Invest Their Money?

Most Canadians keep their money in bank savings accounts. This is a big financial mistake. The bank may love you, but you're just cheating yourself.

There's more than one bank savings account open for every person in Canada. A few of us don't have one at all. A lot of us have two or more.

At an interest rate of half of one percent a year—the rate paid on some savings accounts—you'll double your money every 144 years.

Savings accounts will never pay you enough money in interest to stay ahead of inflation. So you should use them only as a temporary storage place while you decide what to do with your money.

Is Your Money Safe in the Bank?

Keeping your money in Canadian banks, trust companies or credit unions is very safe. Any institution that displays the Canada Deposit Insurance Corporation (CDIC) sticker provides guaranteed protection of all funds deposited up to $60 000. If you don't see any sticker displayed, make sure to request proof of CDIC coverage.

How Does CDIC Insurance Work?

Any money that you have in a savings account, chequing account, guaranteed investment certificate (GIC), or term deposit is guaranteed up to $60 000 per institution, not per branch. If you have more than $60 000 sitting in a bank, you can get around the guaranteed limit by keeping up to $60 000 in your name, up to $60 000 in your wife's name, up to $60 000 in a joint account, and up to $60 000 in an RRSP—all within the same institution and all guaranteed.

What About Credit Unions?

CDIC coverage does not extend to credit unions. However, provincial deposit insurance programs can provide them with insurance coverage of customer accounts up to $60 000 apiece. Ask about this coverage. Many credit unions also allow clients to keep as many RRSPs as they want, guaranteeing the funds in each of them up to $60 000.

Investing for a Rainy Day

In every investment portfolio, between 10 percent and 50 percent of the holdings should consist of cash-type investments. You can call this the *slush fund*.

The slush fund provides a safe haven when the market winds start blowing in the wrong direction. It gives you flexibility, liquidity and peace of mind. If the value of your other investments falls drastically, you can still resort to your slush fund for ready cash to take advantage of other opportunities.

Even though you may not get rich from your slush fund, you can still achieve a respectable rate of return. That's because more financial institutions want to use it, even for short periods. And they compete with one another by offering better rates.

What Are Your Options?

In general, if you don't keep money in a chequing or savings account, you can choose term deposits, guaranteed investment certificates, Canada Savings Bonds, and mortgage-backed securities.

Term Deposits

A term deposit involves a contract between you and the financial institution. It's usually a short-term contract for 30 days to one year, although term deposits can extend over five years. Under the contract, you lend your money to the financial institution for a specified period. In return, the financial institution pays you a fixed rate of interest until the contract expires. In general, the longer the term, the higher the interest rate.

Maturity in life arrives when we know the difference between puppy love and true romance. In finance, maturity comes when a contract expires. This moment is called the **maturity date**.

Sometimes the interest rate on a term deposit is less than the rate on a premium savings account offered by banks. Also, you can cancel a term deposit prior to maturity, but only if you pay a penalty charge.

There is often a substantial spread between the highest and the lowest rates offered for the same term. So shop around for the best rate of return.

GICs

Guaranteed investment certificates—called GICs—are similar to term deposits. But GICs usually have longer terms, maturing in one year or more. Most GICs lock up your money (figuratively speaking, of course) for the duration of the contract. Some financial institutions, however, will allow you to cash in a GIC early, if you pay a penalty. So make sure you understand the terms of the contract.

One-, Three-, or Five-Year GICs

Invest in them all—each at the right time. Here's a strategy to protect you against

51

interest-rate swings. Instead of putting all your money into just one five-year GIC at today's low rates, you should buy five GICs of equal value, but stagger the maturity dates. For instance, if you have $5000 to invest , you should buy the following:

> a one-year GIC for $1000;
>
> a two-year GIC for $1000;
>
> a three-year GIC for $1000;
>
> a four-year GIC for $1000; and
>
> a five-year GIC for $1000.

After the first year

> the one-year GIC will mature;
>
> the two-year GIC will now have one year left until maturity;
>
> the three-year GIC will now have two years left until maturity;
>
> the four-year GIC will now have three years left until maturity;
>
> the five-year GIC will now have four years left until maturity.

As your GIC matures each year, you should reinvest the proceeds in a new five-year GIC, to replace your most recent five-year GIC, which now has only four years left until it matures.

Follow this strategy year after year. No matter what happens, one GIC will mature every year, and you'll continually reinvest the money at the current interest rate.

Index-Linked GICs

Index-linked GICs provide the same reassurance as ordinary GICs that your principal will remain intact, but with the possibility that you'll earn a higher return if stock markets go up. That's because their return is linked to an index such as the TSE 300. If the index goes up, so does the return on the GIC.

So is everybody happy? Well, maybe. Just as you do with a conventional GIC, you pay a price for your peace of mind. For one thing, there's usually a cap on the maximum return you can get from an index-linked GIC. If stock markets rise considerably, your GIC may not provide a comparable return. If stock markets fall considerably, you get back your principal and nothing more; you'd get a higher return from a standard GIC. Investors also don't receive the tax deferral and lower tax rate they'd get from a real equity investment. That's because all gains are taxed as interest income.

CSBs

Canada Savings Bonds (CSBs) are one of the most popular savings instruments. Each fall, CSBs are sold through financial institutions, such as banks and trust companies, to Canadian residents in denominations of $100, $300, $500, $1000, $5000 and $10 000. Currently the limit on the total value of CSBs that you can purchase in one year is $100 000.

Purchasers can choose bonds that pay regular or compound interest. Interest rates for CSBs are set each year when they're issued, and are guaranteed for only one year. Each year, the CSB yield may stay the same, or go up or down, depending upon the current economic climate.

CSB Pros and Cons

The advantages of CSBs are as follows:

➤ They're easy to purchase.

➤ They're extremely safe.

➤ They're highly liquid (which means you can always find someone to take them off your hands if you want to cash them in).

The disadvantages of CSBs are as follows:

➤ They must be held for at least three months before you can collect any accrued interest.

➤ When you go to roll over your CSB—that is, when your CSB matures after one year and you take the money and immediately buy another CSB—you can't predict the interest rate that will prevail at the time.

Regular interest bonds pay you interest each November 1, either by cheque or by direct deposit to your account. **Compound interest bonds** reinvest your interest automatically, so your savings continue to grow until the bonds are cashed or reach maturity.

You can put Canada Savings Bonds in your RRSP at an interest rate that begins at 3.5 percent and rises over the next seven years to 6.5 percent. These interest rates may not seem high, but they're above the rate of inflation, and they're guaranteed.

Do not confuse CSBs with conventional government and corporate bonds. Although they're both called bonds, Canada Savings Bonds do not respond the way conventional bonds do to interest-rate swings. No matter how high or low rates go, you can always cash in your Canada Savings Bond and get your full investment back, even if you cash it in before it matures. That's because the government guarantees the full value of CSBs.

In the United States, MBSs are called "Freddie Mac," "Fannie Mae" and "Ginnie Mae." In Canada, they're just called MBSs.

Because there's so little risk associated with CSBs, no one pays a premium or a discount to buy them. The only risk associated with a CSB comes from inflation.

Mortgage-Backed Securities

Mortgage-backed securities (MBSs) are pools of high-grade residential mortgages. They work like this: Financial institutions put together hundreds of mortgages into a single package, called a pool. Then they sell shares in the pool to investors like you. Theoretically, you're lending your money to a borrower whose mortgage is in the pool. The financial institution is acting as an intermediary.

Each pool comes with its own interest rate and payment schedule. If a mortgage borrower defaults on a mortgage in the pool, you don't lose your money. That's because the interest and principle of the mortgage are both guaranteed by the Canada Mortgage and Housing Corporation (CMHC).

Theoretically, there's a correlation between the dollars loaned in the form of mortgages and the dollars borrowed from investors in MBSs.

The interest rate that you receive from an MBS depends upon the interest charged to the mortgage holders. The financial institution calculates the lowest mortgage rate of all the mortgages in the pool. Then it pays MBS investors one half point below the lowest rate.

An investment in an MBS

> ➤ pays an above-average yield;
> ➤ provides regular cash flow;
> ➤ is government-guaranteed; and
> ➤ is guaranteed regardless of the amount contributed.

How Much for an MBS?

You'll need at least $5000 to purchase an MBS. MBSs can be purchased from brokers, and are issued by banks and trust companies that hold mortgages. Most are issued with five-year terms and can be held in an RRSP or an RRIF.

Can I Sell My MBS Before It Matures?

If you want to cash in your MBS before it matures, you'll have to sell it to somebody else. However, that's not a problem. A lot of people buy and sell MBSs. They form a market, called a *secondary market*.

However, if you sell the MBS before it matures, the amount you receive depends on the current interest rate. When interest rates rise, your MBS will fall in value; when interest rates fall, your MBS will rise in value.

When Is the Best Time to Buy an MBS?

The best time to buy an MBS is when interest rates are high and beginning to fall. That way, you can sell it before it matures for a profit on your original investment. However, if you plan on holding your MBS until it matures, any time is a good time to purchase one.

The Least You Need to Know

➤ Financial institutions insured by the CDIC will guarantee your money on deposit to a limit of $60 000 per institution, not per branch.

➤ Keep between 10 percent and 50 percent of your investments in cash, so you can pay for bargains when they appear.

➤ Term deposits are short-term investment contracts that usually mature in 30 days to one year.

➤ Guaranteed investment certificates are investment contracts that usually mature in one to five years and usually pay a higher yield than term deposits, but carry stricter rules about cashing them in early.

➤ Canada Savings Bonds (regular interest) pay you interest directly each November 1.

➤ Canada Savings Bonds (compound interest) reinvest your interest automatically.

➤ Mortgage-backed securities are pools of high-quality residential mortgages guaranteed by the Canada Mortgage and Housing Corporation.

Part 3
Interest Rates, Credit and Loans

Millions of Canadians can testify that the ups and downs in interest rates make them feel woozy and unsure of their investment decisions. We saw proof in 1994 when short-term interest rates were raised six times in just one year. Just what the heck is going on? And what can you do to time your investment and buying decisions when there's a flip-flop interest-rate market?

One thing you can do is learn more about credit cards and loans. Like it or not, they're necessary in the world of financial planning. The credit world doesn't stop with your credit rating. You 'll also find out how to beat those 18-percent rip-off rates that credit cards offer and save yourself some dough. Plus, you'll discover how to finance a car—without being taken for a ride—and how to shop the real bottom-line costs when you're looking for a mortgage.

Chapter 7

Interest Rate Math

In This Chapter

➤ Think in dollars and cents, not percent

➤ Rate vs. yield

➤ How to ride the roller coaster just right

➤ Heady's Five Critical Laws of Timing

➤ A safe bet: Dollar-cost averaging

Math is the least understood part of managing your money, but you can handle it, make more money and spend less, by learning the ABCs outlined in this chapter.

If you know how financial institutions calculate interest rates, for example, you won't be confused by rate versus yield or by information on compounding.

On a savings account, for example, the longer you agree to lock up your money, the higher the interest rate. Reason: It's an enticement to keep your cash in the bank's vault for a longer period. The bank can count on the money staying there, instead of having to chase after new money day after day. Other factors, of course, also come into play—such as where the banks think interest rates might be months or years from now. They try to balance their savings account maturities against their loan maturities.

Compounding Interest on Top of Interest

Compounding is simply interest added to interest. The more frequently a financial institution compounds your money, the more interest you earn. If the compounding

Which would you rather have? An outright gift of $1 million, or a penny in a savings account that doubles every day for 30 days? Better think this one through before you answer. At the end of the 30 days, the $1 million will still be worth one million bucks. But the penny will have grown to an astounding $5.37 million! That's not a misprint; get out your calculator and check it for yourself.

Before you sign up for an investment or a loan of any type, never let the financial institution get away with only quoting you mumbo-jumbo percentages. Instead, insist that the institution explain the deal in dollars and cents—nothing else. That should apply to both your investing and your borrowing.

is done daily, that's one of the two best methods of all. Compounding is like depositing $1 the first day, and having the bank add interest of one cent on the second day to increase the balance to $1.01. Then on the third day, the bank adds more interest on top of the $1.01 to build the account to $1.02, and on the fourth day it piles even more interest on the $1.02 to build the balance to $1.03.

For example, if you deposit $1000 earning 5-percent interest compounded monthly, your account grows to $1051 at the end of a year. But if the compounding is less frequent (say, on only a quarterly basis), your balance grows to just $1016. Look for frequent compounding when you shop. You'll find one of seven methods used to compute interest on savings accounts: continuous, daily, weekly, monthly, quarterly, annual, and simple interest.

The Chiseling Gets Down to Pennies

We all know that there are 365 days in a year. Well, not all financial institutions use that many days when they compute your interest. Some work with a 360-day year. That shaves your earnings by only pennies—but it saves the institution millions of dollars a year.

Say you deposit $10 000 in an account that pays 7 percent interest. If the financial institution uses a 365-day calculation method, you earn $709.72 in interest; with a 360-day method, the interest comes to $700 on the same account.

The Great Rate Roller Coaster

Interest rate cycles go up and down like a roller coaster. You can accurately call the shots on when—and when not—to buy a short-term or long-term GIC, or when to purchase a new home or finance a new car.

You're usually vaguely aware of when rates are getting higher or lower, aren't you? And you don't have to be a brain surgeon to detect that when you're in a bank or talking to a mortgage lender, the numbers keep changing. The rates they quote you today aren't the same rates as last week.

What you probably don't realize is that if you keep track of interest rates for only a few weeks, you'll see the numbers form a pattern as clear as a bell. They go up and down over time, forming a picture that looks like a roller coaster. And that's exactly what rates behave like—a roller coaster. The rates go in one direction for a long time, and then they change direction and go the other way. But unlike a roller coaster, each trip lasts for a few years instead of a few hundred yards.

Make sure you ask the bank how they will notify you before your GIC matures. Whatever you do, don't let the GIC automatically roll over at the same institution, because its new rate may be too low compared with what others are offering. You may elect to switch your account pronto.

When the roller coaster gets to the top of a peak or the bottom of a trough, it pauses for a short while and then takes off into the next part of the cycle.

Enjoying the Ride

Okay, let's pretend you're on the rate roller coaster. (You're already on one, whether you realize it or not.) To give your investments the biggest money-making ride of all, remember this secret:

Pick the right time to save when rates are high, and the best time to borrow when loan rates are low.

The best sources for tracking changes in the economy are the business pages of your local newspaper, or national newspapers such as the *Globe and Mail* and the *Financial Post*.

By doing that, you can earn more, and cut costs by just as much, when you buy a new home or finance a new set of wheels. But how can you tell whether rates are at a peak or in a valley? Good question.

How Long Has the Roller Coaster Been Going in that Direction?

Roller coaster rate-rides usually last for a couple of years. More precisely, the average ride, up or down, lasts an average of one-and-a-half to three years. To figure out where rates are headed in the future, you need to calculate the amount of time the coaster has been on its current ride. The easiest way is to visit your library or cozy up to your bank and ask them to do a little research for you. Find out what rate the bank paid on one-year GICs last month, six months ago, one year ago, and two years ago.

Aha! Now the roller coaster picture is taking shape! With a little imagination, you'll be able to determine when the current ride began. Match this against the fact that cycles usually last one-and-a-half to three years, and you'll be able to estimate how much farther the roller coaster has to go.

How Fast Is the Roller Coaster?

Economic wizards love to point out that interest rates don't go up and down in a vacuum. Rather, rates are influenced by economic growth that expands or contracts like a rubber band. When the country is in a recession, rates are low, as they were in the early 1990s. When the economy picks up steam and there's fear of inflation, the Bank of Canada steps in and raises rates to slow the economy. If the bank tightens up too drastically, the slowdown could push the country back into a recession.

You need to know this because it will help you figure out, during an up-cycle, how much your GIC rates might rise over the next few weeks. If rates are going up by only two-hundredths of a percent a week (say, from 7.00 percent to 7.02 percent), that's a slow ride. Rates could continue to move up slowly, or even pause in their tracks. If they're rising faster—say from 7.00 percent to 7.10 percent—it means a longer upward ride.

Heady's Five Critical Laws of Timing

Okay, you've done your roller coaster homework. You know how the cycles go up, down, then back up again. Now you're ready to put your new knowledge to work. You're going to invest based on where the roller coaster is on the track. By following these laws religiously, you should be able to add a substantial amount of coin to your personal treasury.

➤ **Law 1: Go short when rates are rising**   If rates just started to take off, say, up by a quarter-percent within a few weeks after the up-cycle started, don't touch a 2 1/2- or five-year GIC with a 10-foot pole. Why? You'll be trapped into a low rate for a long time. Instead, buy a three-month T-bill—no longer—and plan to renew it when it matures.

➤ **Law 2: Go long when rates peak**   When rates peak, it's a sign that rates could start falling in a new down-cycle. Grab a three- to five-year GIC for all it's worth. You'll keep earning that same high rate while all other rates are falling.

➤ **Law 3: Watch the indicators, especially the Bank of Canada, economic data reports, and the banks' prime rate**   At a bare minimum, at least follow your daily news headlines to detect whether the economy is getting stronger or weaker.

➤ **Law 4: When the Bank of Canada changes rates, move quickly behind it**   As an investor, your key is the rate that the Bank of Canada charges banks for loans. Once the Bank of Canada moves, the chartered banks follow suit. Every time the Bank boosts its rates, the banks increase their prime rates within 24 hours. GIC rates follow.

➤ **Law 5: The longer interest rates have been falling, the shorter the GIC term you should select**   Let's say the numbers have been dropping steadily for two years. Odds are that the down-cycle is going to end soon, so you want a GIC that will carry you past the bottom—or trough—of the down-cycle and into the next upward cycle. This would not—repeat, NOT—be the time to buy a two- or five-year GIC, because you'll miss out when rates start rising again.

By obeying the laws of timing, you'll maximize your earnings while the rest of the crowd gets white knuckles from riding the roller coaster the wrong way.

Buy Low, Sell High, etc.

The surest way to make money from investing is to buy low and sell high. Unfortunately, many of us do the opposite. We buy high and sell low. We're afraid to buy. So we wait until the price of our selected investment has risen before we do. Once we buy, we're afraid to sell. So we watch the price of our investment fall before we finally do. This is *not* a good way to make money.

Dollar–Cost Averaging

If you feel uneasy trying to time the cycle of interest rate ups and downs, try dollar-cost averaging. It sounds complicated; most discussions about investments do. But it's actually one of the best strategies for an investor, and one of the easiest to understand.

Here's how it works: Instead of investing all your money in one shot, you invest a fixed amount at regular intervals. You decide when and how much to invest.

You can invest $100 every two weeks, for example, or $500 a month for five months, or $1000 every three months for a year.

With each round, you buy only what your money will pay for. No more, no less.

For example, let's say you have $5000 to invest in GICs. Instead of investing it all in one GIC, you buy five, each worth $1000, each maturing at a different time, and each paying a different yield.

You can do the same thing with stocks, mutual funds or other investments, using

$5000 or $500. For example, you invest $100 a month for five months in a mutual fund.

➤ In January, the fund sells at $10 a share, so you pay $100 for 10 shares.

➤ In February, the fund trades at $5 a share. Your $100 investment now buys 20 shares.

➤ In March, the share price edges back to $7.50. You buy 13 1/3 shares for $100.

➤ In April, the share price is back up to $10. Once again you buy 10 shares.

➤ In May, things really pick up. Your fund's share price rises to $15. With $100, you can buy only 6 2/3 shares.

You now have a total of 60 shares. If you'd invested your entire $500 when your fund was selling at $10 a share, you'd have bought only 50 shares.

At $15 a share, they'd now be worth $750.

Instead, using dollar-cost averaging, your 60 shares are worth a total of $900. You're $150 ahead of the game.

This isn't magic. It results from investing a fixed amount of money at regular intervals. You automatically buy more shares when the price is low and fewer shares when the price is high.

REALLY?

For more detailed information on investing and personal finance, check out *The Complete Idiot's Guide to Personal Finance for Canadians.*

In our example, we applied our theory over five months. But to really maximize your gains, you should invest a consistent amount, on a monthly basis, over a much longer period. The point: Be consistent.

In fact, to invest successfully using dollar-cost averaging, you have to commit yourself to investing for the long term. Once you start, you can't cash in your chips after a month or two because you want the money for a trip to Acapulco. Nor can you cash in when the market starts to fall. You have to stick with it.

In fact, the lower prices fall, the more bargains you'll pick up, and the faster your portfolio will grow.

The Least You Need to Know

➤ The more frequently the bank compounds your money, the more interest you earn. Accounts that compound daily are best.

➤ Get your lender or financial institution to explain the deal to you in dollars and cents instead of percentages.

➤ Interest rates are like a roller coaster—they have peaks and valleys and are in constant motion.

➤ Most up-cycles or down-cycles last an average of one-and-a-half to three years. If you know how long the interest rate has been in its current cycle, you can predict where it's heading in the future.

➤ Watch economic indicators such as the Bank of Canada, economic data reports, and the chartered banks' prime rate to figure out where rates are going.

➤ Buy short-term GICs when the interest rate is rising, and buy long-term GICs when the rate has reached its peak.

➤ Dollar-cost averaging is a good alternative to timing the cycles of interest rates.

Chapter 8

How to Cut Your Credit Card Costs in Half

In This Chapter

➤ A crash course on the credit card jungle

➤ How—and where—to get a card that will cost you nothing

➤ How to avoid the credit card debt trap

➤ Which fees and charges will hurt you most

➤ Where to get a card even if you have bad credit

There's no bigger rip-off than credit cards. Banks are getting away with murder—charging you 18 percent or more because you've become addicted to the convenience of plastic.

The plastic picture is also getting more confusing. More banks and more companies have jumped into the credit card business because it's one gigantic gold mine. But the credit card pie can only grow so big; that's why card issuers are dangling low-rate offers, freebies and rebates to grab your account away.

You need to see through these offers and cut a cheaper deal, including switching your cards to low-rate, no-fee institutions. More important, you should learn how to avoid falling into the card debt trap and hurting your credit record. This chapter explains how credit cards work, who offers the best rates, and how to trim your costs to the bone.

Can't Live With 'Em, Can't Live Without 'Em

Notice how more credit card offers have been bombarding your mailbox lately? Card companies sent out more than 10 million offers to consumers in 1997 alone. Why? Two reasons:

➤ Credit cards represent enormous profits for banks and other card issuers. They sock cardholders with rates of 18 percent or more while they pay minimal interest on savings.

➤ More card outfits are competing for your business, so they're tempting you with lower rates and rebate deals.

Canadians are hooked on plastic, plain and simple. Convenient? You bet. We simply whip out our cards; no money leaves our wallets. That's a good feeling—temporarily. But later, when the monthly bill comes in with all your charges plus interest, it's pay-up time. Sure, the bank will let you get away with a teensy minimum payment. But that practice could keep you in debt forever. And if you fall behind in your monthly payments, you'll wind up with an ugly blemish on your credit record that will haunt you for years.

How Credit Cards Can Cost You

You can make purchases with your credit card up to a certain limit decided by the card issuer. As you use the card, you're constantly borrowing against your limit and repaying the money. Say your credit limit is $1000 and you buy a garment for $100, or take a $100 cash advance against the card. You have $900 left. When you repay the $100 (plus the interest charges), you again have $1000 in available credit.

Most Canadians pay their credit card bills as soon as they come due; but about four in 10 carry an outstanding balance from one period into the next, paying interest on the outstanding amount.

Let's set it straight: Banks and other credit card outfits want you to do this. They make their profits by making it easy for you to finance your balance. If you paid off your bill every month, they'd make money only on the fees you pay for your card.

How expensive can credit cards be? Take the case of a cardholder with a balance of $2500 who pays 18.5-percent interest. If he made only a minimum monthly payment of 2 percent of the unpaid balance—which many card issuers permit—it would take more than 30 years to pay the card off. Even worse, the total interest would come to $6500. All for a $2500 loan!

Using Credit Cards Wisely

Skip credit cards entirely? Just try it. In today's society, a credit card is almost as important as a birth certificate. You need plastic to rent a car, buy an airline ticket,

Among the six billion people in the world, there are now 500 million Visa cards in circulation. They account for volume approaching US$1 trillion. But purchases made with Visa cards account for only 5 percent of consumers' total personal spending.

reserve a hotel room, order from a mail-order catalogue or TV shopping network, or rent movies. A woman we know moved into a new town and tried to deposit $20 000 in a bank. She had her driver's licence and voter's registration card, but the bank insisted on seeing a credit card before they'd accept her as a new customer. She didn't have one, so they declined her business!

Credit cards are definitely useful. The key to avoiding credit card trouble is to be smart about how you use credit. For example, did you know that

➤ You can get a free card if you pay off your balance each month?

➤ You can cut your card costs nearly in half if you have good credit?

➤ You can even get a card if you've had credit problems or haven't had a chance to build up a credit record of your own?

The following sections will help you to become a smart credit card user.

Kinds of Credit Cards

There are five main types of credit cards:

➤ Fixed-rate cards

➤ Variable-rate cards

➤ Gold cards

➤ Secured cards

➤ Credit cards with gimmicks such as rebates

Retail credit cards (such as those issued by department stores) are also big business, but their interest rates tend to be higher than the rates banks charge on their standard cards. We've seen many stores slap customers with rates as high as 21 percent.

Remember that no matter what credit card you use, your payment record on the card is going to wind up on your personal credit report—accessible to any bank or company to which you apply for credit.

Fixed-Rate Cards

This is your ordinary, everyday, plain card. The interest rate is *fixed* at a certain percentage. Whatever you buy, that's the percent interest you pay. This type of credit card has become an ugly duckling because the average rate is about 17.5 percent.

To avoid paying these high fixed rates, shop the best card deals nationwide. You'll find rates as low as nine percent. It's a perfectly safe and smart thing to do; after all, most big card-issuers are national anyway. The only catch is that the lower the card rate, the more difficult it will be for you to get your credit approved, because the financial institution may apply tougher standards. But if your credit is good, give it a shot!

You can also switch banks to get a better deal on your credit card. Make sure you cut your old credit card in half, and enclose it with your cheque and a letter to the old bank. Advise them that you are closing your account, give the number, and keep a copy of the letter.

Double-check the rates and fees you're now paying on your cards. The rate may have gone up over the past year if you're carrying a variable-rate card that is tied to some index. If your rate today is 16 to 19 percent, you're being taken to the cleaners. You might have missed the fine print on a bank notice, stating that the card's annual fee has been raised.

Variable-Rate Cards

Choosing a variable-rate credit card will cost you less in the long run. With this type of credit card, your interest rate changes according to an index used by the bank. Often, the rate is tied to the bank's prime rate plus six percentage points. For example, if the prime is at 8.5 percent, the variable rate on your credit card would be 14.5 to 15.5 percent.

Variable-rate cards are great when the prime rate is low, as it was in the early 1990s. Then, the average variable rate was only 12 percent. But when rates start rising, as they did in 1994, variable-rate plastic becomes less and less attractive. The average today is about 15 percent.

Gold Cards

The secret to shopping for gold cards lies in their perks: emergency roadside service, buyer protection plans, cash back if you spend thousands of dollars, medical insurance for travellers. All too often, though, cardholders choose gold cards as a status symbol. The only thing a gold card *can* promise you is a higher credit limit—and sometimes expensive annual fees. Gold card applicants require a stronger credit record.

Secured Cards for Those with Bad (or No) Credit

Anyone who's been hanging his head because he lost his card and damaged his credit rating during bad financial times now has new hope: a secured card.

69

A secured card works like this: You keep $200 to $500 on deposit with the bank. It issues you a card with which you can make purchases for up to your deposit amount. Some institutions also pay you a small amount of interest on your deposit.

The interest rate you pay on a secured card is a little stiff, anywhere from 17 to 21 percent, but it's temporarily worth it to start rebuilding your credit. Banks may charge an application fee of $20 to $40 on secured cards, as well.

Why the boom in secured cards? Because banks have discovered a huge, new market of people with damaged credit: young people applying for a card for the first time, divorced people who don't have their own personal credit records, and new workers, including immigrants.

Is a secured card for you? Yes, if your credit needs repair and you don't mind paying the high interest. If you mind your manners and make your monthly payments on time, that will be a plus on your credit record. Six to 12 months later, you might be able to ask the bank to increase your credit limit, or apply for a standard card.

Gimmick Credit Cards

Credit cards with bells and whistles are popping up all over, as every card outfit and its brother tries to get a piece of the credit card pie. The main gimmicks are discounts on merchandise and services, and promises of cash rebates. The more you use a particular card, the more rebates and freebies you get. These can range from discounts on new cars to free air travel and cut-rate hotel rooms. Sounds groovy, but following are the questions you must ask yourself:

➤ Could I get a better deal with another card that offers a lower interest rate and lower fees?

➤ Do I really need the "free" merchandise, discounts and whatever? (If the card gives me points toward buying a Chevrolet sedan, but I'm in the market for a Ford pickup, it doesn't make much sense.)

REALLY?

If you're turned down for credit, understand why. Perhaps your salary is not high enough compared with your living expenses. Maybe you haven't lived at your current address or worked for your current employer long enough to show stability. Time may resolve these matters. Reapply for credit when your situation changes.

The offers have lots of different twists, the most popular being money-back gimmicks that return a percentage of your purchases. But as with any credit card, it's not the gifts and pizzazz that count—it's what you wind up with in your pocket. Compare the bottom-line costs—after the rebates.

Key Fee Factors

Okay, you've got the types of cards down pat. Now you need to know the key *cost factors* you could be hit with. The three main ones are interest rate, annual fee and grace period. The kind of card you want depends on the way you pay off your credit card bills. If you're a "revolver," that is, if you finance your balance every month, you want a credit card with a very low interest rate. If you pay your balance off in full every month, you want a card with no annual fee. This card will cost you nothing.

The *interest rate* is what you're charged to borrow the bank's money to finance what you purchased with the card. If you're in the habit of not paying off your monthly balance, you want the cheapest, rock-bottom interest rate you can find. If you don't pay off the full balance, interest keeps accumulating on the unpaid amount. The meter begins ticking the moment you buy something with the card or, more likely, the day the card issuer bills you for what you owe.

The interest could keep you in bondage forever if you don't use your noodle. For instance, it would take eight years and eight months to pay off a $1000 balance at 16.5 percent of you only paid the minimum payment. The minimum is normally 2.5 percent of the amount owed. You'd wind up paying $766 interest on your $1000 loan. But you could pay off the debt in three years and pay $500 less in interest just by adding an extra $10 a month to your payment.

You pay the *annual fee* just to have the right to have the card for one year. The fee is usually $20 to $50, but many banks charge no fee at all. If you're the meticulous type and always pay your monthly card balance in full, you should carry a no-annual-fee card and nothing else. The card will cost you nothing. It will be like having a free card.

The *grace period* is the number of days you have to pay off all new purchases without being hit by a finance charge. The usual grace period is 25 days. Typically, if you don't pay off your entire bill, all new purchases get clobbered by finance charges immediately.

For example, two brothers, Eenie and Meenie, both carry credit cards with an 18-percent rate. Each has a $1000 balance on his card, on which there's no annual fee. Eenie pays off the entire $1000 before the 25-day grace period is up. The card costs him zero. But Meenie only makes a minimum payment of $20, and gets charged 18-percent interest per year on the remaining $980.

If you can't pay off your credit card entirely, always be sure to pay at least the minimum payment on your card before the grace period expires. Late payments will go over like a lead balloon at the next place you apply for credit. You'll probably get rejected.

Other niggling card costs:

➤ **Late fees**   You'll usually be nicked with a flat $15 charge, or 2 percent of your outstanding balance, if you don't make at least a minimum payment by the due date shown on the bill.

➤ **Cash advances**   You can borrow money against the card, but the interest rate you pay for this type of transaction is apt to be higher. Plus, the interest-rate meter starts ticking as soon as you withdraw the money and doesn't stop until you repay your balance in full.

The Biggest Secret of All: Watch Your Habits!

Canadians are up to their ears in debt, and the credit card got them there. Bad card habits have caused divorces, bankruptcies, lost dreams and emotional wreckage. You can avoid the credit trap by following these simple rules:

➤ Know your credit limit based on your income, amount of current debt and credit history. A rule of thumb is that your total monthly debt should not exceed 38 percent of your monthly income.

➤ Carry only the number of cards you need, even though you haven't used up your credit line. When creditors review your record, they look at how much you're able to go into debt.

➤ Don't apply for more than one card at a time. Some creditor may think you're going to charge like mad and take off for Brazil.

➤ Consider joining a credit union to take advantage of their lower interest rates. In 1994, for example, the average credit union offered a fixed-rate credit card at 12.98 percent, versus the national average of 17.95 percent.

➤ Remember that a bad credit record will dog you for years. Nothing can screw up your life faster than going overboard with credit cards. Your card payment record will shadow you in everything you do, including buying a home (or renting), getting a job, and opening a chequing account.

➤ Pay against your balance ASAP. Don't let bills hang around. Every day you wait is going to cost you more in interest.

➤ If you can't make your payments on time, or if you want to dispute a charge, contact your card issuer immediately—and put everything in writing.

➤ Don't get fooled when card issuers lower your minimum payments. It only makes it easier for you to stay in debt, and increases the total interest you'll pay. This is a tar pit if ever there was one.

➤ If you run into severe financial problems, contact a personal credit counseling organization. They've helped millions of people, and can probably help you at no charge, or for a small fee.

More Useful Tips

Here are further useful tips on credit cards from the U.S. National Association of Consumer Agency Administrators:

1. Don't give your credit card number or its expiration date to anyone via the

telephone unless you've initiated the call—even if the caller says it's for "verification" or security purposes.

2. Always keep an eye on your credit card: Ensure that unscrupulous salespeople aren't making two copies of the card imprint.

3. Always sign new credit cards immediately. This helps the salesperson verify your signature. A blank panel allows thieves to forge your signature on the card and receipts.

4. Check your credit card statement against receipts. Act immediately to notify the issuer about errors or fraud. Dispute charges in writing.

5. After making purchases with a credit card, make sure the salesperson returns your card and not someone else's.

6. Never leave your credit cards anywhere at work. Someone can steal your card number.

7. Make sure only one charge slip is imprinted with your credit card number. Always take carbons.

8. Memorize PIN (personal identification number). Never give out personal information on the phone. Don't use your birthdate or commonly used numbers as your access code.

9. Don't leave debit or credit card receipts showing your account number where others could easily find them.

10. The approved "user" on accounts, such as a girlfriend/boyfriend or spouse—when the account is not held jointly— isn't liable for charges. You are!

11. Be careful of limited-use credit cards. Some gold/platinum cards can only be used to purchase specific items from a catalogue.

12. Beware of "easy credit" offers or help to improve your credit history. Your card may have to be "secured" with a large deposit in a no-interest or low-interest bank account. Know what you're getting before paying the application fee.

13. Question any unknown/incorrect charges on your bill immediately. You're not required to pay a disputed amount or any interest until the investigation is completed. If the charge is correct, however, you may be responsible for accrued interest.

14. Shop around for a credit card that best suits your needs. Compare interest rates and annual fees. If you carry a monthly balance, look for a low interest rate. If you pay the entire balance monthly, look for a low annual fee.

15. When shopping for a credit card, compare extra fees for late payments, over limit charges, cash advances, etc. Analyse the total cost of using a credit card.

Please see Appendix A for even more useful tips from the U.S. National Association of Consumer Agency Administrators. There are also a number of consumer credit counselling agencies accessible through the World Wide Web. You can learn more about credit cards at Web sites administered by Canada's major banks. One of the best is the TD Bank's, at www.tdbank.ca.

Establishing Credit

Here are more tips for individuals with credit problems from Experian Information Solutions, a North American credit agency:

➤ Start small and build up

➤ Pay your bills on time

➤ Ask a family member or friend to help you get credit

➤ Apply for a secured credit card

➤ Understand why you're denied credit

Start Small and Build Up

A local department store or local lending institution is a good first step. Even if you don't have other credit, you may be able to obtain a credit card with a small credit limit—perhaps $200 or $300.

Before you apply, ask if the credit grantor will regularly report your bill-paying history to a credit bureau. Since your intention is to build a positive credit history and obtain higher credit limits in the future, avoid lenders who don't report your information to credit bureaus.

Why? Because credit grantors who do not report your bill-paying performance to a credit bureau will not help you achieve your financial goals.

Pay Your Bills on Time

When you get a credit card or loan, use it. Consistently pay your bills on time. Each month, your credit grantor will report this information to the credit bureau. In this way, you'll establish a history of responsible credit use.

After six months, apply for another card. Continue using your credit and paying your bills. Before you know it, you won't have to ask for credit—credit grantors will come to you.

Ask a Family Member or Friend to Help You Get Credit

Another option is to ask a parent or friend with an established credit history to co-sign your loan or credit card application. If granted, the account will appear on both your credit report and that of your co-signer.

Take extra care to repay your co-signed debt promptly. Failure to do so will hurt your co-signer's credit, as well as your own. After a few months, try again to get credit on your own.

This strategy can also work in reverse. You can co-sign a parent's or friend's application—or be added to an account they already have. You then will benefit from their good credit history.

Apply for a Secured Credit Card

If none of the above options work for you, consider applying for a secured credit card.

To obtain a secured credit card, you must open and maintain a savings account as security for your line of credit. Your credit line is a percentage of your deposit. (For example, if you deposit $1000 into a savings account, you may receive a credit card with a $500, $750 or even $1000 spending limit.)

Before you apply for a secured card, be sure to ask if the card issuer will report your use of the card to credit bureaus. If the issuer doesn't report your use of the card, having the card will not help you obtain credit in the future.

Also, beware of the extra fees you may have to pay to obtain secured credit. Secured credit cards typically have higher interest rates than do unsecured cards; annual fees are also common.

Use extreme caution before calling a 900 telephone number for a credit card. The call itself can cost as much as $50, and there's no guarantee you'll receive the card.

Don't jump at the first secured card offer that comes along, no matter how plastic-hungry you are. With so many banks beating the bushes for business, you should shop for these cards as you would anything else.

Beware of third-party outfits that "guarantee" to get you a secured card. The company may be a fly-by-night scam, and besides, you can easily handle your application by yourself and deal directly with the bank.

75

The Least You Need to Know

➤ Credit cards are so profitable that competition for your credit card business has increased dramatically in recent years. You can use this to your advantage by shopping for a card that best meets your needs, such as a low interest rate, no annual fee, or rebates that could save you money.

➤ The basic types of credit cards are fixed-rate cards, variable-rate cards, gold cards, secured cards, and credit cards with gimmicks such as rebates.

➤ To figure out how much a credit card is costing you, you need to be aware of the interest rate, annual fee, and grace period. Extra fees are also involved when you get cash advances, or are late with a payment.

➤ Don't carry more cards than you need, and always pay more than the minimum monthly payment to avoid drowning in credit card debt.

Chapter 9

Inside Those Credit Rating Agencies

In This Chapter

➤ How much personal data the credit agencies already know about you

➤ How to get a copy of your credit report

➤ How agencies "score" your habits and predict your future behaviour

➤ How to improve your chances of getting credit and removing errors from your credit record

Like it or not, it's a nosy credit society that you live in. Your ability to borrow money or get a new job can swing on the information contained in your personal credit report. Who has the data? Two giant companies that have the goods on just about every person in Canada.

People with bad credit? They get stung over and over again because of what's on their credit report. Even those with good credit can easily become victims of erroneous information that somehow gets on their report without their knowing it.

More credit applicants get turned down for a loan than get approved. Yet—shockingly—most consumers don't even bother to get a copy of their own credit report to see what's on it. They remain in the dark, never realizing how much negative stuff the credit agencies have dug up on them: the info can range from their date of birth to their income, payment habits, and the people they owe.

This chapter goes inside the shadowy world of credit bureaus, and explains how they score your credit history. It tells which mistakes to avoid, as well as how to strengthen your credit file and greatly improve your chances of getting a loan.

Big Brother Is Watching You

You can forget about how private you think your personal financial life is. The odds are 25-million-to-1 that if you have a credit card, department store account, savings or chequing account, auto loan, student loan or mortgage, there's a computer file on you. Everything is in it: your job, how much money you make, where you've lived, and how you've paid your bills.

Your file will show the name and date of any company that nosed its way onto your credit report over the past two years.

Despite the fact that credit agencies have 25 million consumer credit reports on file, last year only 3 million Canadians bothered to peer into their own files to see the often shocking information on their credit records. Of those, one in four discovered an error that they eventually had corrected.

A little scary? You bet. Big Brother is watching you like you wouldn't believe. Its computers sit in a company you've likely never heard of, run by people you've never met. Make that two companies instead of one—Equifax, and Trans Union. They're the two big guns of the credit-agency business, and both probably have the same info on your life.

They supply personal credit data about you to any place you go for credit—from credit card companies and auto dealers to, yes, even the company that's considering you for a job. And whenever you apply for credit, those outfits feed your latest personal information into the computers of the Big Two.

The Big Two agencies aren't the ones who decide whether you'll get a loan or be hired. They only compile the data and provide it to organizations that determine whether they'll extend you credit. It could be a department store, bank, or credit card issuer. And to confuse the issue, they all evaluate your credit history differently. Little wonder the Big Two are a mystery to the average consumer, who knows zip about how the credit system operates.

You Wouldn't Believe What They Know About You

Here's what you're up against—those credit agencies look under every rock. They gather information on you from hundreds of thousands companies such as retailers, banks, finance companies and credit card issuers. In turn, those companies feed monthly updates on consumers back to the Big Two. The info includes, for example, the following: names, old and current addresses, Social Insurance Numbers, birth dates, employment information, and how people pay their bills. The Big Two also get information from public records from provincial and municipal courts. But this information is limited to tax liens, legal judgments, bankruptcies and child-support payments.

With the tap of a few computer keys, an agency can pull up your credit life story and send it immediately to Megabuck Bank or Bubba's Auto Emporium where you're sweating out a loan. In turn, the information you filled out on your credit application at Megabuck and Bubba's also winds up in the computers of the Big Two for the next place you apply for a loan. They get you coming and going.

As you sit in the loan officer's or car dealer's office, she may call up your credit file on the computer on her desk. Ask her to show you what's on the screen. You can see if the information's accurate.

How Predictable Are You? The Big Two Think They Know

Credit agencies work with outside mathematical experts to develop what they call predictive models—computer programs that try to estimate your future credit behaviour based on your previous behaviour. Einstein would have trouble understanding these complicated computer whatchamacallits. They involve far-out terms such as regression analysis and neural networks—concepts that are way above the heads of average people.

These programs can predict the probability of someone going bankrupt—three, six or nine months down the road—or they can determine the likelihood of a person stiffing his creditors by never paying bills.

How are these predictions applied? A bank makes a list of the kinds of new customers it's seeking. It goes to a credit bureau and says, "Tell us who has two credit cards and has never been 90 days late on a payment." The bureau prints a list of people who match those criteria. The bank sends a promotional mailing to everyone on the list, offering each credit. The approval rates on these applications are higher than if the bank were to simply mail to everybody in town.

The Bad Stuff Comes Off...Eventually

Fortunately, negative information on your report can't hang around forever. The agencies are *supposed to* wipe off any bankruptcy data 10 years after it was entered. They're also *supposed to* erase after seven years any tax liens, lawsuits, judgments or accounts put up for collection.

But don't assume that will happen, or that everything on your report is accurate. The agencies, like every company, are working with the human factor. A data clerk can easily hit the wrong computer key when he enters your information. Or the people down at Bubba's may have misread the info on your credit application.

With more and more organizations using national credit reports to make decisions, erroneous data could wind up costing you a job, or get you turned down on an insurance policy. One couple we know got rejected for credit because they made a late payment of $10 on a department store bill five years ago.

Here's another unpleasant possibility: An agency could just plumb forget about eradicating your negative information when it's supposed to.

The Three Cs: An Old-Fashioned Pipe Dream

There was a time when you could go into a bank, and the banker—who was your friend and neighbour—had known you since you were in pigtails or knickers. He'd okay your loan with no credit check or other hassle. You can kiss those days good-bye. Banking has become big business, and people move around a lot. Big business today doesn't want to take any risks. You and your habits are now impersonal numbers in a Big Two computer. Oh, sure, banks still maintain that they lend money the old-fashioned way—on the basis of what they call the Three Cs:

➤ **Character**   It may not have anything to do with what kind of person you really are. More than likely, admit the credit agencies, it means how long you've lived at the same address and worked at the same company.

➤ **Capacity**   How much debt can you afford, based on your current income? The lender looks at your living expenses, current financial obligations, and the payments that your new loan would require.

➤ **Credit**   How long have you had credit accounts such as credit cards, mortgages and personal loans? What is the credit limit you're allowed on each one? How close are you to those limits now? Have you made your payments on time?

Nobody's perfect, and lenders know that. But if you've had a car repossessed, or another lender has given up trying to collect on what you owe, the Three Cs have probably gone down the tubes in your case.

Knowing Your Credit Rating—It's More Important than Ever

With the development and application of new technologies, Canadian banks can now process a small-business loan application within hours. And the application itself is no more than a page long, whether the applicant needs $1000 or $30 000.

Banks rely on a combination of techniques to provide such prompt and efficient service. One is called *credit scoring*. Comparing the applicant's household income, the annual sales of the applicant's business, and other information, with a standardized database of customer profiles, the bank can determine the risk that the applicant might default on the loan. If the applicant's score is sufficiently high—the risk low—the bank can approve the loan within a single day.

Credit scoring works by evaluating patterns of behaviour of groups of customers and measuring risk accordingly. Using this approach, a lender can determine the precise level of risk involved in a particular loan, without evaluating the individual behaviour of each member of the group.

What Does Credit Scoring Mean for You?

Credit scoring provides benefits for borrowers as well:

➤ It drastically reduces the amount of paperwork and information required on a loan application. In fact, for unsecured loans of up to $35 000, lenders require only a single page of information.

➤ It reduces the time required to process a loan application. Most applications can be processed in a single day.

➤ Lending decisions become more equitable as individual characteristics about the borrower become less significant. If your credit history is sound and you meet the expectations of the lender, you can anticipate receiving a loan, even if your particular company operates in an unusual industry.

The thing that creditors examine like a hawk is your debt-to-income ratio. This is the percentage of your average monthly income that goes toward repaying the debts you owe. To arrive at the ratio, add up your monthly payments, including your mortgage or rent, and divide it by your monthly gross income. A ratio of more than 35 percent is a signal to lenders that you may be stretched to the limit and may not be able to handle any more debt. Here's an example:

Your monthly income is $3000, and your monthly debts are $1000.

Divide $3000 by $1000 and you get 33 percent. That's your debt-to-income ratio.

Before they approve a loan, lenders still evaluate an applicant's business and personal credit history, through electronic links to one of Canada's two national credit bureaus. All Canadians who have borrowed money have established a credit history that reflects their repayment habits, current address and employer's name. This information is gathered from public records and lenders such as financial institutions, department stores and oil companies. Your credit history includes information on former loans, mortgages and outstanding credit card balances. It indicates the nature of the loan, how quickly you repaid it, whether a lender has ever turned over a loan to a collection agency, and whether you've ever gone bankrupt. Unfavourable information, such as a bankruptcy, is kept on file for about seven years. Multiple bankruptcies are recorded permanently.

The Credit Rating

Your individual credit rating consists of two elements, indicated by a combination of letters and numbers.

Letters indicate the type of loan.

➤ "R" stands for revolving credit, such as a credit card, which enables a borrower to make purchases up to a specified limit and repay the balance over time.

➤ "I" stands for installment credit, such as a mortgage or car loan, with a defined term and regular payments.

➤ "O" stands for open credit, such as an American Express card, on which the borrower pays the balance in full each month.

Numbers indicate the borrower's promptness in repaying debts.

➤ "Zero" represents a new, unused account.

➤ "One" indicates that the borrower pays within a specified payment schedule, usually within 30 days.

➤ "Nine" identifies a bad debt that has been written off by the lender.

If you plan to apply for a loan, your credit history will play a critical role in the process, so you should make sure that yours is accurate. Errors can occur when you move, for example, when you obtain a new credit card, or when you get married or divorced. There's also a good chance that someone else has the same name as yours, without necessarily sharing your good judgment and prudent spending habits. If you find an error, the credit bureau must correct it and notify lenders of any changes. If you and the lender disagree about your credit rating, a note is attached to your history explaining the difference of opinion.

When you need to dispute any information on your credit report, remember that you have a legal right to insert up to 100 words into your file at the credit agency. Explain your side of the story. State all the facts—the names, numbers, dates and places concerning what really happened. Believe it or not, credit grantors will take your statement into consideration when they check your file because the statement says something about your earnestness and character.

Check Your Credit Rating

You can obtain your own credit history by contracting the bureaus directly. Usually you'll need photocopies of two pieces of identification, along with proof of your current address taken from a utility bill or credit card invoice. Mail this information to the following address: Equifax Canada Inc., Box 190, Jean-Talon Station, Montreal, Quebec H1S 2Z2 (1–800–465–7166) or Trans Union, Consumer Relations Department, P. O. Box

338–LCD1, Hamilton, Ontario L8L 7W2 (416–291–7032). They will mail the appropriate information to you in about two weeks.

Are You Good, Bad or Grey?

Lenders have a habit of lumping you into one of three ranges—"good," "bad" and "grey." Its computers make the first cut. The top scores are considered "good," and these customers are automatically approved for a loan. The "grey" scores are for people who score somewhere in the middle of the range. These are personally reviewed on an individual basis. The "bad" group might just as well have leprosy. But occasionally the lender may move a person into the "grey" group to give her "another chance."

An example of a person who would immediately be placed in the bad category is someone who has had charge-offs in the past. Charge-offs are loans that creditors eventually have to wipe off their books because the loans have never been paid. "If we see someone who has had charge-offs greater than $300 in the last four years, we just immediately decline it," explained one credit agency executive. "I don't want anyone in my office spending any more effort on that one."

If you've been habitually 30, 60, or 90 days late in making your payments, you could be hurting your credit record even more. All late payments are bad, but 90 days is worse than 30, as you might guess. Credit card companies are a little looser when you don't pay on time because, after all, those guys want you to go past the due date so they can charge you interest on your balance!

It's Thumbs Down in Most Cases

The most closely guarded secret of all? The lenders' **approval ratio**. It's the percentage of applicants who do or don't get approved for their loans. Sources at the Big Two agencies give this picture:

➤ If a credit card issuer sends a mailing to consumers that says they have preapproved status for credit, the odds are nine in 10 that they'll actually be approved. But if the card company somehow finds out that the person's credit has deteriorated lately, it may conclude, "Hey, this guy is not as good as we thought he was." Result? He'll get approved, all right, but the creditor may bust his credit limit down to $200–$500. He also may pay a higher rate of interest on the money he borrows.

➤ The person who just picks up a credit application at a store, then fills it out and mails it in, has a two in 10 chance of getting approved.

➤ The person who applies for a "gold" credit card (with a $5000 credit line and other perks) has a four in 10 chance of being okayed.

➤ New car loan applicants also have a four in 10 possibility.

For a plain-vanilla credit card, credit scorers used to look for someone with an annual income of at least $12 000. Now, some have dropped the requirement to as low as $8000. To obtain a gold credit card, a person needs an income of about $30 000.

Why are the minimums falling? Because of fierce competition for customers. The credit card pie is just so big, and more and more outfits want a piece. To cover their higher risks, creditors may charge a higher interest rate (plus special fees) and monitor these new customers once a month. Another reason for easier credit is that the percentage of delinquencies—people who fall behind in their payments—is decreasing.

Boost Your Chances of Getting Approved

It's not easy for a lot of people, but the sure way to increase the odds of obtaining credit is to follow these basic rules:

➤ Pay your bills on time.

➤ Pay down the debts you owe.

➤ Don't take on more credit than you need and can afford.

➤ If, say, you have an auto loan and several credit cards, reduce the number of cards immediately.

➤ Use the credit you have wisely. Don't live up to your credit limit.

➤ Ask the credit agencies for a copy of your report every year or two, so you'll know what kind of picture they have of you.

➤ Correct any errors on the report.

Certain inquiries won't show up on your report. Examples include inquiries made by you to monitor your report (or to obtain a copy of it) or inquiries made by companies who want to send you an unsolicited credit offer through the mail.

Credit Inquiries Can Haunt You

Let's say you've been pretty good about paying your bills on time. You earn a nice income, and you've lived at the same address for two years. You can't think of anything that could possibly prevent a lender from giving you credit. No tax liens, no bankruptcies, no nothing.

You carry one credit card, but in the past three months you've applied for two more, and are now in the process of also trying to borrow money to finance Junior's college education. You've also contacted a couple of companies about changing jobs.

That makes six new inquiries on your credit report in a very short time. What happens? The two credit card companies check you out at one of the Big Two credit agencies and count four inquiries besides their own. Alarm bells ring in their minds. They figure that all those inquiries mean you're about to plunge into big debt. They look like red flags to a bull. *Whammo!* You get turned down.

Guard Against Mix-Ups

Almost one in four credit files contains an error. A lot of them undoubtedly were the credit agencies' fault, but there are tons of horror stories of errors created by consumers themselves. You can prevent errors and mix-ups on your credit report by following a few simple guidelines.

1. Always use the same name. If your full name is Jeremy C. Bullwhistle III, don't write J. C. Bullwhistle or Jeremy Bullwhistle (without the C). Don't use Jerry, or your last name without the three Roman numerals after it. The reason for this is that you don't want inconsistencies appearing on the report. You could get tagged with the bad credit of Jerry Bullwhistle-the-Credit-Card-Maniac who lives 2000 kilometres away. You'd be amazed at how many folks commit that simple mistake, and wind up spending months or years fighting the credit agencies to prove they're the *real* Jeremy Bullwhistle III.

2. Always use your social insurance number. You've got the only one like it in the world. This will help you prevent your name from being confused with folks with the same name.

3. Always list your home addresses for the past five years. It will help you in the future if you move.

Protecting Yourself from Fraud

Canadians lose more than $200 million each year to credit card fraud artists. You can protect yourself by doing the following:

➤ Sign your new cards as soon as they arrive.

➤ Treat your cards like money. Keep them in a safe place.

➤ Shred anything with your account number on it before throwing it away.

➤ Don't give your card number over the phone unless you initiate the call.

➤ Don't write your card number on a postcard, or on the outside of an envelope.

➤ Remember to get your card and receipt immediately after every transaction, and double-check to be sure it's yours.

➤ If your billing statement is incorrect or your credit cards are lost or stolen, notify your card issuers at once.

Beware of "We'll Fix Your Credit" Operators

You may come across these bozos in classified ads or even on television. They offer to "fix your credit" by claiming to be able to remove any negative information from your credit report, "even if you have bad credit."

Forget those pitches. Otherwise you'll learn a painful lesson that could cost you hundreds or thousands of dollars. The truth is, those credit-repair clinics can't do anything for you that you can't do yourself, for free or at a minimum cost.

If the information in your report is correct, by law no one can remove it. You, yourself, can have inaccurate information removed at no charge. Credit agencies will supply you with a simple dispute form. It's easy to fill out and mail back.

Maintaining Good Credit

Follow a few simple rules to maintain a healthy credit rating:

➤ **Pay your bills on time** Almost all lenders will look at whether you're on time or late with your bills. Most lenders are lenient and will tolerate a maximum of 30 days late. If you are currently behind on your accounts, catch up before you apply. This is how you can make the grade to get credit: Fit the profile of the people who pay their bills on time.

➤ **Don't be too close to your credit limits** Typically, lenders will compare your credit card balances to the total amount of credit you have available. The more cards you have close to the limit, the more of a risk you are to lenders.

➤ **Cancel any credit cards that you don't use** If you already have five or six major credit cards (even if they have zero balances), you will have a tough time getting additional credit. Why? Because lenders will think that you already have more than enough.

➤ **Get a copy of your credit report and correct any errors on an annual basis** As many as 40 percent of all credit reports contain errors, so get out your red pen.

➤ **Find out how many inquiries there are on your credit report** The more inquiries there are, the less likely you are to get the credit you're seeking. For example, every time you apply for a credit card, an inquiry about your credit application is included in your credit report. If too many credit card companies inquire at once, they may be suspicious about your intentions.

Statistics show that people who have recently applied for a lot of credit are less likely to keep up with their payments on a timely basis. If you have five or more inquiries in the past six to eight months, wait a few months before you apply for credit again.

The Least You Need to Know

➤ Most of your financial information—your salary, bank accounts, credit cards and loan information—is stored in computers at the Equifax and Trans Union credit agencies.

➤ When deciding whether or not to approve you for a loan, lenders use items from your credit report to come up with a score that determines how big a credit risk you are. Employers may also use your credit report to verify employment history.

➤ To improve your credit report, pay your bills on time, cut down the number of credit cards you carry, don't live up to your credit limit, and pay off your outstanding debts.

➤ Review your credit report periodically to check it for mistakes. One in four credit files contains errors.

➤ Be sure to dispute any errors on your credit report by inserting up to 100 words on the report to explain your side of the story. Also, show your lender any copies of paid invoices and letters that document your position.

Chapter 10

Variations on a Mortgage

In This Chapter

➤ How home equity loans pay off high-rate bills

➤ Which type of loan is best for you

➤ Tricks and traps your banker won't tell you about

➤ How to figure the real cost of your loan

The ultimate financial goal of every homeowner is to build equity in the property. That simply means owning an increasingly larger portion of the place yourself, until it's all yours—free and clear. At that point, your equity has reached 100 percent.

When you first buy a home, the money you use as your down payment represents your initial equity in the property. The mortgage (along with any other loans you might have arranged to pay for the property) is your debt. Look at it this way: when you start out, you may only own the equivalent of one bedroom and the front driveway of the house. As you repay the principal of your mortgage, and the proportion of your debt to your equity declines, you gradually assume ownership of a bedroom, the kitchen, the living room, the deck, etc. As long as the home retains its value, you'll effectively own a little more of it each year.

Initially, it's a slow process, because most of your early mortgage payments consist of interest. But as time passes, interest charges decline and you repay principal more quickly. Your equity increases accordingly.

The amount of your equity also depends in part on the current real estate market. If property values fall, your equity in your home will also fall, although your mortgage remains the same. For example, suppose you made a down payment of $25 000 on a house worth $100 000. You have $25 000 worth of equity, and you're carrying a $75 000 mortgage. Times are bad, and the market value of the home falls to $95 000 at the end of the first year. During that time, you paid off $1000 of the principal, so your outstanding balance is now $74 000. But the value has fallen, so you end the year with equity of only $21 000 ($95 000–$74 000 in debt). Through no fault of your own, the equity in your home has actually dropped.

In extreme cases, your equity can disappear entirely, so that you owe more money than your property is worth. Even if you sold your home, you wouldn't recover enough from the sale to pay off your mortgage completely. In the meantime, you'd likely have difficulty renewing your mortgage unless you could add enough money of your own to restore the balance of debt to equity to a level acceptable to the lender.

There's Value in Your Home

As property values rise, the opposite happens: The proportion of your equity compared to your mortgage debt increases. In other words, if the value of your property rises over the term of your mortgage, your equity in the property increases, while your mortgage remains the same.

Let's go back to our previous example and assume the home's value rose to $105 000 at the end of the first year. Even though you paid only $1000 against the principal, your equity in the property has moved ahead to $31 000 ($105 000 – $74 000 debt). If you sold the property immediately, you could pay off the mortgage and have $31 000 left—a 24-percent gain on your initial $25 000 investment, in just one year. (Of course, you had interest expenses as well, so your net gain wouldn't be as much. But you get the idea.)

Of course, unlike a stock or bond, a home can't be easily exchanged for cash. Nor would many people readily sell their homes just to cash in the equity they've accumulated. As a result, individuals may have a high net worth, but hardly enough cash to pay their bills.

In recent years, financial institutions and other lenders have tried to address this predicament. They've developed mortgage-based programs that let homeowners take advantage of the equity in their homes and convert it to cash to meet their immediate financial needs. Governments have also developed plans that let homeowners pay their bills without jeopardizing their homes in the process.

There are other ways to cash in the equity in your home. In some cases, you can work with a purchaser to obtain cash for your equity while remaining in your home for a specified period after the sale.

Here are some of the options available to people who own their homes but require more cash flow to meet their financial needs.

Reverse Mortgages

In a reverse mortgage arrangement, you get cash in return for a mortgage on your home, which you use as security against the loan. The lender provides the cash through a line of credit, or in monthly payments, or in a lump sum—or a combination of any of these. There are no repayments against a reverse mortgage while you are alive.

When you die, your home is sold, and the proceeds are used to pay off the mortgage. This includes the original principal plus all the compound interest that has accumulated over the years since the contract was written. (Since there are no payments against the loan, the interest charges are tacked on to the principal and compounded each year.) Any money that remains goes into your estate. In the case of a married couple, the arrangement can be set up in such a way that the home is not sold until the last spouse dies.

If you decide to sell the property, you have to pay off the mortgage balance. The remaining proceeds are yours.

In the U.S., where these arrangements have become increasingly popular, some reverse mortgages provide monthly payments for life, no matter how long the homeowner lives. In fact, the total value of the monthly payments may eventually exceed the value of the mortgaged property. When the homeowner dies, the lender can recover the value of the home but can't seek the remaining amount from the homeowner's estate.

Most lenders will provide a reverse mortgage only to homeowners over a certain age. In fact, the advantages of a reverse mortgage depend to an extent on how long you live. The older you are, the more a lender will provide in the form of a reverse mortgage.

With this in mind, lenders provide loans corresponding in value to the homeowner's age. At the age of 65, for example, a borrower who owns a $300 000 house may obtain a reverse mortgage of around $50 000. At the age of 80, the same homeowner could obtain a reverse mortgage of more than $100 000.

How Reverse Mortgages Work

Under most reverse mortgage arrangements, you can use some of the money to buy an annuity, which then provides you with a fixed monthly income for life, and for the life of your spouse as well if you set up a joint and survivor annuity. The advantage of this kind of arrangement is that income from the annuity is effectively received tax-free.

The math is complicated, but the principle is simple: the reverse mortgage is treated as an investment loan (the annuity being the investment). So the imputed interest cost is tax-deductible. Since that cost is almost always more than the annuity payment (which is partially taxable), the net result is tax-free income.

Reverse mortgages are only available in certain parts of Canada at present, and only a few lenders offer them. However, it is likely they will become more popular as the baby boomers age and need more money to pay for their living expenses.

If you are interested in this type of plan, wait as long as possible before applying. The older you are, the greater the mortgage you will qualify for. Plus, your annuity payments will be higher as well.

It's also a good idea to have any reverse mortgage agreement carefully reviewed by a lawyer before proceeding. You need to be sure there are no clauses that could trigger a sale of your home before you're ready or could affect the income you're relying on.

Also, talk over your plans with your children before going ahead. The equity in your home will form a large portion of your estate. If you place a reverse mortgage on it, that part of the inheritance will be lost to your children and grandchildren. If you're in financial need, your children may prefer making regular payments to you themselves, in exchange for keeping the house unencumbered so it can pass to them at some time in the future.

Life Estate

In a life estate, a purchaser pays a reduced amount for your home in return for allowing you to live there rent-free for the rest of your life. When you die, the purchaser takes ownership of the home.

In the meantime, you maintain the home as if it were your own, paying all the bills and insuring it against damage. You can even move out and rent the property.

The reduction you make in the price of your house to obtain a life estate depends on your age, health, marital status, and any other factors that might affect your prospects for living to a ripe old age.

If you're contemplating such an arrangement with someone outside your family, be careful, however. There was a case in France recently of a man who died in his eighties after making this type of deal with an elderly woman many years before. She was in her 110s and still living in the home when he passed on. So he never was able to take title to the property.

Home Equity Loans

If you need cash, a home equity loan may provide a more convenient alternative to a mortgage on your house. A home equity loan comes in a variety of forms. You can arrange a line of credit, for example, secured by the equity in your house. You can also arrange a term loan against your equity.

In both cases, you'll have to go through most of the same steps and incur the same costs as if you were obtaining a regular mortgage. That's because your home equity becomes the security for the loan. However, you probably won't have to pay for a home inspection, a survey or an environmental inspection, all of which are included in the closing costs of a normal mortgage. The lender will certainly want a current appraisal, however.

The real advantage of this type of loan is flexibility. Let's look at a home equity personal line of credit (PLC), which is the most common way in which this type of arrangement is set up. A PLC gives you access to a large amount of ready cash, but, unlike a regular mortgage, you don't receive the money up-front. Instead, it works like a chequing account. You receive a chequebook that you can use to draw against your PLC. As you make use of the money, interest is charged, usually at prime rate or slightly higher. However, you pay interest only on the outstanding balance each month, not on the entire amount available through the PLC. You also have repayment flexibility. Some plans allow you to repay as little as the interest due each month. Others require a small repayment of principal as well. In all cases, you can make much larger payments at any time to reduce the principal, without penalty.

There is no amortization, and no term. The plan can run for as long as you own the property. You can draw an amount, repay it, and do it all over again. In most cases, you never have to reapply. The interest rate is based on the prime rate, which means it can fluctuate from month to month. However, it will always be highly competitive, making this one of the cheapest ways to tap into your home equity.

Some municipalities allow senior citizens to defer payment of property taxes so they can remain in their homes. When the individual sells the home or the individual's executors settle the estate, the municipality collects the deferred taxes plus interest.The deferred taxes constitute a loan, secured by the senior's equity in the home. This arrangement is available only in certain areas, so you should check with your local government offices to see if they have such a plan, and if you qualify.

Tax-Deductible Mortgage Interest

Under Canada's tax regulations, a taxpayer can't deduct the interest paid on a mortgage from taxable income. But in some cases, you can deduct your mortgage interest if you use the proceeds from the mortgage loan to buy Canadian securities such as stocks or bonds rather than property. You have to prove to Revenue Canada that you've used the mortgage funds to earn income rather than to pay for your home.

There are a number of ways to take advantage of this opportunity. If you've paid down your mortgage, for example, you can arrange a second mortgage to invest in stocks, bonds or other securities. Let's say you've prepaid $20 000 of your principal. You then borrow $20 000, secured by the equity in your house, at an interest rate of 8 percent. You invest the money in stocks, bonds or mutual funds and deduct the interest payments on the loan from your taxable income. In the first year, your interest payments would amount to $1600, which you can deduct.

You might also sell stocks, bonds or other securities that you currently own to pay down your mortgage, then borrow the same amount—secured by a mortgage on your home—to reinvest in the stocks, bonds and other securities that you sold. This enables you to deduct the interest payments from your taxable income. To gain Revenue Canada's approval, it helps if you let some time pass between the sale and reacquisition of the securities. To be sure that you execute this manoeuvre properly to comply with the government's tax regulations, you should get the advice of a financial adviser or a tax lawyer before you proceed.

You can also borrow money from your own self-directed RRSP, secured by a mortgage against your principal residence. Then you can invest the money in securities and deduct the interest on the loan from your taxable income.

All this manoeuvring comes at a cost. You have to pay for the mortgage, for administering your RRSP, and for legal and other costs. But in the long run, the money you save in lower taxes will probably compensate for the cost of arranging the mortgage.

If you use your reverse mortgage to buy an annuity, there's another benefit aside from your not paying tax on the income. The federal government has also agreed that the payments won't affect your ability to collect the guaranteed income supplement or other government payments geared to income.

Life estates are commonly used within families. Children might purchase their parents' home for a reduced amount, allowing the parents to remain in the house rent-free for the remainder of their lives. When their parents die, the house belongs to the children, not to their parents' estate.

If you use a home equity loan for business or investment purposes, the interest charges will be tax deductible in most cases. So keep a careful record of all your expenses and claim a deduction under "carrying charges" when you file your tax return. You don't have to send documentation of your investments, but have them available in the event that Revenue Canada asks for more information.

The Least You Need to Know

➤ As property values rise, the opposite happens: The proportion of your equity compared to your mortgage debt increases.

➤ In a reverse mortgage arrangement, you get cash in return for a mortgage on your home, which you use as security against the loan.

➤ Under most reverse mortgage arrangements, you can use some of the money to buy an annuity, which then provides you with a fixed monthly income for life, and for the life of your spouse as well if you set up a joint and survivor annuity.

➤ In a life estate, a purchaser pays a reduced amount for your home in return for allowing you to live there rent-free for the rest of your life.

➤ If you need cash, a home equity loan may provide a more convenient alternative to a mortgage on your house.

➤ Under Canada's tax regulations, a taxpayer can't deduct the interest paid on a mortgage from taxable income. But in some cases, you can deduct your mortgage interest if you use the proceeds from the mortgage loan to buy Canadian securities such as stocks or bonds rather than property.

Chapter 11

Financing a Car—Without Being Taken for a Ride

In This Chapter

➤ Avoid the biggest rip-offs of all

➤ Where's the cheapest financing?

➤ Buying vs. leasing

You'll probably buy many cars in your lifetime, but how much are you really paying? If you're like most consumers, you'll never learn the nervy, shocking back-room tactics used by car dealers to drive up the cost of your car. Their rip-off tricks run into the hundreds, beginning the moment you walk into the showroom. A dealer can trap you with overcharges on things you don't need, from undercoating to credit life insurance—and inflate your financing costs without you ever knowing it. Result: You can be scammed into paying thousands of extra dollars on that shiny new set of wheels.

The same goes for leasing a new auto instead of buying it. Although leasing today may appear to be the cheapest way to get behind the wheel, leasing is loaded with mathematical schemes that the average person doesn't understand. This chapter strips away the mystery surrounding buying a car versus leasing one, explains the key steps of shrewd buying, and points out how not to be taken for an expensive ride!

Knowing the Biggest Rip-Offs

When you go into a store to buy a television set or washing machine, the salesperson tells you the price and maybe the cost of an optional service contract. And that's about it, right? Not so with a new car. Auto dealers are the gimmick-and-add-on champions of all time. Besides the financing rip-offs, which we'll discuss a little later, the list includes the following:

A Web site called ToFindACar.com lists over 2000 used cars with their suggested prices.

You probably can't do much to avoid setup-and-prep charges, but this chapter does discuss other ways you can foil a dealer's attempts to add to the price. For one thing, the window sticker on most new cars shows a Manufacturer's Statement of Retail Price at the bottom. That's what the car maker has determined to be the optimum retail price for the options shown on the sticker. You won't be able to escape the delivery (freight) charge on the MSRP, but the dealer's charge for setup-and-prep is a tip that the dealer has that much room within which to discount the selling price. (You can always shop another dealer's window stickers for comparison.)

➤ Invoices and stickers that could have been created by somebody in the back room, not the manufacturer.

➤ An outrageous delivery charge. Shouldn't the cost of hauling the car from Detroit or Windsor be included in your price?

➤ The dealer's setup and preparation charge. What did they do besides a wash and vacuum? After all, the car didn't arrive in bits and pieces from the manufacturer, did it?

➤ A whole bunch of options—a power sun roof, for example, or power seats—all priced sky-high.

➤ Dealer maintenance, which you can buy more cheaply somewhere else.

➤ Extended warranty plans that they scare you into buying because Nick, the mechanic, does work at $70 an hour.

➤ Dealer interest rates that have been booted up higher than what you could get from a bank.

➤ Vehicle undercoating. Forget it. You don't need to spend the extra couple of hundred bucks. Do you think manufacturers are stupid enough to build new cars that rust out overnight?

➤ Credit life insurance. You're not required to buy it, and you shouldn't. Insurance experts have pointed out that of every $1 people spend on this scam, only 40 cents is paid out in the form of claims. Most people are already covered by life insurance policies or other assets if the borrower dies.

➤ Trade-ins. The dealer promises to lower your monthly payment if you trade in Old Betsy. But he's already figured how much it will cost him to spruce up the car and how much he can get for it at auction. He knows exactly how much money he has to play with to get your business. He'll take his cost of that old clunker out of your hide one way or another.

You don't need any of the rip-off extras that the salesperson will try to load on you. They only increase the debt you'll have to finance and boost the salesperson's commission. Even so, consider options carefully, and make your own decisions. You may wish to include certain attractive options if you plan to sell the car a few years later. Reason: Today many options—for example, power windows, cruise control and a cassette player—have become almost standard equipment that your future buyer will expect when she buys the car from you.

Used Cars: Buying Right and Selling Right

A new car depreciates the moment it's driven off the dealer's lot. The amount of depreciation can vary, but we've heard of as much as 20 to 30 percent in the first year.

When you finance a used car, expect to pay an interest rate of two to three percentage points above the rate you pay on a new car. If a new car costs 9.5 percent to finance, chances are a used car will cost 11.5 to 12.5 percent in the same town. (If your credit is bad, prepare to get hit with a rate that may be 18 percent or higher.)

How to Get Top Price When You Trade In or Sell a Used Car

Look at the vehicle you're trying to trade or sell. Ask yourself, "Would I buy this car if someone offered it to me?" If not, invest a few bucks at an auto detail shop, a complete car wash (including wax), and a mechanic if necessary. On many used autos, this couple of hundred dollars of investment could bring an extra $500 to $1000 in the selling price or trade-in value.

On a trade, the new car dealer is saying to himself, "Let's see, if I accept this clunker against the price I'm going to try to get from this customer on a new car, there's some fixin' I'm gonna have to do. Like new carpets, a couple of tires, wash and wax, maybe an engine tune-up and other stuff." The dealer figures he'll sell your slightly renovated car for, say, $5000 at an automobile auction; he offers you $4000 for Old Betsy. He spends $300 to get it in shape, and pockets the $700 difference.

The dealer may try to low-ball you by saying that it will cost him much more to get your car into ready-to-go condition. Don't believe it.

Now you know rule number one when you trade your car in on a new one: Do some preliminary shopping around before you let a dealer know that you have a used car to trade.

First try to negotiate a new-car price at a discount off the dealer's sticker price. Dealers tell us that this discounted price may be between $1000 and $1500 less than what the sticker price (MSRP) shows. (Don't expect a big discount if there is an industry shortage of a particular model. In that case, the discount will be less.)

Then, using the discounted price, ask the dealer how much he'll pay you for the car you'll trade in. This strategy will go over like a lead balloon with the dealer, but at least he'll know you're no idiot.

Stifle Those Emotions When You Go to Buy!

Follow these rules whenever you are buying a new or used vehicle:

You'll probably come out ahead if you negotiate the lowest possible price on a new car and sell your old car by yourself. Consider running a classified ad in the Used Cars section of your local newspaper, plus an inexpensive ad in *Auto Trader*, a small publication you'll see offered free at newsstands, supermarkets and other locations.

➤ Don't get excited about the vehicle. The salesperson can read you like a book. If she senses you're falling in love with that little two-seater with the stick shift and double carburetor, it's going to cost you.

➤ Don't be anxious to close the deal on the same day.

➤ Shop at least one other dealer who offers the same car. Dealers know from experience you're going to do this, and that's what will give you clout in negotiating the cheapest price.

➤ As mentioned before, start negotiating a discount off the sticker price right off the bat—before you reveal that you have a car to trade.

Getting the Best Financing

Competition in the new car market is so ferocious that many dealers earn more of their living from the finance charges than from the profit they make off their autos. This section explains how you can avoid the pitfalls and walk out with the best deal.

Avoid Dealer Financing

Want to save 1 to 2 percent on your loan right off the bat? Avoid dealer financing altogether. And don't even think about going to an independent finance company where the rates are even higher—unless, of course, your credit is so shot that there's no other way out.

Go to a bank or trust company and obtain a preapproved loan for the amount you plan to finance. Better yet, join a credit union if you're not already a member. CUs are big in car loans, and their interest rates always beat what banks charge.

When you walk into the dealer's showroom armed with a preapproved loan, you'll have enormous clout for two reasons. First, the dealer knows you're a red-hot, live prospect—and he won't let you out the door until he gives you his best deal. Second, he won't try to flim-flam you with his own financing (which is more costly), because you already have the cheapest one in your pocket. A nice position to be in.

Get a Simple Interest Loan

With a simple interest loan, you'll be paying interest only on the remaining amount of the loan. How come? As you make your payments month after month, you'll be steadily paring down what you still owe on that original $15 000. Say you make 10 monthly payments of $373. At 9-percent interest, your first payment of $373 is on the whole $15 000. Of the $373, $112 is interest and the other $261 reduces the principal you still owe to $14 739.

Simple interest loans are commonly offered by banks, whereas many finance companies will charge higher interest through front-end loans. If a finance company does offer a simple interest loan, it will probably be at higher interest rates than what you'd pay at a bank. If the applicant has a poor credit history, the rate could shoot up even higher.

After the tenth payment, you'll have whittled the principal down to $12 302. But your monthly payment will stay the same. Here's why: When the bank sets up your simple interest loan, it figures a flat amount of how much total interest you'll pay on the, say, $15 000 that you're borrowing. You can arrange your payments so that they'll still be $373 every month. That's easier for you, because you wouldn't want to start out with a gigantic payment and have it get smaller every month. You might not be able to afford the payment in the early months.

Example: On a four-year (48-month) loan, the total interest comes to $2917. Divide 48 payments into $2917 and you get a monthly interest payment of $61. The bank gets its $15 000 back, plus the $2917 interest. You can budget for a steady monthly payment figure.

What you should avoid is a "front-end installment loan." Unlike the simple interest example you just read, with the installment loan **you pay interest every month on the original $15 000 you borrowed**. In this case, your total interest cost would work out to $5400, or $2483 more than with the simple interest loan. Your monthly payment would be $425 instead of $373. Better that money goes into your pocket instead of the dealer's (or the bank's).

Other Financing Secrets

The following tips will help you stay focused on the bottom line of buying a car:

➤ **Don't slide into the low payment mentality**   This is where many folks never learn. Car dealers are no idiots. They know the average person is more concerned about being able to afford their monthly payments than they are about the total cost of the loan. So what do dealers—and banks—often do? Suggest you stretch the loan term to five years instead of three. They say it will "make it easier on you." Humbug. All lower monthly payments do is jack up your financing cost.

Here's an example: A $15 000 loan financed through a bank at 9 percent for three years comes to $477 a month, with a total cost of $2172. But over five years, though the monthly payment drops to $311, your loan cost jumps to $3683. Not much of a deal, eh?

➤ **Make as big a down payment as you can**   Generally, you'll be required to make a down payment of 10 to 20 percent when you buy a new car, although we've seen credit unions finance 100 percent of the price. Some banks will do that, too, but only on luxury models. Why a bigger down payment? Because the more you put down, the less interest you pay.

➤ **Be wary of manufacturer financing**   Boy, are they enticing—those car dealer ads with low-ball financing and the promise that you can drive the car home by five o'clock! Car manufacturers have captive finance companies to help their dealers wheel and deal. They desperately want your business, and they'll turn cartwheels to get it—including offering a super-low interest rate and same-day credit approval, even on Sundays.

However, this type of financing has several downsides. First, the low-ball rate may only apply to certain models, like that little convertible over there with the purple stripes and no trim. Other regular models may cost more to finance. Second, if you do get the dealer's low manufacturer rate, the dealer may take it out of your hide by charging you more for the car. Third, manufacturer financing is less apt to give you a simple interest loan.

➤ **Stay away from variable-rate loans**   Most car loan rates are fixed—that is, you're charged the same interest during the entire loan term. Some car financing rates are variable—meaning the rate can go up or down, depending on which direction all bank rates are going. If rates rise, your car loan rate could go up by as much as two to three percentage points in a year.

If that happens, the bank may make it easier for you by keeping your monthly payment the same—but stretching the term of your loan. Result: Your 48-month loan could turn into a 50-month loan. You wind up paying a higher finance cost.

➤ **Take advantage of car rebates**   If Bubba's Auto Showroom says the manufacturer has a special $1000 rebate offer, you may want to grab it—that is, if the rebate applies to the exact auto you want. Here's why: Say you're working with that same $15 000 example at 9-percent bank interest for four years. The loan payment is $373 per month. The total cost of the car is $17 917. On the other hand, if you take the $1000 rebate and apply it to your down payment, you'll reduce your monthly payment to $348. The total cost of the loan will be cut to $16 723.

➤ **Check whether you can pay off your loan early** Some lenders will let you do it, others won't. So before you sign for a loan, ask if you can prepay the loan without a penalty. Are there any extra fees or charges? If a prepay is okay, be sure to note on your payment cheques how much is going toward reducing the principal and how much is going toward the interest. This way you'll have proof if you're ever challenged by the dealer or the bank.

Some lenders have a complicated little gizmo built into the way they calculate your payments. It's called the Rule of 78s. It's complicated as heck, but it simply means that most of your early payments are going toward the interest, not the principal. In that case, you won't save very much by paying off the loan in advance.

Buy or Lease?

How popular has leasing gotten? Today, about one-quarter of new car deals are leases, up from three out of 100 a decade ago. And leasing will get bigger. Why?

There are several reasons. Auto prices have been going up: The average car cost about $20 000 last year versus about $12 000 a decade ago. It's now cheaper to get into a leased vehicle. Consumers also have less disposable income to play around with, and there's more competition for the dollars they do have.

Banks like home equity loans because they're protected by holding a lien on your house. This means that if you can't meet the payments, the bank could take your home, never mind the car.

Knowing that, dealers have learned how to gouge people with complicated lease agreements that only an accountant can understand. Leasing was no problem when big corporations did most of the leasing, but now Joe is the key customer—and he knows zip about the subject. This section will help you figure out whether leasing is for you—and how to get the best deal on a lease.

How a Lease Works

In a nutshell, leasing is just like buying a car except that you pay only a portion of the principal with your monthly payments. When the lease expires, you can do one of two things:

Dealers may talk you into a lease by using language that sounds like you're purchasing the car instead of leasing it. For example, one Detroit auto maker instructs its dealer sales staff to never use words like *lease*, *interest rate* or *residual* when they chat with you in a showroom. Instead, they're instructed to use words such as *buying*, *equity*, and *guaranteed future value*. And you have the option to *trade or sell* after a couple of years.

Some dealers figure the residual value in two or three years instead of four or five. That tips the scales in his favour. Why? Because a car can depreciate by 10 percent the moment you drive it home, and maybe by another 20 percent two or three years later. The younger the car, the higher the residual value. If you get a three-year lease and the dealer has figured the value after two years, you'll have to spend more than you should to buy the car when the lease expires.

➤ Walk away from the car and owe nothing. That's called a closed-end lease. It's the most popular type of lease.

➤ Consider buying the car. That's an open-end lease. Your monthly payments may be lower, but you could wind up on the short end of the stick, as you're about to find out.

At the beginning of the lease, the dealer has figured how much your car will probably be worth at the end of the lease, say, in three or four years. That's called the *residual*—what the dealer thinks the street price of the car might be at that time. When the lease is up, you can buy the car for the residual value, or *buyout price*.

Look at the Bottom Line

Let's say you're deciding between leasing or financing a $15 000 vehicle, but don't have the $3000 down payment (20 percent) to go the financing route. Under a lease, the dealer will typically want—up front—the first month's payment of, say, $250 plus $15 in taxes—and another $250 as a refundable security deposit. That makes a total cash deposit of $515. Assume the lease is for four years, and the residual value is $8000.

If you finance the car, you'll be borrowing $12 000 for four years after making your $3 000 down payment. Assume you pay federal and provincial taxes up front, and that your interest rate is 10 percent. Your monthly payment will be about $350. So far, the lease gets the nod. But how will your wallet really make out in the long run?

With the straight loan deal, in four years you'll own the car outright after paying a total of $4800 in interest, $2250 in taxes and $12 000 on the principal. Had you leased, you'd probably make a $240-per-month payment and could simply turn the car in after four years and say good-bye. You wouldn't own a dime's worth of the vehicle and would still need new wheels. To buy the leased car, you would have to pay the dealer the $8000 residual value.

But suppose the street value of the car has declined to only $6500? You'd be out the $1500 difference, because you could probably buy a similar car for $6500. It would be a good deal only if the residual value was less than the street price. In that case, you'd be foolish not to pay the residual value and keep the car. You could sell it at a profit and use the money as a down payment on another set of wheels.

The key to getting the best deal on a lease is to do your homework. Check out these sources before and after you lease:

➤ Using a search engine on the Internet, check the listings under used car guides.

➤ Check the site called www.cartrackers.com.

➤ Check the classified ads in your local paper to determine your car's value.

Don't Sign that Lease Until You've Read This

Before you sign any lease, go over these points as though your life depended on them:

➤ Lease for no more than three years. That's the most you want to get stuck with if something unforeseen happens.

➤ Dealers are pushing shorter and shorter leases, such as two years. One reason: Their warranties from manufacturers to cover any possible problems with cars may only be for that long.

➤ If you turn the car in before the lease expires, the dealer will sock you with an early termination charge of $250 to $500. Insist that the charge be calculated by the level yield method, which means the dealer only recovers his charges for services and depreciation—no more.

➤ Say you lose your job and can no longer make the payments. When you turn the car in, that's called voluntary early termination. You'll still be responsible for all remaining monthly payments, plus the pre-set residual value. In that case, the total due could be twice the value of the car!

➤ How many kilometres a year do you drive? If you've exceeded that estimated mileage when the lease ends, the dealer will hit you with an extra-cents-per-km. charge. Be honest up front. If they tack on a higher mileage cost at the beginning, it will probably be less than what you would be charged when the lease is up.

➤ A lease may require higher insurance limits. Insurance is your responsibility, not the dealer's.

➤ What does the dealer mean by "normal wear and tear"? If the car is dented and dinged all over, and the seat cushions are ripped and torn, it's going to cost you.

➤ You may have to keep documents to prove the car maintenance was done by a reputable outfit.

➤ Check all the fees and payments under the lease. You have a right to see them.

The Essential Guide to Buying and Selling a Car in Canada, by Kendrew Pape and Mel Wise, offers advice on how to get the deal that will suit your needs as well as your pocketbook. The book includes tips for striking the best deal and negotiating for extra options; the meaning of the fine print in leasing and financing; and other tips.

➤ Negotiate. Dealers can wheel and deal on leases just as on a sale.

The Least You Need to Know

➤ Just say "no" to vehicle undercoating, credit life insurance, extended warranties and other unnecessary charges the car salesperson will probably try to talk you into.

➤ When you negotiate a low price on a new car, get the dealer's discounted price before you mention that you have a trade-in.

➤ Whether you're trading in your old car or selling it yourself, spend a few bucks to get the vehicle into top cosmetic and mechanical shape. You'll make more money on the deal.

➤ Don't show any emotion when you inspect a new car, and do not close the deal the same day you visit the dealer's showroom.

➤ Always shop the same vehicle at more than one dealership.

➤ Get pre-approved for a loan through a bank or credit union before going to the dealer. Not only will you save money on interest rates by not financing through the dealer, you'll have more negotiating power because you have the money in hand.

➤ Other ways to save on finance costs include getting a simple interest loan, paying a higher down payment, and taking advantage of manufacturers' rebates.

➤ Leasing a car is not as simple as your dealer may lead you to believe. Make sure you're aware of all the terms of the lease and compare the lease to the cost of buying the car outright.

Chapter 12

Better Homes and Mortgages I: Taking the First Step

In This Chapter

➤ Do you really want to own a home?

➤ Buying blunders to avoid

➤ Reducing your real estate tax

➤ Understanding how lending works

➤ Understanding mortgages

➤ The importance of prepayment

It's May 1st and you're writing out the cheque to pay your rent, again. Exactly $950 down the tubes, and you can't even wallpaper the walls, change the colour of the carpeting or hang a chandelier. You've been living like this for three years, paying rent (on time, of course) on the first of every month. Where has it gotten you? Some $34 200 in the hole. Of course you need a place to live, but at one point or another in your life you're going to have to make a decision: whether to continue to rent or to buy your first home.

It's the Canadian dream: a place you can call your own, where you can hang as many chandeliers as you want and install green carpeting if you want. After all, it's your home and your decision! When most folks look to buy a home, what they really buy is the cozy Norman Rockwell idea of owning a home, which is what many real estate professionals use to hook potential homebuyers.

If you want to learn more about buying a home, check out *The Complete Idiot's Guide to Buying and Selling a Home*, by Bruce McDougall and Shelley O'Hara. It's packed with helpful information.

What some of these real estate pros won't come out and tell you about is all the headaches that go along with home ownership. It's more than just a leaky faucet or a broken air-conditioner that you are now responsible for. This chapter helps you determine whether or not you should buy a home, how to seal the deal, and how to arrange the best financing to pay for it all.

So You're Thinking of Taking the Plunge

Whether you buy or rent a home, the decision is based on more than just finances. It's also based on your expectations for your future lifestyle. Do you mind having to mow the grass every Saturday? Would you rather have the building engineer fix your stopped-up toilet? You are the only person who can answer those questions.

The Ups and Downs of Home Ownership

The major advantage to buying a home is the equity or ownership you build over time as you pay off your mortgage (as long as your home appreciates in value). If your home appreciates in value as a result of good maintenance and it's in a good location, congratulations. You have a chance of considerable appreciation over time.

Other advantages? If you sell your home, you don't have to pay a capital-gains tax on the profit. And you can borrow against the equity in your home if you need money.

But there are disadvantages, too. Because a home is considered an illiquid investment, you may not be able to sell your home if the real estate market takes a turn for the worse. Homeowners who have variable-rate mortgages risk higher mortgage payments if interest rates shoot up.

Also, some people may have difficulty affording the large chunk of money initially required to buy a home. It goes beyond the down payment; there are closing costs, mortgage application fees, and taxes to pay. And because people often sacrifice their entire lifestyle by sinking 40 to 50 percent of their income into home ownership costs, they tend to lead stressed lives.

When to Keep Renting

Renting does have some advantages over buying. For one, the extra money you save from not paying a down payment and home maintenance costs can be invested in stocks, bonds and mutual funds, which often rise in value faster than do house prices. Also, if your housing needs are constantly changing, either because of your career or family additions, renting doesn't lock you into the same long-term commitment as a home can.

Of course, renting also has a downside: no ownership, for one.

If you decide to continue renting, keep the following points in mind when choosing a place to live:

➤ Make sure you can afford the monthly rent *and* have money left over to invest, so that someday you can afford to buy a home with the money you've saved.

➤ Don't rent the first home or apartment you find. Do your homework. The more time you take to do your research, the more likely it is that you'll come across a better deal.

➤ Unlike an inspection you'll get before you buy a home, you have to do your own rental inspection. Make sure you check all the appliances from top to bottom. So what if the rental agent thinks you're goofy because you check the water pressure in the shower. You are the one who has to live there and get the thing fixed if it doesn't work.

If you decide to keep renting but someday want to own a home, consider waiting until the real estate market has bottomed out to try to get a good deal on a house.

If you like your rental home, you can always ask your landlord whether she would consider renting with option to buy. Rent-to-own agreements are gaining popularity, and the beauty of them is that you are not obligated to buy if you don't want to. If you do consider a rent-to-buy option, make the term as short as possible. If another prospective buyer comes along with ready cash, you won't be encumbered by a long-term contract.

Three Times, My Foot

People say that you typically spend about a third of your income on housing. Maybe that's true, but potential homebuyers often take that one step further and assume that they can afford a house that is three times their annual income.

Wrong! Why? You need to take into account your assessments and taxes and any other outstanding liabilities you have now. For example, a lender will ask you if you own a car. "Sure," you say. "But I have five more years' worth of payments on the car." The lender then says, "Then you don't really own the car—the bank does."

You must consider all your outstanding liabilities when determining how much you can afford to pay for a house. Otherwise, you'll inflate the true value of your buying power.

Figuring out how much you can afford to buy shouldn't be a long, involved process. Complete the following worksheet to determine what you can manage to buy.

A. Gross Annual Income: $_____
   (before taxes)

B. Gross Monthly Income: $_____
   (Line A divided by 12)

C. Monthly Allowable Housing Expense and Long-Term Obligation
   (Line B multiplied by .36): $_____

D. Monthly Allowable Housing Expense: $_____
   (Line C minus long-term obligations or Line B multiplied by .28, whichever is less)

E. Monthly Principal and Interest: $_____
   (Line D multiplied by .80; estimate since taxes and insurance will vary)

F. Estimated Mortgage Amount: $_____
   (Line E divided by the appropriate factor from the interest rate chart—see the table below—and multiplied by 1000)

G. Estimated Affordable Price Range: $_____
   (Line F divided by .80 or .90, depending on down payment)

When in doubt, check these out! Here's a list of figures you need to check at your real estate closing:

➤ The broker's commission

➤ Monthly payments

➤ A charge for loan fees that have already been paid

➤ A charge for utility bills that have already been paid

➤ A professional (such as a lawyer, contractor or appraiser) who has not yet been paid

Buying Blunders to Avoid

The following are common buyers' mistakes:

➤ **Keeping your real estate agent on board even if you don't like him**   If you don't like your agent, don't keep him. You're not obligated. If you're in the process of looking for a new home and your realtor just doesn't cut the mustard, make the switch.

➤ **Not getting prequalified**   Forget scouting the real estate section of your newspaper to see what you want to buy. Get prequalified first! Talk to a lender (a bank, credit union or mortgage broker) about all the costs involved. Although the worksheet on the previous page gives you a good start, a lender will help you determine not only what you can afford based on your income and debt obligations, but also what you can afford including taxes, condo association assessments, or private mortgage insurance—depending on what you're looking for and the amount of your down payment. The lender will provide a preauthorized loan, which lets you know exactly how much you can afford to pay.

➤ **Not shopping around for a lender**   Basically, you're buying money when you apply for a mortgage, right? Because you'll be giving this person the most intimate details of your financial life, you should find someone you're comfortable with and who will offer you a good deal.

➤ **Thinking that a large down payment will cancel out any previous blemishes on your credit report**   Wrong! In fact, a lender would rather choose someone with little to no money to put down and a squeaky-clean credit report than someone who has a 20-percent down payment and black marks up to his ears. The down payment for people with credit problems may be larger; it depends on the lender. Correct any erroneous information on your credit report and give explanations for the blemishes that you can't get rid of.

➤ **Getting emotionally involved if you miss an opportunity**   One real estate maven tells us that potential home buyers become so emotionally involved when they miss out on one deal that they often botch up the offer on the next home they want to buy.

➤ **Not doing your homework**   The best way to avoid this glitch is to get a printout of all similar homes in the potential area that have sold in the past six months. Your agent can give you such a list. The house you want should be selling in the same price range. If not, maybe the homeowner upgraded too much and the price is not justified.

Inspector Clouseau, I Presume

Anyone see the movie *The Money Pit* with Tom Hanks and Shelley Long? It's a home inspector's nightmare. Detecting problems is what a home inspector does. What you, as a potential homebuyer, hope for is that there aren't too many problems.

You should make a conditional offer on the property you want to buy. The condition: You won't proceed with the purchase until you have the property inspected and the inspector says the property's okay, or the seller corrects any defects.

Inspections usually cost around $250 to $500, and the buyer pays for the inspection to find out if anything's wrong. If you're feeling squeamish about taking your real estate agent's word for "this really good guy I know," you can find a professional inspector by contacting your province's association of home inspectors. Keep in mind that your realtor can recommend an inspector too, or just comparison shop using the *Yellow Pages*. You can get out of the contract if the inspector finds things wrong with the property, such as leaking plumbing or a malfunctioning furnace. (Or you could have the homeowner agree to fix the problems before you buy the house.)

Challenging the Tax Collector

If homeowners could have one wish, many of them would wish they didn't have to pay property taxes. These taxes can amount to thousands of dollars. You can't eliminate them altogether, but you do have an alternative. Challenge your assessments.

➤ Show that the property is overvalued or that your assessment is higher than that on comparable properties in your area. How? You can have your real estate agent pull up all the nearby listings on the Multiple Listing Service to compare properties. Do it before you make any necessary repairs to damage or deterioration on your property that have lowered its value.

➤ Check the tax records for a description of your property and income. Local tax records often show big boo-boos in overstating size or income.

➤ Figure out the ratio of the assessed value to the current market value. You may have to consult a real estate agent to help you compare this ratio with the average ratios of similar properties sold in your area recently.

Then take your case to your provincial tax court. You can find out more about this from your province's ministry of housing.

And Now...the Mortgage

Once the seller has accepted your offer, you have a piece of paper saying you're buying that property. Now you have to put your money on the line. For most of us, that means getting the financing in order.

How Lending Works

Banking is a business, just like any other, that involves buying and selling. What bankers and other lenders sell is money.

Here's one example of how it works: Your aunt Betty deposits $500 in her savings account, and the bank agrees to pay her 2-percent interest on her money. The bankers then take Aunt Betty's $500 and lend it to you. In exchange for letting you use the money, the bank charges you 7-percent interest.

The 7-percent interest rate covers the 2 percent that the bank has to pay Aunt Betty, the cost of moving the money around, and a profit for the bank. The difference between the savings interest and lending interest is called the *spread*.

When money is tight, more people want money, and rates go up. When money isn't tight, there's more money than there are borrowers, and rates go down.

Principal: The Big Kahuna

Unless you have enough money of your own to pay for a property, you'll have to borrow some money while using your own money as a down payment. The amount you borrow is called the *principal* of the mortgage. As you repay the loan over time, the amount of the principal declines.

Interest Rates, or What's the Charge?

If all lenders offered money to all buyers at the same rates and on the same terms, selecting a lender would be easy. But lending is a business, and lenders compete for your business by adjusting the terms of a loan. How much you pay for the loan, how often you pay, and over how long a period, can vary from one lender to the next.

Lenders differ in how much they charge you to use their money. This charge, called the interest rate, depends on the lender, the economy, the type of loan and other factors. The interest rate has a huge effect on how much you pay for an item.

If you borrow $100 000 at 7 percent for 25 years, your monthly payment will be $701. If you borrow the same amount of money for the same amount of time but at 10 percent, your payment increases to $895 a month. The difference is $194 a month.

Amortization: Everything You Need to Know in Three Sentences

The lender calculates your monthly payments based on the total length of time it will take to pay the mortgage in full. The customary amortization period is 25 years, but you can arrange for shorter amortization periods as well. The shorter the amortization period, the larger your payments—but the more you save on interest.

Over a 25-year amortization period, for example, a borrower would make 300 payments. Over a 10-year amortization, the borrower would make only 120 payments, but each payment would be much larger.

Term: If the Amortization Period Is the School Year, the Term Is One Semester

Mortgage lenders provide money for a certain period, ranging from six months to 10 years. This period is called the *term* of the mortgage. If you think interest rates will soon fall, you might want a short-term mortgage. If you think they're going to remain steady or go up, you might want a longer-term mortgage.

On a $100 000 mortgage, at 7-percent interest, amortized over 25 years, you'd make a monthly payment of $701. Amortized over 15 years, you'd pay $894 a month. But it would take you 10 years less to pay off your mortgage, and you'd save more than $20 000 over the entire amortization period.

The word **mortgage** is derived from the Latin word meaning "dead" (mortuum) and the Old Teutonic word meaning "pledge" (*wadjo*, which also provides the root for "wage"). Writing in the 17th century, the English jurist and legal scholar Lord Coke suggested that the word came into being because if the individual providing the pledge defaults on the mortgage, the property used to secure the mortgage "is taken from him forever" and so "becomes dead to him."

At the end of the term, the principal and interest on the mortgage come due. Unless Great Uncle Hughie dies and leaves you an oil well so you can pay off the mortgage, you'll likely renew it with the same lender or look around for another lender who can give you a better deal.

Types of Financing

Your mom and dad may live in the same house that you grew up in. They've been paying for the house for almost 25 years. They pay the same monthly payment now as they did in 1975, when they bought the house. (Their house payment is less than your car payment!) Back when they purchased their home, most people selected this type of financing, which is called fixed-rate financing. Most people expected to stay in their homes for 25 years and wanted the stability of fixed payments.

Times have changed! First, people don't stay in the same spot so long and, second, lenders have become more creative with the financing they offer. Now you can shop around for different types of loans.

Mortgage loans vary depending on who offers the loan and how it's backed. The two most common types of loans are conventional and government-assisted. You can get your loans from Bill Banker or from Bill Banker with Ottawa backing you. Loans also vary depending on how the payments are structured. The two most common structures are fixed-rate mortgages and variable-rate mortgages.

A mortgage actually consists of two legal documents: The note specifies the amount of the loan, the repayment terms and other conditions of the agreement; the mortgage itself gives the lender claim to the property if the borrower defaults.

Conventional Loans

We're not sure where the term "conventional" originated. Perhaps this term got tagged on this type of loan because most conventional loans are made by bankers, and bankers are known to be conservative, traditional—yes, even conventional. Think blue suits, white shirts, boring ties.

Conventional loans are secured from a lender, usually a bank or trust company. Conventional loans require a down payment of at least 25 percent of the price of the home. The value is determined by an appraisal or by the purchase price, whichever is less.

High-Ratio/Insured Mortgages

If you can't scrape together 25 percent of the cost of the home, you might still qualify for a high-ratio mortgage, insured by the Canada Mortgage and Housing Corporation (CMHC), a crown corporation, or the Mortgage Insurance Company of Canada, a private company. You can obtain up to 95 percent of the purchase price, depending on the price of the house, whether you've bought another home within the last five years and other conditions.

The insurance protects lenders. It enables them to lend money to people who might not qualify for a mortgage under ordinary circumstances. To obtain a conventional uninsured mortgage, for example, a borrower needs enough money for a down payment of 25 percent or more of the value of a property. Some people don't have that much cash available. By applying for an insured mortgage, they can still buy a home. The borrower's happy; the lender's happy; and everyone wins.

Depending on the amount of personal money you use for a down payment, you'll have to pay an application fee of $75 to $235 and a premium of 0.50–2.50 percent of your loan to obtain a CMHC-insured mortgage.

Vendor-Take-Back Mortgages

Sometimes vendors will offer to help potential purchasers who want to buy a property by lending them a portion of the purchase price. Called a vendor-take-back (VTB) mortgage or purchase mortgage, such a loan often comes with favorable or flexible terms, depending on the inclinations of the individual vendor. The loan may be open, for example, which means you can repay the loan at any time, without penalty. The vendor may charge an interest rate lower than the prevailing market rate. Or the vendor may negotiate with you about the term of the loan.

By obtaining a VTB mortgage, you can avoid a lot of red tape and administrative charges. You don't have to sit in a bank, waiting for a loans officer to look you over and examine your credentials before approving your mortgage. You can sit down with another person at the kitchen table and work out the specific details of your loan, without waiting for approval from a higher authority.

Open and Closed Mortgages

With a fully open mortgage, you can pay off all or part of your mortgage at any time during the term of the loan, without penalty. In return for this privilege, you'll

If your mortgage agreement doesn't specify the penalty you incur if you prepay the entire amount before it comes due, you could have a problem if you sell your home in the meantime. You might have to pay a penalty of three months' interest or more. In some cases, the lender may not let you prepay the mortgage at all. So you could sell your house and still have a mortgage to pay.

probably incur a slightly higher interest rate. If you have a fully open mortgage and interest rates fall below the rate that you're currently paying, you can refinance at a lower rate, without penalty.

During the 1980s and early 1990s, interest rates fluctuated drastically. As a result, most lenders stopped offering open mortgages, because they wanted to maintain some stability and predictability within their own loan portfolios. With interest rates stabilizing, however, a few lenders have started offering two-year or three-year open mortgages. Many more offer open mortgages for very short terms of six months or less.

Some lenders offer partially open mortgages that allow you to repay a portion of the mortgage without penalty. Others will negotiate a prepayment penalty in advance, so you'll know, for example, that you have to pay an additional three months' interest if you prepay your mortgage.

A closed mortgage restricts the borrower from refinancing, repaying or making other changes to a mortgage agreement over the full term of the loan. Even if interest rates fall below the rate of the loan, the borrower must continue to repay the mortgage at the higher rate until the mortgage comes up for renewal. If you sell your property and can't transfer the mortgage, you'll have to negotiate with the lender and hope you can repay the mortgage at all.

To pay off a closed mortgage, you'll almost certainly have to pay a penalty. The penalty usually amounts to three months' of payments, but the lender can charge more or refuse to let you pay off the mortgage at all.

Some mortgage agreements allow you to prepay a certain percentage of your mortgage, but not the entire mortgage. Under the terms of some mortgages, you can pay off the balance only after you've repaid a specified proportion of the principal. Others allow you to pay off a percentage of the total loan, once a year, but not the remaining balance.

You should make sure that your agreement covers both portions. If it allows you to repay 10 percent or 15 percent a year prematurely and without penalty, for example, what penalty will you incur if you prepay the remainder? Don't neglect this portion of the agreement until you need it. By then, it will be too late to negotiate.

Fixed vs. Floating Rates

With a fixed rate, the interest rate that you pay on your mortgage remains stable over the entire term of the mortgage. A floating rate fluctuates according to the prevailing interest rate set by the Bank of Canada.

Individuals who think mortgage rates might drop usually choose a floating rate; others who think interest rates might rise select a fixed rate, which protects them from the impact of rising interest rates. But certainty comes with a price: A fixed-rate mortgage usually carries a higher interest rate than does a floating-rate mortgage.

Variable-Rate Mortgages

With a variable-rate mortgage, you pay interest at the prevailing rate each month, although you make a fixed monthly payment over the term of the agreement. This means that the proportion of principal and interest changes from one payment to the next. Your monthly interest is calculated according to the prime rate. If interest rates go up, your payments remain the same, but the additional interest is added to your total debt. If interest rates go down, your payments remain the same, but the amount that goes toward the principal increases.

You can pay off all or some of a variable-rate mortgage at any time, usually without penalty, or convert it to a fixed-rate mortgage at any time.

Portability

Some mortgage lenders allow you to take your mortgage with you if you buy a new home before the mortgage's term expires. This can save you money in several ways: First, you avoid a penalty for paying off your current mortgage prematurely. Second, you avoid paying any fees involved in discharging the mortgage. Third you avoid many of the costs involved in obtaining a new mortgage.

If your new home requires a larger mortgage, you can add the required amount to the existing mortgage and blend the interest rates to determine your total monthly payment.

If you have a fixed-rate loan, you may not be stuck with that loan for the rest of your life. You can refinance the loan to get a better interest rate. Generally, it's a good idea to refinance if interest rates drop by 2 percent or more. You'll probably have to pay a penalty if you refinance before the term of your mortgage ends. But calculate the costs to see how long you must have the new loan to break even on the cost of refinancing.

An **index** is a known benchmark used by a lender to set its mortgage rate on a variable-rate (as opposed to a fixed-rate) loan. The lender adjusts the homeowner's rate when the index goes up or down. When the index rises, the interest rate increases; when the index declines, the rate is adjusted downward.

115

A uniquely Canadian concept, a **convertible mortgage** usually carries the lowest interest rate of any available mortgage. You pay interest at a fixed rate over a short term of no more than six months. As with a variable rate mortgage, you can convert the mortgage at no cost to a longer, closed, fixed-term mortgage at any time.

With a convertible mortgage, your repayments are applied to principal and interest in equal proportions over the entire term, even if interest rates fluctuate.

Prepayment

The faster you can pay off the balance of the principal, the less interest you'll pay over the course of the mortgage. In the early years of the mortgage, your payments consist primarily of interest. To reduce the size of the principal, especially during these years, you have to make additional payments.

Few lenders will provide a fully open mortgage, but most will allow you to make partial repayments of the principal, usually once a year; by making two payments of equal amounts in the same month; or by increasing the frequency of your payments—to biweekly from monthly, for example.

Increased Payments

Some lenders allow you to increase the size of your monthly payments at any time during the term of the mortgage, by a certain percentage. This is similar to making an annual lump-sum payment, except that you spread the payments over 12 months. The additional amount goes toward the principal of your mortgage, which considerably reduces the amount of interest you pay over the life of the mortgage. You should make sure this privilege is described in writing in your mortgage agreement.

Do You Qualify?

Institutional lenders such as banks, insurance companies and trust companies will usually lend up to 75 percent of the appraised value of a home in the form of a conventional first mortgage. In most cases, your Gross Debt Service (GDS) Ratio—your monthly payments on a conventional first mortgage, plus property taxes and heating costs— can't exceed about one-third of your total monthly income. Your Total Debt Service (TDS) Ratio—your GDS plus payments on all other debts—can't exceed about 40 percent of your total monthly income.

If you're applying for a government-insured loan, you'll need a down payment of 10 percent of the home's appraised value. (Qualified first-time buyers need only 5 percent.) Under Canada Mortgage and Housing Corporation (CMHC) guidelines, you can't devote more than 32 percent of your gross household income toward the payment of the mortgage principal plus interest, property taxes, heat and 50 percent of condo fees, if applicable. Nor can you commit more than 40 percent of your total household income to your total debt repayment—including mortgage principal, interest, property taxes, heat, plus 50 percent of condo fees if applicable, plus payment on all other debts such as credit cards, car loans and leases.

Optimal Size of Mortgage

Most lenders will provide a mortgage, the monthly payments for which—including principal, interest, taxes and heat—require no more than one-third of your total income. Within this limit, the size of the mortgage you negotiate will depend on your current and future income, your credit rating, your tolerance for debt, and your outlook on the property market.

If you think you'll earn an increasing amount of money every year, then the size of your mortgage will fall in proportion to your total income. Presumably, this will make it less onerous to repay your mortgage as time passes. A large mortgage today may not seem so large in three or four years, as your income increases.

Some people simply don't like owing money to other people. They like to stay free of obligations, financial or otherwise. The larger their debt, the greater their discomfort. If you're one of them, a small mortgage makes sense. Likewise, if you feel unsure about your job and your income, you may choose a smaller mortgage to reduce your anxiety if the worst happens.

If you expect property values to fall, however, you may think twice about borrowing a

When interest rates are low, you might consider borrowing as much money as you can to buy a house. That way, you'll get the highest return on your investment. In fact, you should never pay cash for a house, but use borrowed money instead, even if the cash is available. Here's why:

If you pay $200 000 in cash to buy a house, and property values rise by 5 percent a year, your property will appreciate by 50 percent in 10 years. It will be worth $300 000, and your equity will have increased by $100 000.

That may sound attractive, but you could have increased your equity even further by borrowing money to buy a bigger house. If you'd taken your $200 000, borrowed another $300 000, and bought a house worth $500 000, whose value appreciates at 5 percent a year, in 10 years it would be worth $750 000. Your equity would increase by $250 000. By borrowing money, you'd have $150 000 more than you'd have if you'd paid cash.

lot of money to buy a property. As we've mentioned, the farther the value of your property falls, the greater the proportion of your debt to your equity.

Don't Forget the Hidden Costs

As part of your application for a mortgage, you commit to pay the lender's costs of preparing and registering the mortgage. These costs include application fees, appraisal costs, legal fees and disbursements. Your lender will provide details of these costs when you apply for the mortgage.

Most of these costs can be incorporated into the loan, so that you don't have to make any unanticipated payments when you acquire the property. Of course, that just makes them less apparent; it doesn't make them less painful to pay.

➤ **Appraisal fee**   Appraisal fees range from $150 to $500. Lenders don't usually provide a copy of the appraisal to the borrower, but you should ask anyway.

In some cases, a seller may commission a professional appraiser to evaluate the property before putting it on the market. If the lender will accept the appraisal, you may avoid the cost of obtaining another one.

➤ **Survey fee**   A survey should cost $150 to $400. Lenders want a survey to confirm that the property you've used as collateral for your mortgage complies with all relevant by-laws, that new additions don't extend beyond the boundaries of the property, or that a neighbour won't dispute those boundaries. In some cases, a lender will accept a survey provided by the seller of the property, if it's up to date. In other cases, you'll have to arrange for the survey, either yourself or through your lawyer.

➤ **Mortgage insurance**   If you obtain a high-ratio mortgage, you'll have to pay about 0.5 percent to 2.5 percent of the total amount for mortgage insurance provided by the Canada Mortgage and Housing Corporation or the Mortgage Insurance Corporation of Canada. This guarantees the lender that the loan will be repaid even if you default. The premium is usually added proportionately to your monthly mortgage payment.

➤ **Mortgage life insurance**   Lenders often provide optional mortgage life insurance. If you die, your mortgage will be paid off. As an alternative, you might choose to obtain term life insurance that pays a lump sum in the event of your death equivalent to the size of your mortgage. Mortgage life insurance covers the remaining principal and interest outstanding on your mortgage and declines as you pay down your mortgage. For about the same amount, you can obtain a term life policy that pays an amount equivalent to the original mortgage, even if you've paid off most of your mortgage before you die.

➤ **Fire insurance**   Lenders require coverage of a mortgaged property against fire and damage. The policy must cover the replacement cost of the property and specify that the lender of the first mortgage has first rights to the proceeds of the policy. The mortgage lender will require proof of insurance before you receive any funds under the mortgage.

➤ **Provincial fees**   Most provinces require a fee for registering a mortgage and for transferring title of the property. These fees will usually appear on your lawyer's bill, and can amount to $100 or more.

➤ **Land Transfer Tax**   While it has nothing to do with your mortgage, provinces apply a tax to property transactions called a land transfer tax. It's usually calculated as a percentage of the total cost of the property. In Ontario, for example, you'll pay 1 percent of the first $100 000, up to 4 percent of any amount over $400 000.

> Some lenders suggest strongly that a borrower use the lender's lawyer to execute the transaction. But it usually works to your advantage to use your own lawyer, and you should dig in your heels if the lender tries to talk you out of the idea.

➤ **Legal fees**   Lawyers charge a fee equivalent to about 1 1/4 percent of the price of an average house. They usually deduct their fees for preparing and filing mortgage documents directly from the mortgage loan.

➤ **Goods and Services Tax**   You'll have to pay GST on your lawyer's services and on any other services involved in obtaining a mortgage. You also have to pay GST on a new house or condominium, but not on a resale property. If you live in the property, and you pay no more than $350 000 for it, you're eligible for a rebate. This will ultimately reduce the GST you pay to 4 percent of the total value. Ask your lawyer about the procedures involved in obtaining this rebate.

The Least You Need to Know

➤ Buying a house can be a good investment. But if you don't have a nice chunk of cash available up front and aren't willing to devote a lot of time and money to upkeep, you may want to continue renting for a while.

➤ Avoid common buying blunders by getting prequalified for a loan, not letting your agent boss you around, and doing your homework.

➤ Once you find a house you like, make sure you have it inspected before you commit to buying it.

➤ There are a number of factors, from fixed and floating rates to prepayment options, that affect the size of your monthly payments and the total amount you pay for your mortgage.

Chapter 13

Better Homes and Mortgages II: Making Decisions about Financing

> **In This Chapter**
>
> ➤ How much can you afford?
>
> ➤ How to find a lender
>
> ➤ How a lender looks at you
>
> ➤ What happens if you're rejected?

When you approach a lender for a mortgage, you should be prepared to answer some probing questions about your personal finances. The lender will look at your income, your savings, your debts and your future earnings—among other things—as well as the property you intend to buy, to determine if you can really afford it. And, as you'll find in this chapter, if you get turned down by a lender, you can take a few steps to make sure you're approved next time.

How to Decide on the Type of Financing

Deciding on the type of loan you take depends on several factors, including your current financial situation and your future plans.

How Much Can You Afford for a Down Payment?

Money, as usual, is the first consideration. If you have piles and piles of money sitting in your closet, you can pick and choose among the different lending options. If you're like most people, though, you probably have just a dinky little pile, and it affects the type of loan you can get.

For example, conventional loans require a 25-percent down payment. If you can't come up with that amount, you have to consider a different type.

If you can afford a higher rate with higher monthly payments, some lenders may offer you a no-points deal.

How Much Can You Afford for a Monthly Payment?

You can adjust your monthly payments by selecting a loan with a lower interest rate or longer amortization, or by putting more money down. By selecting a loan type with the lowest initial interest rate, you may qualify for the house.

For example, suppose that you can pay no more than $700 a month. This amount includes principal, interest taxes and insurance. A fixed-rate loan at 8 percent may require monthly payments of $733. You won't qualify for this type of loan.

On the other hand, if there's a variable-rate mortgage available at 6 percent, the monthly payment for principal and interest is $600. You could qualify.

The way the math works out, the higher the interest rate, the greater the amount of your early payments that goes toward interest. Conversely, the lower the interest rate, the less the amount of early payments that goes toward interest.

Condominium Mortgages

The purchaser of a condominium unit receives legal title to the unit as well as an undivided interest in the common areas of the development. An undivided interest gives a purchaser the legal right to sell his share of the common area without the consent of the other purchasers.

The first mortgage registered against the entire condominium project is a blanket mortgage. As we discussed earlier in this chapter, that means the mortgage is registered over the entire property. The blanket mortgage is placed on the project by the developer, who uses the funds from the mortgage to build the project. As the developer sells individual units, the mortgagor discharges the mortgage off the individual units. Meanwhile, the purchaser places a condominium mortgage on his title, if required.

The condominium mortgage resembles a conventional mortgage, with a few additional details. These include the following:

➤ a clause giving the lender the right to use the borrower's vote in the condominium corporation. The corporation operates and manages the development. Theoretically, the lender could participate in all meetings of the corporation and vote on all decisions. In practice, this seldom happens.

➤ a clause allowing the lender to pay the common area costs of the condominium if the borrower fails to pay them. The lender then adds these costs to the principal amount of the mortgage, which is repaid with interest.

➤ a clause giving the lender the right to demand that the borrower comply with all the terms of the condominium by-laws. By breaching any of the by-laws, the borrower also defaults on the mortgage.

A Weighty Decision

Here the decision being weighed is the type of mortgage that's best for you. None at all would be best. But most of us don't have that option.

Pluses

A fixed-rate mortgage gives you the benefit of knowing your exact payment for the term of the loan. What you pay on a 10-year loan in 1994 will be the same amount you pay in 2004. To some buyers, the financial security of having a set payment greatly outweighs any savings they might gain from getting another type of mortgage.

Fixed-rate mortgages are especially sensible when interest rates are low. Why take the chance of playing "spin the interest rate" when you can lock into a favorable rate now? If you plan to stay in your home for a long time, a fixed rate becomes even more desirable.

Finally, keep in mind that if your income is likely to rise, the burden of making payments will not be so great. While you're making twice the money, your house payments will still be the same as they were three years ago. That's a plus. And if your income is likely to decrease or remain steady (for instance, if you're retiring) a fixed-rate mortgage might also be the best bet. Your payments will be the same, so you can plan accordingly.

Minuses

When interest rates are high, the picture changes. In this case, the rates for a fixed-rate mortgage may be so high that you can't qualify for a fixed-rate loan. Also, why lock into a higher rate for the life of the loan? Instead, consider a variable-rate mortgage, which is usually offered at a lower rate. If interest rates rise, you can convert the mortgage to a fixed rate, usually for a fee.

Is the Shorter Amortization Better?

Some real estate professionals advise buyers to take a 15-year rather than a 25-year amortization. You end up saving a considerable sum if you stay in the home for a long period.

123

You don't save much money by locking into a long-term mortgage, even when interest rates are rising. Economist Peter Norman compared homeowners who obtained a mortgage in January 1987, when interest rates reached their lowest point in several years. On a mortgage of $122 700, the borrower who chose a five-year term at 10.75 percent ended up paying $52 216 in principal and interest. The borrower who chose five one-year terms, at interest rates of 9.5 percent, 10.25 percent, 12.13 percent, 12.65 percent and 12.2 percent, paid $52 321, a difference of only $105 over five years. In the meantime, the borrower with the shorter terms could take full advantage of all available prepayment options.

During other periods, when interest rates were more volatile and did not rise or fall steadily, according to Norman's analysis, short-term borrowers saved as much as $28 000 by choosing a one-year term and renewing annually over five years, compared to borrowers who locked into a five-year mortgage. When interest rates are low, Norman explains, more of your payment goes toward the principal.

Other experts disagree. These experts say that you may not want to tie up your money for housing expenses. You can always make double payments on the 25-year loan, but if you find yourself in a financial bind, you're not locked in to these higher payments.

Or you can put the extra money in a savings account or mutual fund that earns more money than your mortgage rate. This leaves the money readily available in case of an emergency.

Whether or not to go with a shorter amortization is up to you. If you can't afford or qualify for the higher payments of a 15-year loan, you should consider a 20- or 25-year loan. You'll still get to decide, though, how often you'd like to make those payments.

Biweekly payments can save you a lot of money, but they may also be more of a headache. You have to make twice as many payments, and some lenders charge a handling fee for this type of mortgage.

Go Short

A short-term mortgage makes sense, especially if it's closed, because it gives you a chance to make a large repayment, when the term expires, without incurring a penalty. If you anticipate a large inheritance or a windfall from another source, you should choose a short-term mortgage, unless a lender will agree to an open mortgage.

Prepaying Your Mortgage

When you're shopping around for a mortgage, inquire whether you can prepay the mortgage without penalty. Why prepay? Remember that the lenders want their money first, so most of your money in the first few years of the loan goes toward interest.

On a $115 000 loan at 8 percent, for example, you pay around $10 000 in monthly payments in the first year, but less than $1000 of that goes toward the principal. After one year, you still owe $114 000.

Here's where prepaying can be beneficial. When you prepay, the money goes directly to the principal. If you have an extra $1000 after paying your monthly bills (yeah, right), you can pay that $1000 toward the mortgage. That money goes directly toward the principal.

Again, financial experts disagree on whether prepaying the mortgage is beneficial or not. It does reduce the amount of money you pay for the home. You'll pay off the home more quickly if you prepay.

Critics of prepaying argue that you can put extra money to better use. For example, if you prepay that $1000, you get no tax benefit. If you put that money into a registered retirement plan, you'll get a tax break. If you put the money into a savings account, you'll have access to it if you need it. If your mortgage rate is 7 percent, and you invest in a mutual fund paying 10 percent, you can make 3 percent on your money rather than paying off your mortgage.

Keep in mind that prepaying does not reduce your monthly payment obligations. You can't tell the lender that you paid an extra $1000 last year, so this year you are going to skip the first few payments. You *must* still make the regular payments.

It's a good idea to pay for your house and pay off your mortgage as quickly as you can. In this way, you pay as little interest as possible. That means you should take advantage of opportunities to make double-up payments and annual lump-sum payments.

Assumable Mortgages

Certain mortgages are *assumable*, which means the buyer can just assume the responsibilities of the seller's mortgage. The buyer doesn't have to pay for obtaining a new mortgage and, if the mortgage has a lower-than-market or reasonable interest rate, the buyer can save a lot of money on interest.

For example, suppose that a seller has a 7-percent fixed-rate mortgage and has a buyer that is interested in assuming the payments on this loan. If the loan is freely assumable, the buyer can save the costs of applying for a loan and other associated costs. (The buyer usually must get the lender's approval for the loan.)

The buyer assumes payment on the existing mortgage and pays the difference between the mortgage balance and the selling price. For example, if the seller sold the home for $100 000 and still owed $80 000, the buyer would assume the $80 000 mortgage and pay the seller $20 000. You can see that even if you don't have the expense of closing on a loan, you may still have to come up with a considerable sum of cash. In this example, to raise the additional $20 000, the buyer could obtain a mortgage from the same lender, who would blend the rates and terms together with the assumable mortgage.

You may not want to assume a mortgage, but you'll want to ask whether the mortgage you're securing is assumable. An assumable mortgage may be more attractive to buyers when you sell your home.

Selecting a Lender

A lot of buyers are so grateful that someone is willing to lend them the money to buy a home that they don't realize they should shop around for a lender. Don't forget, you're a customer. You're giving the lender your business, and you should be sure to select the lender that offers you the best deal and best service. The mortgage process can make or break a transaction.

Who's Got the Money?

It can get confusing when you apply for a loan. There are so many lenders to choose from. A mortgage broker may interview you, then submit your application to another lender. Or your local bank branch may provide you with a loan. Here are some common sources of loans:

➤ Commercial banks

➤ Trust companies

➤ Credit unions

➤ Insurance companies

➤ Canada Mortgage and Housing Corporation (CMHC)

➤ Vendor take-back

➤ Personal sources

➤ Mortgage brokers

Mortgage Brokers

A mortgage broker is an intermediary who matches the particular needs of a borrower with the specific criteria of a lender. There are more than 2500 of them in Canada, primarily in B.C., Alberta, Ontario and Quebec.

In addition to dealing with conventional lenders such as banks, trust companies and insurance companies, mortgage brokers also have access to sources of funds that aren't always apparent to the individual borrower, such as pension funds, private lenders, foreign banks and syndicates of investors who regard mortgages as a secure form of investment.

In the past, borrowers used the services of a mortgage broker if they had problems finding a lender on their own. More recently, however, individuals have started to rely on mortgage brokers to intermediate on their behalf, just as home buyers rely on real estate agents to help them buy and sell property. A qualified mortgage broker can negotiate more effectively than can the average loan applicant— especially a first-time home buyer—who doesn't spend every day keeping track of all the bells and whistles that mortgage lenders use to attract customers, and who may not have much experience in evaluating mortgage programs.

Doing business at a bank where you have a chequing account or another loan can be an advantage. Why? You may be able to apply at the same branch where people already know you. Plus, because you have the other accounts, the bank may discount your mortgage rate by (say) one-quarter of a percentage point if you agree to have your monthly payments debited automatically from chequing.

Before the borrower signs the mortgage papers, a broker must disclose in writing all the fees, costs and deductions associated with the loan. For conventional mortgages, brokers do not charge the borrower a fee. Instead, they receive their payment from the lender. For borrowers who may not qualify for a conventional mortgage, however, a broker charges a fee of 1 percent to 2 percent of the mortgage itself. The broker usually collects the fee only after finding an acceptable mortgage.

Mortgages on the Internet

Canada's major banks all operate Web sites on the Internet that answer questions about mortgages, calculate mortgage payments according to several variables such as amortization, interest rate and frequency of payment, and determine the maximum loan for which you can qualify. The Canada Mortgage and Housing Corporation also operates a Web site describing CMHC's products, including its mortgage loan insurance programs (www.cmhc-schl.gc.ca).

In February 1997, CIBC (www.cibc.com) and Bank of Montreal (www.bmo.ca/mortgage) posted online mortgage applications on their Web sites that enable potential borrowers to apply for mortgage approval over the Internet. Borrowers can complete a mortgage application in about 45 minutes, then send it to the bank by e-mail or fax and receive a response within two days. Or they can take it in person to the nearest bank branch and get an immediate response. Royal Bank now provides a similar service (www.royalbank.com).

Through another Web site operated by a national mortgage brokerage called The Mortgage Centre (www.mortgagecentre.com), you can submit your mortgage application to the Mortgage Market and receive bids for your evaluation from major banks, trust companies and life insurance companies.

In March 1997, Royal LePage Ltd. set up a similar service that lets a customer shop for a mortgage through the company's electronic network. The customer has to go to a Royal LePage office. By telephone or video teleconferencing system, the customer provides relevant information to a Royal LePage mortgage specialist. Within four hours, the customer can choose from the nine lending institutions that bid on the mortgage.

The nine lenders are as follows:

1. The Associates—Ford Motor Credit (USA)

2. Beneficial Canada

3. CIBC Mortgage Corporation

4. Cooperative Trust—a collection of credit unions across Canada

5. First Line Trust—CIBC

6. M.R.S. Trust—Mackenzie group of funds

7. Mutual Group—Mutual Life of Canada

8. National Bank of Canada

9. Sun Life Trust—Sun Life Insurance

Meanwhile, through Online Mortgage Explorer Inc. (www.themortgage.com), you can fill in an electronic form, answer about 20 questions and find out if you qualify for a mortgage from the Mutual Group, a group of 18 companies that offer financial services in Canada and the U.S.

New mortgage-related Web sites seem to be appearing almost daily. You can locate them through Yahoo Canada (www.yahoo.ca) or another search engine.

Applying for the Mortgage

Once you select a lender, you face the agonizing process of applying for the loan. First, you have to gather and complete so much information. You may think you need everything from your second grade report card to your library card.

Second, you're bombarded with foreign terms and concepts dealing with financing. You should be a step ahead here, though.

Third, you have to wait. Waiting for approval is the worst.

But Officer...

Depending on the type of lender you approach, you can expect to deal with a loan officer. This person is responsible for taking down all your financial information, and is usually your primary contact at the bank, trust company or credit union. This person makes sure that all the needed information is ready for review.

How the Lender Decides Whether to Lend You Money

How does a lender decide that Buyer A gets the loan, but Buyer B is rejected? The lender will look at a number of factors, including your current financial situation, your payment history, the current lending guidelines, and the property being purchased.

Here's the basic process the lender goes through: the lender takes your application, verifies your employment and income information and source of down payment, checks your credit report and appraisal, and finally approves or rejects the loan.

Taking the Application

In the application process, the lender will ask you for a lot of information about your financial situation, such as your current income, your current debt obligations, and more.

Here are some of the things you'll have to provide:

➤ Copies of all bank statements (savings and chequing) for the past three months. If an account shows a large deposit in the past few months, be prepared to explain where this money came from.

➤ Copies of all stock accounts and other assets (life insurance).

➤ Your most recent pay stubs as well as the names and addresses of your past employers.

➤ Your tax returns for the past two years. If you're self-employed, you'll need to provide additional tax returns and all your schedules, including profit-and-loss statements for past years as well as year-to-date.

➤ A copy of the purchase agreement. You may also need a copy of the front and back of the cheque for the deposit.

➤ If you're selling your current home to buy a new one, you'll need a copy of the listing agreement. If you've sold your house, bring a copy of the purchase agreement.

➤ If you're making the down payment with money given to you as a gift, you may be required to bring a gift letter, which states the money is a gift and does not have to be repaid.

➤ It's a good idea to bring a list of your addresses for the past five to 10 years. You'll be asked to complete this information on the application.

➤ Collect the addresses and account numbers for all credit cards and other debts. For example, if you have a car loan, you'll need the lender's name, account number and address. You should also know the monthly payments and balance owed.

129

➤ If you're renting, bring in copies of the past 12 months' rent cheques.

➤ If you have credit problems, be prepared to explain them.

Verifying Information

The lender then reviews and verifies your information. Have you been employed at the place you listed for the amount of time you said? Is your salary what you say it is? Do you have a serious criminal record? Do you have the money you say you do in your bank or other accounts?

Accuracy is the key. The lender wants first to be sure the information is accurate, and second, to be sure that the information is honest (so if you want the loan, it's best to tell the truth).

If you have more than enough assets, you may not want to list them all. If you do, the lender will have to validate each asset you list, which can be time-consuming. Instead, list only enough to qualify for the loan and down payment you want. If it turns out you need additional assets to qualify, you can always mention them later.

Ordering Your Credit Report

In addition to verifying your income and employment, the lender will order a credit report. This report will tell the lender about your credit rating and credit history. How have you managed past debts? Have you recently filed for bankruptcy? The lender will look for any trouble signs, such as a history of late or missed payments, and will check to see whether you listed all your debts. Not including some debts on an application can raise a red flag to the lender.

Finally, the lender will check to be sure you don't have *too much* credit available. Lenders may think that too much credit can be too tempting.

It's a good idea to check and clean up any credit problems before you apply for a loan. Also, most lenders run two credit checks (an initial check at the time of application and one later, right before closing). For this reason, it's not a good idea to take on any new debt during the loan process. That debt is likely to show up on your second credit report.

Getting an Appraisal

In addition to checking out *you*, the lender will also check out the property you intend to purchase. You may be silly enough to pay $125 000 for a house that's worth only $75 000, but the lender isn't going to lend you the money to do it. All loans require an independent appraisal, which you, as buyer, usually pay for. The appraiser determines the market value of the home.

To determine the value, the appraiser will look at the neighbourhood. How many homes are currently on the market? How desirable is the area? The appraiser will also look closely at the condition of the home, the size and number of rooms, the type of construction, and the condition of the property. After reviewing the home and property, the appraiser will provide a value as well as supporting information on how that value was reached.

Request a copy of the appraisal in writing from the lender at the time of the application. This appraisal can give you solid information that backs up the value of the home. Note that you can't get the appraisal until the closing.

Usually, the lender hires the services of the appraiser, and you pay for the appraisal through the lender.

If you've ever shopped for a diamond, you may know that the four Cs determine a diamond's worth. Lenders also use four Cs to qualify an individual for a loan:

You can obtain your own credit history by contacting the companies that compile such documents. Usually you'll need photocopies of two pieces of identification, along with proof of your current address taken from a utility bill or credit card invoice. Mail this information to the following address: Equifax Canada Inc., Box 190, Jean-Talon Station, Montreal, Quebec H1S 2Z2, or Trans Union, Consumer Relations Department, P.O. Box 338-LCD1, Hamilton, Ontario L8L 7W2. They will mail the appropriate information to you in about two weeks.

Capacity   Will you be able to repay the debt? Lenders base the answer to this question on your current income and employment record. Lenders also look at your other financial obligations.

Credit history   Being *able* to repay the debt doesn't mean you *will* repay the debt. Lenders look at your past record of making payments. Did you make them on time?

Capital   How much money do you have right now? The lender will look at your assets. For instance, do you have money for the down payment? Do you have enough money after paying the down payment and closing costs or will you have to scrape by for a few months?

Collateral   What can the lender get from you if you default on the loan? The house, of course—but lenders want to ensure the house is worth the amount you're paying, hence the appraisal.

Approving or Denying the Loan

Once he has all the details about your income information, credit history, appraisal and so on, the lender will decide whether to give you the loan.

If the loan is approved, you should receive a commitment letter stating the loan amount, amortization, term, interest rate and monthly payment. If you agree to these terms, you sign the letter. If you don't, you shake hands, say good-bye and go somewhere else.

Read the commitment letter carefully. Lenders sometimes make mistakes. You'll want to be sure the terms are exactly as you intended. If the letter is not accurate, do not sign it.

If the loan is not approved, your loan officer will let you know. See the section What to Do If Your Loan Is Not Approved.

Preapproval

What if rates rise or fall during the period when you're looking for a home? To eliminate this uncertainty, most lenders will preapprove a mortgage, based on the criteria that we've just described, but without the appraisal.

The lender's preapproval should protect you from any increase in interest rates during a specified period, usually 90 days. It should also allow you to take advantage of a decline in interest rates. This may seem obvious, but some lenders, especially private ones, don't always extend this consideration to preapproved borrowers.

Some institutional lenders allow an unlimited number of adjustments, while others restrict the number of interest-rate adjustments they'll allow after they provide their preapproval. In some cases, a lender will reduce the interest rate on a preapproved mortgage, but will charge the borrower an administrative fee. Rather than paying such a fee, you should look for another lender, unless there are other, more compelling reasons not to change.

Even with a preapproved mortgage, you should not be surprised if the price that you've offered on a property differs from the lender's appraised value. As we've explained, lenders tend to be conservative in their evaluations of property. If the appraised value is lower than the price that you've offered for the property, you'll need a larger down payment.

Ensuring a Smooth Process

You may feel as if the entire loan process is out of your hands. That out-of-control feeling can be uncomfortable when so much is at stake. There are some things that you can do to ensure a smooth loan process:

Clean up your credit report Be sure to clear up any credit problems before you apply for a loan. If problems turn up later, a lender won't want to hear your explanation after the fact.

Provide all requested information quickly If the loan officer asks you for a pay stub, get the stub to her as quickly as possible.

Get copies of everything to protect yourself For instance, if you locked in a rate, get it in writing.

Call your loan officer periodically to check on the progress If there are problems, you should know immediately, not at the end of 60 days. Perhaps the lender requires additional documentation. You should make sure that there are no holdups that you're responsible for.

Don't make any big purchases right before or during the loan process

If you go out and buy a new car right before you apply for a loan, that debt will show up on your record. If you buy the car after you apply, the debt may also show up, because most lenders run *two* credit checks: one when you apply, and one right before the closing. So, if you're contemplating a big purchase, it's best to wait until after your loan is approved.

Be careful. Some lenders lock you in the day you apply for a loan. Others start the clock the day you receive your credit approval.

What to Do If You Can't Get a Loan

If you're denied a loan, the lender will usually explain the decision, often in writing. You should talk to the loan officer and find out what went wrong. If you can clear up the problem, the lender may reconsider. If not, you may have to secure other financing.

Ask the loan officer for suggestions on how to improve your chances of getting approved. A loan officer has experience dealing with many successful and unsuccessful loans. He may be able to give you some advice on improving your chances.

Sometimes the institution itself simply doesn't want to lend money on the conditions or terms that you require. If that's the case, the lending officer will tell you, and you should go to another lender.

The following section discusses some of the problems that can cause a loan to be denied.

Income Problems

If you don't have enough income to qualify for that loan, you can try the following to correct this situation:

Secure other financing   If you can't obtain financing through a traditional lender, you may try a different type of financing. Maybe the seller can help you with financing. Also, you should ask your agent for suggestions.

Point out extenuating circumstances to the lender   For example, if you're about to get a raise, you may ask your employer to give the lender a letter saying so. This may improve your financial picture enough to qualify.

Shop for a less expensive home   If you can't qualify for a mortgage on the home of your dreams, perhaps you can qualify for a less expensive home and then trade up when you're more financially secure.

Start a savings program   If you don't have enough for the down payment, start saving now. You may not be able to afford a house today, but that will change if you save enough. Create a budget and start saving money for your home. You could even consider temporarily taking a second job. You could determine the amount you have to save for a down payment, then deposit each pay-cheque from your second job directly into your savings account. When you reach your savings goal, quit your second job and start looking for that dream home!

Examine your current debts   If that dream home is important enough to you, try lowering your existing debts by making some sacrifices. You could trade in your car for a less expensive model; you could sell one car if your family has more than one, then carpool or take public transportation; you could consolidate some outstanding loans so your monthly payments are lower. Be creative and brutal. Trim the fat. If you're spending a lot each month on concerts, movies or restaurants, cut back. You'll be surprised how quickly all of this adds up.

Credit Problems

If your credit report comes back with problems, you should ask to see a copy. If there are errors, have them corrected. If there are problems, correct them or add your explanation. Doing so may or may not change the lender's mind.

If you have too much debt to qualify for a loan, consider paying off some of the debts if you can. If you can't, but have a good credit history, ask the lender to reconsider.

If you have serious debt-management problems, consider getting some financial counseling.

Appraisal Problems

Most lenders will give you a loan for only a certain percentage of the appraised value. If the appraisal is higher than what you're paying, you won't have to worry. If the appraisal is less, you will qualify for a smaller mortgage. In this case, you can come up with a larger down payment to cover the difference. Or, if you made the sale contingent on an acceptable appraisal, you may be able to renegotiate the price.

The Least You Need to Know

➤ There are a number of ways to reduce the total amount you pay for your mortgage, including shorter amortization and prepayment options.

➤ A number of lenders provide mortgages to home buyers, so you don't have to take the first deal that comes along.

➤ The better prepared you are to apply for a mortgage, the better your chances of getting the loan.

➤ If you don't get a loan, ask the lender why. It might have something to do with your income, your credit history or the home you intend to buy.

Part 4
Simple Investment Strategies

"Simple investment strategies"—sound like a financial oxymoron?

Finding your way through the investment jungle can be simple... as long as you pay attention and do your homework. You can easily avoid paying exorbitant fees to Bay Street sharks—and possibly reap better investment rewards—if you concentrate on some of the strategies and secrets revealed in the following chapters.

You don't need to be a financial Einstein to understand (and also roll the dice on) Bay Street. In this part, you'll learn about the pluses and minuses of taking the plunge, the top investment strategies of the 1990s, and some strategies designed especially for senior citizens.

Are you ready to begin?

Chapter 14

Taking Stock

> ## In This Chapter
>
> ➤ What are stocks, and why should we buy them?
>
> ➤ Why do companies issue stock?
>
> ➤ What are dividends?
>
> ➤ How to read the stock tables
>
> ➤ Selling short

If you own a share of a company's stock, you own a part of the company. There are basically two types of stocks: common stocks and preferred stocks.

Common stock represents part-ownership in a company. As a shareholder, the investor can participate in the company's growth by electing its board of directors, voting on corporate policies, and attending its annual meetings.

Preferred stock also represents part-ownership, but investors in preferred shares participate in the company's growth in only a limited way. For example, owners of preferred shares often cannot vote on corporate policies.

How Common Are They?

Thousands of companies would like nothing more than to have you as a part-owner. You don't need a college education. You don't need any special job skills. You don't have to be an upper-middle-class male graduate of an established prep school or the

In Canada, there are three major stock exchanges, where stocks are bought and sold publicly:

- The Toronto Stock Exchange (TSE) is the largest and best known.

- The Montreal Exchange (ME) is a big player in certain areas.

- The Vancouver Stock Exchange (VSE) specializes in low-priced, more speculative stocks, including a lot of mining stocks.

There's also a stock exchange in Alberta called the Alberta Exchange, and a commodities exchange in Winnipeg.

daughter of the president. You don't even need a resume. You just need to buy some of these companies' common shares.

Think of a company's stock as a big piece of pie. If the pie represents the total amount of a company's stock, then each slice represents a share. The more common stock you own, the larger your slab of pie. It's up to you to find out whether the pie is filled with apple, cherry, lemon—or just crust.

Public Companies

Companies that sell shares of their stock to the public are called public companies. Any idiot can walk off the street and buy a share of a public company. And many do. These companies have to follow a lot of strict rules—such as publishing an annual report and reporting insider trades—that are designed to prevent companies from taking the public's money, then packing up and moving to Panama.

Private companies can sell shares as well, but they can't sell them to the public. So if you buy a share of a private company, you might have a hard time finding anyone else who will buy it from you.

The shares of public companies are traded in public markets around the world called stock exchanges. Using the telephone or a PC, Canadian investors can trade stocks 24 hours a day, seven days a week, 365 days a year.

How Stocks Work

Say Uncle Harry wants to start his own company, Acme Buggy Whips. His market research has shown that buggies are making a comeback. Harry's all set to capitalize on this up-and-coming market. However, he lacks one important start-up ingredient: money.

Uncle Harry needs at least $10 000 to pay the rent, buy the equipment and pay the staff to get the business up and running. He tries the bank, but the bank lends money only to people who don't need it.

So Uncle Harry decides to sell shares in Acme Buggy Whips. After jumping through a lot of hoops that we won't describe here, he ends up running a public company, which can sell shares to the public.

He charges $10 a share. That price—$10—is called the **par value**.

To raise $10 000, Uncle Harry has to sell 1000 shares. The number of shares that a company issues is referred to as the shares outstanding.

An investor who buys one of Acme's 1000 outstanding shares will own 1/1000 of the company.

As proof of ownership, Uncle Harry gives each stockholder a certificate that shows how many shares she owns in Acme. A brokerage firm will usually hold the certificates for safekeeping. But investors can ask for the certificate to be sent to them directly.

The stockholders are responsible for electing a company's board of directors. The board oversees the operations of the company. The board members approve the hiring and firing of the company's top executives. They approve or disapprove if the company's managers want to buy another company or sell a piece of the existing business. They also appoint executives to run the company, such as the president and the chief executive officer.

The **balance sheet** shows what the company owns (assets) and owes (liabilities). It also shows the value of all the shares owned by the company's shareholders, and the value per share.

The **statement of income** is a record of the company's sales, costs and profits for the year.

Once a year, the company holds a stockholders' meeting, where it provides investors with its annual report. This report contains two important pieces of information: the balance sheet and the statement of income.

If investors are dissatisfied with the way the company is being run, they can say so at the meeting. For every share owned, the stockholder gets one vote. The more shares owned, the more votes the stockholder gets.

Why Buy Stocks?

Once you invest in a company's shares, how do you earn a profit? There are two ways: dividends, and increases in the stock's value.

Dividends

After one year in business, Acme Buggy Whips has earned $1000 in profits. With the approval of the board of directors, the company can either divide the $1000 equally among the stockholders, in the form of dividends, or keep the profits and use the money to buy new machinery or expand the business.

With the board's approval, Acme Buggy Whips decides to put $500 back into the business. This $500 is called retained earnings.

The company pays the remaining $500 to investors. Each shareholder receives 50 cents

Investors look more closely at a company's earnings per share than at any other financial figure. A business calculates its earnings per share by dividing the company's net earnings by the number of shares outstanding.

For example, if a company has net earnings of $100 million, and it has 20 million shares outstanding, then the earnings per share are $5 ($100 million/20 million = $5).

for every share owned. That 50 cents per share is calculated by dividing the total amount allotted to the company's dividend ($500) by the number of shares outstanding (1000).

The Bottom Line

Why do the prices of stocks go up and down like yo-yos? And why do people seem to care so much about the price of their shares?

The actual value of a stock is determined by the powers of supply and demand. A stock is worth only what somebody else is willing to pay for it. When 15 people all want to buy the stock and only one person wants to sell it, the stock price will rise. That's supply and demand. "You want it, then pay me more for it than those other 14 people beside you will pay."

On the other side of the coin, when 15 people want to sell a stock and only one wants to buy, the stock price will fall until the buyer agrees with the price. "I won't pay you a penny more for that garbage."

But there's more to the story of a share's ups and downs. Buyers and sellers pay attention to corporate earnings, for example. If earnings rise steadily, so does the stock price. When earnings fall, the stock price generally falls too.

Just to make matters interesting, though, sometimes earnings go up as stock prices fall. Sometimes earnings will fall as stock prices go up.

True Value and How to Figure It Out

Here are two calculations to determine the value of a stock:

➤ the price/earnings ratio

➤ the dividend yield

The Price/Earnings Ratio

Also referred to as the P/E ratio or P/E multiple, the price/earnings ratio measures the current price of the share in relationship to the earnings per share. It is calculated by dividing the current share price by the last 12 months' earnings per share.

For example, if a company's stock is trading at $30 a share, and the company earns $2 a share, the P/E ratio would be 15. That's because $30/$2 = 15.

The ratio of price to earnings indicates the premium that an investor will pay to own a piece of the company. A P/E ratio of 15 indicates that an investor will pay 15 times as much as the company earns in a year to own a share. Investors figure the company will grow and that they will recover their investment in less than 15 years.

When the stock market turns down, the stocks that decline farthest in price are the ones with high P/E ratios. As a general rule, stocks that have a P/E ratio above 30 represent a higher risk.

The P/E ratio tells us how much the stock could potentially grow. The higher a company's potential for growth, the more value the market places on its stock. A P/E ratio of 20 indicates that investors will pay the equivalent of 20 years of profits for the stock. A P/E ratio of 40 means the market is much more optimistic about the company's growth prospects and will pay the equivalent of 40 years of profits for a share.

The market doesn't expect to wait for 40 years to get its money back. It expects the company to grow so quickly that it will recover its investment in a much shorter time.

Sometimes the market is right. Sometimes it's not.

A low P/E ratio implies that a company has low potential for growth. It also tells us how much risk is associated with the stock.

The market may not expect much growth from a company whose stock has a low P/E ratio. But it also doesn't see much risk in investing in the company. So its stock price will remain relatively stable.

A large decline in the P/E ratio of a company's stock is a warning sign. It indicates that all may not be well with the company. For example, if a stock's P/E ratio falls from 30 to 20 in less than a year, investors have lost confidence in the stock.

The Dividend Yield

The dividend yield is a stock's indicated dividend for the next 12 months divided by the current share price.

For example, if a company pays its stockholders a cash dividend of 50 cents, and the share price is currently $20, then the dividend yield will be 2.5 percent.

Here's the calculation: $\dfrac{\$0.50}{\$20} \times 100 = 2.5\%$

In other words, the dividend yield indicates the annual return that an investor receives from a stock's dividends. It lets you compare the annual return on different kinds of investments.

141

Generally speaking, the higher the dividend yield, the better the value. However, you have to consider other factors:

- Is the dividend payout secure? (A company that's not in business doesn't pay dividends.)

- Is it likely to be increased in the future?

- What proportion of profits are paid out in dividends, and what proportion are reinvested in the company?

The yield from your savings account may be 3 percent, for example. The dividend yield from your shares in Uncle Harry's buggy whip company might be 2.5 percent. However, yield isn't everything.

A company that passes all its profits to shareholders in the form of high dividends may not last long. To compete with other companies, a business has to reinvest at least some of its profits in buildings, equipment, employees and expansion plans. It can't give all its profits to its shareholders.

P/E vs. Dividend Yield

Some people invest in safe secure companies whose stock has a low P/E ratio but a relatively high dividend yield. These companies may not grow quickly, but nor will they go down the tubes next week.

Other people invest in more risky stocks with high P/E ratios but low dividend yields. These companies may grow so fast that their stock will double in value overnight. Or they may go broke tomorrow.

The P/E ratio and dividend yield fluctuate constantly. When the stock price rises, the P/E ratio rises, but the dividend yield falls. As the price goes up, then there's more P to be divided by E.

The dividend yield—the dividend divided by the share price—works the opposite way. This time, the P is on the bottom of the equation. The bigger the P, the fewer times it goes into the dividend, and the lower the resulting percentage.

Book Value

If Uncle Harry's company goes out of business and he sells off all its assets—the plant, the equipment, the buggy whips—how much would the stock be worth? The answer is called the **book value**.

A company's book value is calculated by taking the value of all the company's assets, subtracting the liabilities, and dividing that number by the number of shares outstanding. (You can find all these figures in a company's annual report.)

But book value can be misleading. When a company has to liquidate its assets, it rarely receives full value for them. Nevertheless, stocks trading near their book value usually present good buying opportunities.

Preferred Shares

Even though they're bought and sold just like common shares, preferred shares are different in several significant ways.

➤ Preferred shares carry a fixed dividend rate that's higher than the common stock.

➤ If the company that issues preferred shares goes belly-up, any money left after its creditors are paid must go to the preferred stockholders first, then to the common stockholders. That's why they're called *preferred* shares.

➤ Preferred shareholders often do not enjoy the same voting rights as common shareholders. But because they receive higher dividends, they're not supposed to care.

Why Choose Preferreds?

Compared to common stock, preferred shares pay higher fixed yields. But their value is far less affected by a company's growth—or lack of it. So the preferred share price is more influenced by prevailing interest rate trends than by the company's earnings. If you could get 6 percent on your money in a GIC and only 4 percent from a preferred share, where would you invest?

The best time to buy preferred stock is when interest rates have peaked and are beginning to decline. At that time, dividend payouts will be high, and stock prices low.

A company's earnings become a factor in the price of its preferred shares only if they fall to the point where they jeopardize dividend payments. Then the preferred share price drops like a stone.

At all other times, the price is based on interest rate trends. When interest rates rise, the price of preferred stocks falls. Similarly, when interest rates fall, preferred stocks rise.

Convertible Preferred Shares

Corporations issue preferred shares that holders can convert into regular shares. The holder of a convertible preferred share can convert it at any time into a specified number of common shares. Say a company sells its convertible preferred shares for $100 each. A conversion clause allows you to convert each convertible preferred share into 10 shares of the company's common stock at any time within the next five years.

At the time, its common stock is trading at $9 a share. Since 10 shares at $9 apiece are worth $90, there's no benefit in exercising the conversion clause at current prices, unless you really want to lose $10. But when the price of a common share rises above

You should consider purchasing convertible preferred shares during periods of rising inflation.

Think of it this way: When inflation is low, the fixed payment that you receive from the dividend on your preferred share retains its value. But when inflation rises, it erodes the value of your dividend payment. If you convert the shares to common stock, the value of your shares may go up, and the money you make in the process won't be so vulnerable to the ravages of inflation.

$10, then it makes sense to convert. For example, if the price of a common share rises to $12, you can convert your convertible preferred—for which you paid $100—into 10 common shares, and get $120.

Unlike regular preferreds, the convertible's price tends to move in line with the price of the common stock. This can be good or bad, depending on which way the common stock moves.

Stock Splits: Two Nickels for a Dime

If shares are low in price, individual investors tend to buy more of them. When the price of the stock rises, individuals don't buy so many shares. For example, they'll buy 20 shares at $1 apiece. But they won't buy four shares at $5 apiece. Instead they'll buy only three, or even none at all.

So when a company's stock goes up in price, the company often splits its stock to lower the unit price. For example, if a stock appreciates from $20 to $60, the company might then consider a 2-for-1 stock split. At that point, each stockholder receives twice as many shares, each valued at $30.

A stock split increases the number of shares outstanding, while leaving unchanged their total value.

The Stock Market Indices

The TSE 300

Every day, news announcers on radio and TV refer to the TSE, which stands for the Toronto Stock Exchange. They may say it's up 10 points. Or they may say it's down 25 points.

In fact, they're talking about the Toronto Stock Exchange 300 Composite Index, also called the TSE 300. This index measures the general performance of the most important stock market in Canada. It's based on the value of 300 stocks trading on the Toronto Stock Exchange.

The index began in 1977, when the total value of all 300 stocks was $34 billion. Rather than juggle all those zeroes, the TSE allotted an arbitrary number of 1000 to represent the value of the TSE 300 at that time. After that, every time the value of shares represented by the TSE 300 Composite Index rose $3.4 million from the previous day's value, the index itself rose by one point. So the news announcer would say, for example, that the TSE rose one point today—to 1001.

The Dow Jones Industrial Average

The TSE 300 is the most popular market index in Canada. In the U.S., the most popular market index is the Dow Jones Industrial Average—known as the Dow.

Started by Charles H. Dow in 1896, the index originally included only 12 stocks. On the first day of trading, the Dow Industrial closed at 40.94. Today the Dow Industrial contains 30 stocks, and the index is currently around 4000.

REALLY?

A market index represents a general market movement, not the movement of individual stocks.

The TSE index would have to rise 45 points for the value of those 300 companies to increase by 1 percent. But even if the TSE 300 rose by 45 points, it would not mean that the value of each of those 300 companies increased by 1 percent as well. Some may have gone up 2 percent. Others only 1/2 percent. And others may have lost 2 percent.

REALLY?

Of the original 12 Dow Industrial stocks of 1896, only General Electric remains as a Dow stock today. The other 29 stocks are as follows:

2) AT&T
3) Allied Signal
4) Alcoa
5) American Express
6) Bethlehem Steel
7) Boeing
8) Caterpillar
9) Chevron
10) Coca Cola
11) Walt Disney
12) Dupont
13) Eastman Kodak
14) Exxon
15) General Motors
16) Goodyear
17) IBM
18) International Paper
19) McDonalds
20) Merck
21) Minnesota Mining
22) J.P. Morgan
23) Philip Morris
24) Procter & Gamble
25) Sears
26) Texaco
27) Union Carbide
28) United Technologies
29) Westinghouse
30) Woolworth

In talking about the value of a share, a dollar is frequently referred to as a point, as in, "Acme shares rose 3 points today."

Standard & Poor

Some people think the Dow, with only 30 stocks, cannot possibly reflect accurately the activity of the entire U.S. stock market. For these nonbelievers, there's Standard & Poor's 500 Index—the S&P 500. It's based on the ups and downs of 500 large industrial stocks.

It's in the Chart

Everything you need to know about a company's day-to-day financial performance, you can find in the stock tables. You just have to know how to read all that seeming gibberish. Here's how:

52 Weeks						Yld	Vol				Net
Hi	Lo	Stock	Sym	Div	%		100s	Hi	Lo	Close	Chg
50.25	42	BCE Inc	B	2.68	5.4		21680	50.25	49.10	50.10	+1.10

- ➤ **Hi and Lo**   These show the highest and the lowest price that the stock traded at over the previous 52 weeks.
- ➤ **Stock**   This is the name of the company whose stock you're looking at.
- ➤ **Sym**   This is the symbol that represents BCE's stock on the ticker. (You can see the ticker in action in brokerage offices.)
- ➤ **Div**   This is the company's estimated annual dividend per share.
- ➤ **Yld %**   This is the stock's dividend yield.
- ➤ **Vol 100s**   This is the number of shares that have been traded throughout the day.
- ➤ **High, Lo, Close, Chg**   The last few columns represent the highest price throughout the day, the lowest price throughout the day, the closing price at the end of the day, and the percent change from the previous day.

Money Talks

Look at a few consecutive annual reports for BCE or go through back issues of a newspaper's stock pages. You'll see that BCE's expected dividend of $2.68 is 31 cents more than the $2.37 per share in 1986, and $1.49 more than the $1.19 dividend per share payment in 1976.

BCE stockholders have benefited over the years as earnings more than doubled, while the company's directors steadily increased the dividend payment. That helps to explain why BCE's share price increased over 16 years from $16.75 in 1982 to more than $60 today.

Bid and Ask

As with most things in life, the people who want to sell stock usually want more than anyone else will pay for it. Likewise, as with most things in life, the people who want to buy stock usually want to pay less than anyone wants to sell it for.

Buyers bid; sellers ask.

A stock may have an ask price of $10 and a bid of $9.75. If you wanted to sell the stock right away, you'd have to accept the bid price of $9.75. If you wanted to buy the stock right away, you'd have to pay the ask price of $10.

You can also place an order to buy or sell a stock at a price in between the bid and ask, say at $9.85. But if you do, there's no guarantee that your order will get filled.

Bid and ask prices are constantly changing in relation to supply and demand.

Board Lots

When you go to the supermarket to buy eggs, you see a price listed for one dozen. When it comes to eggs, one dozen is the standard unit.

When it comes to stocks, the standard unit is 100 shares. Just as 12 eggs are called a dozen, 100 shares are called a *board lot*. For stocks trading over $1, the bid and ask prices are quoted per board lot. A purchase of under 100 shares is known as an *odd lot*.

To Place an Order

All investors should know how to place an order properly with a stockbroker to buy or sell stocks. First, tell the broker that you want to place one of three main types of order.

A market order   You want to buy a particular stock at the current market price. For example, let's say you want to buy 100 shares of BCE Inc. You would call up your stockbroker and ask, "What's BCE trading at?" She'll say, "50 bid, 50 1/4 ask." If you find this range attractive, you say, "Buy 100 shares of BCE at the market." Your broker will repeat the order to you and then place it. *Bing, bang, bong...* you now own 100 shares of BCE at 50 1/4.

A limit order   You want to buy or sell a stock only if it trades at a specified price. You also have to set a time limit for your order. You could set the time limit for one day, one month, or any duration in between. Or you could place an order "good till cancelled," in which case the order stays in effect until it's either executed or cancelled by you.

For example, if BCE is trading at $50, but you don't want to pay more than $48 for it, you would tell your broker, "Buy BCE at $48, good for the week." At the end of one week, if the trade isn't executed, it's automatically cancelled.

A stop order   You want to sell a stock whose price has gone up and is now starting to fall. So you instruct your broker: "Place a stop order."

For example, if you bought a stock at $20, it rose to $40, and it's now starting to head lower—$39...$38...$37...you don't want to lose your profits. So you phone your broker and say, "Place a stop order to sell 100 shares at $35." Now if the stock drops to $35, your shares will automatically be sold.

Once the price of a stock increases by 40 percent to 50 percent profit, it's prudent to place a stop order at 5 percent below the stock's most recent high. This way you protect your profits.

Stock Sense

Over the long term, the average stock price rises by 10 percent to 12 percent a year. But the prices of individual stocks do not always follow that average. The price of a stock can fall so quickly that it will eliminate gains accumulated over the entire previous year.

With this in mind, you should not regard individual stocks as long-term investments. Instead, think of them as trading vehicles—like chestnuts, marbles, baseball cards and Elvis Presley memorabilia. Once you've made a substantial profit on a particular stock, sell it.

One Way to Select Winning Stocks

Companies typically report their earnings per share every three months. Each three-month period is referred to as a quarter.

The most important factor for picking a winning stock is an increase in the company's earnings per share.

Buy a stock only if it records an increase in earnings per share of at least 30 percent to 50 percent in the most recent quarter, compared to the same quarter last year.

Here's another way to put it: A stock earned 30 cents a share in the quarter ending in March of the previous year. You should consider buying it only if, in the quarter ending in March of this year, it earns 39 cents or more per share.

Yearly earnings are also very important. Top-performing stocks should have at least a four-year to five-year track record of back-to-back increases in annual earnings per share.

For example:

YEAR	1993	1994	1995	1996	1997
EARNINGS PER SHARE	$0.14	$0.34	$0.80	$1.29	$1.42

Industry Groups

Compare two stocks with similar earnings. One is involved in a leading industry—electronics, for example. The other operates in a lagging industry—say, buggy whips. The stock of the company in the leading industry will beat the other hands down, every time.

High Interest

Of all the stocks listed on the TSE, 45 percent are sensitive to changes in interest rates. These include the following:

➤ banks

➤ utilities

➤ insurance companies

➤ construction companies.

When interest rates fall, these interest-sensitive stocks tend to do well.

The other 55 percent are sensitive to the economy in general. As inflation comes alive, companies involved in the following become the new market leaders:

➤ steel

➤ gold mining

➤ forestry and lumber.

More Interest

Lower interest rates encourage people to spend money. So when interest rates have been low and are starting to rise, good companies in the following sectors perform well:

➤ retail stores

➤ cosmetics

➤ restaurants

➤ tobacco.

Never invest using a rearview mirror. Last year's big sector seldom wins again this year.

Near the end of a cycle, when interest rates have peaked and are starting back down, companies perform well in sectors such as the following:

➤ pharmaceuticals

➤ chemicals.

"Thar's Gold in Them Thar Hills!"

Here we are, prospecting in specific sectors for companies that will perform well. We start with sectors that have suffered badly over the past few years. Now they're just starting to turn around.

For example, in December 1992, gold had been beaten down to a seven-year low. Even though no one was buying gold shares, we could have made a bundle if we'd moved against the crowd and bought shares in gold-mining companies. Over the next year, most gold stocks rose more than 80 percent. Today, they're back down again, lower than they were even in 1992. Are you willing to buy now and hang on till they rise again?

Is the Price of the Stock Important?

With stocks as with anything else in life, you get what you pay for. With this in mind, never buy penny stocks whose shares trade for less than $1, unless you're looking for nifty wallpaper for your spare bedroom.

Some people believe that a stock that trades for less than $1 can double in value faster than a stock trading at $15 or $30. That's a big mistake. What causes a stock to double is money, and these days, the big money is coming from the institutional investors such as pension funds and mutual funds. These investors almost never buy penny stocks.

Avoid Hot Tips

If something sounds too good to be true, it usually is. For moderate risk-takers like you and me, and anyone else who reads books before making an investment, blue chip companies make the best investments. (But even they can stumble. General Motors has. So has IBM.)

Strategies

Look for profitable companies. Then check the stock tables. If they're trading at the low end of their spectrum, now's the time to buy. (Unfortunately, some may keep on going down.)

Bargains usually emerge when the whole stock market turns down about 5 percent or 10 percent. These short dips are known as corrections. They generally occur once or twice a year.

Bulls, Bears, Crabs

When a bull attacks a matador during a bullfight, he thrusts his horns upward. An upward thrust in the stock market is called a bull market. That's one explanation. Another is that bull markets resemble bulls charging full steam ahead.

A bear attacks by swinging his paw downward. A ferocious downward swing in stock prices is called a bear market. That's one theory. Here's another: In colonial America, grizzly old coots, called bear jobbers, used to find a buyer for a bearskin, collect the payment up front, then go out and shoot a bear and deliver the skin. This resembles the activity of a short seller. Short sellers borrow stock at a high price, sell it and wait for the price to go down. Then they buy the shares back at a lower price, return them to their owners and keep the difference in price.

A crab market moves sideways.

REALLY?

In the 40 years between 1956 and 1996, there were 13 bull markets and 12 bear markets.

- The bull markets lasted 7 to 44 months.

- Each was followed by a bear market lasting between two and 36 months.

- The gains during the bull markets ranged from 22 percent to 150 percent.

- The losses during bear markets ranged from 16 percent to 45 percent.

Conclusion: Over time, the market gains more than it loses.

Asset Allocation, or Don't Put All Your Eggs in One Basket

About 75 percent of stocks follow the general stock market trend. The other 25 percent march to a different drummer. The challenge is to figure out which are which, so you can get in at the bottom and ride a stock to the top, rather than getting in at the bottom just as the bottom falls out.

That's why the "Don't-put-all-your-eggs-in-one-basket" theory comes in handy. This theory is also called *asset allocation*.

Asset allocation means you always put some of your money in cash, some in income-producing investments, and some in stocks or stock funds. If a bear market comes along, you can limit your losses.

Selling Short

An investor can profit if a stock rises in value. You can also profit if a stock declines in value.

When you buy a stock hoping that it will rise in value, you are said to be investing long. If you think the price of the stock will fall, you can sell short.

Instead of buying a stock and then selling it, short sellers sell a stock, then buy it back later, when the price is lower (they hope). They do this by borrowing stock through a brokerage firm, then selling it at the current market price. They wait for a while, tensely biting their nails. Then, if they've predicted correctly, they go out and repurchase the stock at a lower price. They return the shares to the original lender and keep the difference in price. Sometimes short sellers are wrong, and the stock's price rises. Then the short seller has to buy back the shares at a higher price, suffer a loss.

It's a lot easier to pick a stock that will rise than to find one that will decline. That's because the stock market, over time, goes upward, not downward. If you bet a stock will drop, the cards are automatically stacked against you.

For quick access to information on stocks and financial data, check www.fin-info.com or www.investor-corner.com.

Foreign Stocks

You can buy shares in foreign companies that don't list their shares on Canadian stock exchanges either by purchasing units of a mutual fund that invests in foreign companies or by purchasing American depository receipts (ADRs). ADRs are negotiable certificates issued by U.S. banks, which represent the shares of a non-U.S. company on deposit with the bank's overseas custodian. You can't deduct the dividend tax credit on ADRs, and you may also have to pay a withholding tax on the dividends. But if you think the future prospects of Gucci shoes look good, call your broker and order Gucci's ADRs.

The Least You Need to Know

➤ Stocks represent part-ownership in a company.

➤ You shouldn't invest more than 35 percent of your money in stocks.

➤ Corporate profits that are returned to investors are called dividends.

➤ Two of the best measures of a stock's true value are the price/earnings ratio and the dividend yield.

➤ The three most important stock market orders are the market order, limit order and stop order.

➤ Beginning investors should stick to the well-known, blue-chip type companies.

➤ Never buy penny stocks.

➤ Never buy hot tips.

Chapter 15

Everything You Ever Wanted to Know About Bonds

In This Chapter

➤ What's a bond?

➤ How are interest rates related to bonds?

➤ The different types of bonds

➤ The best time to buy bonds

➤ Bond mutual funds

What Are Bonds?

Quite simply, a bond is a loan. If you lend me $1000 and I write a promissory note that explains when I will pay you back and what rate of interest I will pay, that note represents a bond.

Whenever you lend money, you must make sure not only that you get repaid, but also that you earn interest on your money.

Before people lend money in the form of bonds, they want some reassurance that the borrower can repay them. Only then do they proceed to lend the money. That's why bonds tend to be stable, conservative investments.

Who Sells Bonds?

Bonds are sold by governments and corporations. They're big, stable, conservative and reliable, and they usually repay their debts.

When you lend money to the government, you receive a government bond. When you lend money to a corporation, you receive a corporate bond. The bond says the government or corporation will repay you, with interest.

Usually the interest is paid twice a year, at a fixed rate. On the date when the entire amount has to be repaid—called the *maturity date*—you will receive back the bond's face value.

The performance of the bond market is closely tied to movements in interest rates.

Face value, par value, and **principal amount** all describe the amount of the loan to be repaid. People say a bond has a face value of $1000, for example.

The **coupon rate** is the rate of interest paid annually on a bond.

The **maturity date** is the date when the bond matures and you receive your loan back.

All You Ever Wanted to Know About Coupons

A bond consists of two parts:

➤ a piece of paper, which is the actual bond (also called the *residual*);

➤ a number of smaller pieces of paper called *coupons*.

At one time, almost all bond certificates came with coupons attached. To collect your interest, you just cut off a coupon and cashed it in every six months or so. Rich people with wads of bonds in their bedside tables sat around all day clipping coupons.

In bond talk, the word **coupon** means interest payment.

A bond's annual interest rate is also called its coupon rate. In most cases, a bond's coupon rate is fixed for the duration of the term. (But just to complicate matters, some bonds are issued with variable rates.)

The standard price for an individual bond when it's first issued is $1000. That's the bond's face value.

Once you pay for the bond, you can wait until it matures to get your $1000 back. Or you can sell it to somebody else in the open market.

Bond Trading

Once bonds start trading on the open market, their price is quoted at 1/10 of their actual price.

For instance, if a bond sells at par for $1000, then it will be listed in the newspaper as 100. If the bond sells at a premium for $1200, then it will be listed as 120. If the bond

At Par If a bond trades at its face value, it trades at par.

Premium If a bond trades above its face value, it trades at a premium.

Discount If a bond trades below its face value, it trades at a discount.

Coupon The little piece of paper that's attached to the bond represents the bond's interest payments.

Residual Another term for the value of the bond itself, the residual is the amount you'll receive when your loan is paid back.

Bonds are issued with maturity dates ranging from three months to 40 years.

- Short term bonds mature in two years or less.

- Intermediate term bonds mature in two to five years.

- Long term bonds mature in five years or more.

sells at a discount for $850, then it will be listed as 85.

Ups and Downs

When interest rates rise, the price of bonds falls. When interest rates fall, the price of bonds rises.

More specifically, when the prime rate rises by 1 percent, bond prices fall about 10 percent. When the prime rate falls 1 percent, bond prices rise about 10 percent.

Here's why: In January 1997, a corporation issues a $1000 bond that matures in 30 years with an interest rate of 10 percent. Having read this book, you decide to purchase it. (Meanwhile, other corporations are issuing bonds at similar rates for 20 years or 10 years or even 40 years. Keep this in mind for later.)

In doing so, you agree to lend to this corporation $1000 of your hard-earned money. In return, the corporation will give you a nice little certificate. It also promises to pay you 10 percent a year on your $1000 investment, for a total of 30 years. After 30 years—but not before—the corporation will pay you back your $1000 in full.

In the year 2007, 10 years after you buy the bond, you decide you no longer want to keep it. You have two choices:

1. You can sell it back to the corporation.

2. You can take it to the bond market and sell it to somebody else.

If it's 2007, your bond is now 10 years old. It's no longer a 30-year bond. It's now a 20-year bond.

You originally paid $1000 for it. So you should be able to sell it for $1000, right?

Well, not exactly. Because money is harder to borrow in the year 2007, companies are issuing 20-year bonds with an interest rate of 12 percent. And there you stand with a bond that matures in 20 years but pays only 10 percent in interest. (If you can get 12 percent a year for 20 years on one bond and only

10 percent on another, would you pay the same price for them?)

There's only one way out. You'll have to sell your bond for less than $1000 to compensate the buyer for taking the crummy 10-percent interest rate. (In fact, you'll get about $830 for it. This price is based on a calculation involving the bond's net present value.)

However, if interest rates have fallen to 8 percent in 2007, your bond will increase in value, because it pays 10 percent. Now you can demand *more* than the bond's face value of $1000. In fact, you can sell it for about $1250.

> When interest rates rise, bond prices fall. The extent of the decline is related to the bond's term to maturity. With a 2-percent rise in interest rates, a three-year bond will fall 5 percent in value. A 10-year bond will fall 12 percent in value. A 30-year bond will fall 18 percent in value.

The Yield

When a bond is first issued, the yield is usually set at a fixed rate for the life of the bond. That fixed interest rate is based on prevailing economic conditions.

Once a bond starts trading on the open market, its current yield is constantly adjusted to keep it competitive with other bonds.

The current yield is the actual rate of return on a bond purchased in the open market. It is calculated by dividing the bond's coupon rate by the bond's current price. For example,

> ➤ When sold at par, a bond with a face value of $1000 that pays a coupon rate of 8 percent ($80) will provide a current yield of $80/$1000 = 8%.

> ➤ If the bond's price rises to $1100, its current yield will be $80/$1,100 = 7.3%.

> ➤ If the bond's price falls to $900, its current yield will be $80/$900 = 8.8%.

The Yield to Maturity

If you buy a bond at a discount, you'll have a capital gain when the bond matures and you collect its face value. The capital gain is equivalent to the difference between the price you pay for the bond and its face value.

For instance, if you buy a bond with a face value of $1000, and you pay only $900, you will have a capital gain of $100 when the bond matures.

The yield to maturity involves comparing the capital gain with the years to maturity to arrive at the actual purchase price.

When you look at bond tables in the financial pages, the column showing the yield represents the yield to maturity.

When a bond is purchased at a discount, the yield to maturity will be higher than the current yield. When a bond is purchased at a premium, the yield to maturity will be less than the current yield.

Who's Calling?

Most bonds are issued with a provision known as a call. A call gives the bond issuer the right to call in the bond before it matures.

This might happen if interest rates fall. Say a company issues bonds in 1997 yielding 10 percent. In 1999, interest rates fall to 8 percent. If the corporation can call in its old 10-percent bonds and replace them with new 8-percent bonds, it will save itself 2 percent in annual interest payments.

In return for calling the bond, the corporation will usually pay the bondholder a premium above the bond's face value, usually equal to a year's interest.

If you originally paid $1000 for a bond paying 10 percent, the issuer would likely pay you about $1100 to call it back before it matured.

Most bonds cannot be called in for at least the first five or six years after they're issued.

Give Them Credit

People who buy bonds like to know the risks involved. Is there a risk that the bond issuer will default on its payments? Will the bond issuer still be around when the time comes to cash in the bond?

To measure the risk of investing in a bond, investors rely on credit ratings. The credit rating of a company or government reflects its stability and trustworthiness. The higher the rating, the lower the risk and the safer the bond.

Federal government bonds usually have the highest rating. (Not always, though. If governments keep borrowing like there's no tomorrow, they end up owing so much money that they can't possibly pay it all back, and their ratings fall.)

Next in line are the provincial government bonds, followed by municipal and corporate bonds. The ratings range from AAA (the best) down to C.

Who Rates?

Bond rating services in Canada include Dominion Bond Rating Service (DBRS), Canadian Bond Rating Service (CBRS), Standard & Poor's, and Moody's Investor Service. Your broker can tell you the rating for any bond that interests you.

Bond issuers pay interest for the privilege of borrowing your money and also to compensate you for your risk. The lower a bond's rating, the higher the interest paid by the issuer.

First in Line

A corporation is legally obligated to repay its loans from its bondholders whether it makes a profit or not. If it cannot meet its payments, the bondholders can force the firm into bankruptcy.

If bankruptcy occurs and the company sells off its assets, bondholders must be paid first, before the holders of preferred or common stock.

Last to Profit

Unlike a shareholder, a company's bondholders do not share in the company's growth. They receive no dividends, and their capital gains are not related to the rise or fall of the company's stock price. Bondholders are loaners, not owners.

Convertible Bonds

To make their bonds more attractive to investors, many corporations offer convertible bonds. These give the bondholders the privilege of converting their bonds into a specified number of the company's common shares at a specific conversion price.

These bonds still carry all the features of regular bonds, such as coupon rate, face value, maturity date, and call date. But because they're closely tied to the company's common stock, their price rises and falls in relation to the stock price. When the common stock rises in value, so does the price of the convertible bond.

The performance of these bonds is much more volatile than that of regular bonds. Convertibles also tend to carry lower yields than do regular bonds.

Debentures

Debentures are a type of bond issued frequently by large industrial corporations. They are not backed by real estate or property that can be sold to repay the bondholders if the company goes under. Instead, they're backed only by the general credit of the corporation.

First Mortgage Bonds

These bonds are backed by a first mortgage on the company's property. They offer investors first claim on the company's assets if it defaults on the repayment of its loan. They're generally quite safe.

159

Strip Coupon Bonds

Uncertainty makes investors nervous. For example, they get nervous when they feel uncertain about the direction that interest rates will take.

Before you go to the bank or the trust company to reinvest a GIC or Canada Savings Bond that reaches maturity, you have no guarantee that the new interest rate will be as good as your current one.

One way to obtain such a guarantee is to buy a strip coupon bond—known as a "strip." It will let you know exactly what you'll earn this year, next year, and every year until the bond matures.

Say your typical long-term government bond has a face value of $100 000, a 20-year term to maturity, a 10-percent yield, and coupons that pay $500 in interest every six months. Instead of selling these bonds intact, brokerage firms buy them and separate the coupons from the rest of the bond.

Now they can sell either the bond without the coupons or the coupons without the bond.

If you buy a bond without the coupons, you won't earn any interest. To compensate the investor, strip coupon bonds sell at a discount. Instead of paying the full face value for a $100 000 bond, for example, you pay about $15 000.

When the stripped bond matures 20 years down the road, you can cash it in and collect the face value—$100 000. That's $85 000 more than you paid for it, which represents your earned interest.

The Advantages of a Strip Coupon Bond

➤ When rates are high, you can lock your money away to earn high yields year after year.

➤ Once you buy a strip, you can forget about it until it matures.

➤ You'll have no more worries about reinvesting your money at lower rates.

➤ You're buying the bond at a discount, so you don't need a lot of money to invest up front.

➤ You know exactly how much money you'll have when the strip matures.

Tax Concerns

Even though you won't receive any money until the strip matures, Revenue Canada will tax you each year on the interest. That's why the best place to hold your strip bonds is inside a tax-free account, such as an RRSP or RRIF.

Up Is Down, Down Is Up

The rules that apply to regular government bonds also apply to strip coupon bonds: When interest rates fall, strips rise in value. When interest rates rise, strips fall in value.

However, strip coupon bonds are about 60 percent more vulnerable than regular bonds to changes in interest rates. Say you invest $20 000 in a 20-year strip coupon bond when current rates are 8.5 percent. Then rates rise to 10.5 percent. Your strips will fall in value by about 25 percent. So you would lose about $5000 if you suddenly had to cash in your strip before it matured.

Ordinary bonds that pay cash interest allow you to reinvest the interest at the new higher rates. Strip bonds offer no such luxury.

The reverse is also true. If rates fall, your strips will rise correspondingly in value.

The Long-Term Scoop

Over the past seven decades, bonds have returned average annual gains of less than 5 percent. Yet many investors still believe the best strategy is to hold on to their bonds until they mature, regardless of the direction of interest rates. After all, they reason, no matter which way interest rates go, they'll still continue to receive their interest payments. And when the bond matures, they'll get its full face value.

When interest rates are declining, that rationale makes sense. But when interest rates rise, bondholders lose.

That's because they lose the opportunity to invest their money in new higher-yielding bonds.

When Is the Best Time to Buy Bonds?

Rising interest rates mean lower bond prices. Falling rates mean higher bond prices. So we should buy bonds when interest rates reach a peak and begin to decline. We should sell bonds when interest rates hit bottom and begin to rise.

Now all we have to do is accurately predict the future movement of interest rates.

REALLY?

In June 1977, the Canadian prime rate was 8.25 percent. By August 1981, just over four years later, the prime reached 22.75 percent. By April 1983, it was back down to 11 percent.

When interest rates fluctuate so widely, bond traders can easily earn double-digit returns. But when interest rates are low and relatively stable, single-digit returns are the best you can hope for.

Strategy

Never buy bonds unless interest rates are high. That's the cardinal rule of the bond market. As a general rule, when long-term Government of Canada bonds are yielding at least 10.5 percent and inflation is under 5 percent annually, it's safe to start putting some (15 to 20 percent) of your money into bonds or bond mutual funds.

Long-term Government of Canada bond yield statistics are available in most financial newspapers such as the *Financial Post.*

Use Your Age

An effective way to decide how much of your portfolio to invest in bonds is to use your age as a guideline:

Age 34 or younger	5 percent	in bonds or bond funds
Age 35 to 49	15 percent	in bonds or bond funds
Age 49 and up	30 percent	in bonds or bond funds

The bond market is five times larger than the stock market. It's also a leading indicator of the stock market. That means it indicates the direction that the stock market will take.

Market Trends

During major stock and bond market advances, bond prices usually start rising first, followed by stocks. Similarly, at the end of an advancing market, bond prices usually begin declining, followed by stock prices.

Over the past 80 years, the bond market has always undergone a major downturn either before or at the same time as every major downturn in the stock market. At the end of each of the last six recessions, when the stock market reached bottom, bonds began rising an average of four months prior to stocks.

What ties the two markets together? Interest rates.

The very thought of rising interest rates sends shivers up the spines of many bondholders. Then, as interest rates rise, people pull their money out of the stock market and put it into GICs yielding double-digit returns. Thus, when bonds turn, stocks follow the leader and turn too.

Bond Funds

Rather than investing with the aim of increasing the value of their holdings, bond funds focus on income.

They usually invest in government, corporate and strip coupon bonds.

Like individual bonds, bond mutual funds respond to interest rates. When interest rates rise, bond mutual funds fall in value. When interest rates fall, bond mutual funds rise in value.

Short-Term and Long-Term Bonds

The price fluctuations (volatility) of a particular bond fund is directly proportional to the average maturity of all the bonds held in the fund's portfolio.

The longer it takes for its bond holdings to mature, the more sensitive the bond fund will be to changes in interest rates.

In general, funds that invest primarily in long-term bonds (maturing in 20 to 25 years) will be more volatile than funds that invest primarily in intermediate-term bonds (maturing in 5 to 10 years).

A short-term bond fund that invests primarily in bonds maturing in one to three years will be the least volatile.

Foreign Bond Funds

The Canadian bond market represents only 4 percent of the world's government bond market. So if you're limiting your bond investments solely to Canada, you may be missing out.

➤ **1986**   Japanese bonds earn 37 percent; Canadian bonds earn 13 percent.

➤ **1987**   United Kingdom bonds earn 35 percent; Canadian bonds, 3 percent.

➤ **1988**   Australian bonds earn 18 percent; Canadian bonds, 9 percent.

➤ **1989**   Canadian bonds are the top performers, earning around 13 percent.

➤ **1990**   United Kingdom bonds earn 23 percent; Canadian bonds, 20 percent.

➤ **1991**   Australian bonds earn 23 percent; Canadian bonds, 20 percent.

Dollars to Drachma to Deutschmarks

Before you can purchase another country's bonds, you must convert your money into that country's currency. For instance, if you want to purchase German bonds, you must first convert your Canadian dollars into German marks.

That doesn't guarantee a profit, even if you're right on your timing, and German bonds appreciate in value. The mark could fall in value faster than the Canadian dollar. So when you sell your German bonds for marks, then use the marks to buy Canadian dollars, you end up with fewer dollars than you started with.

This is called *currency risk*.

Never invest in bond mutual funds when interest rates are rising. And if you've already invested in a bond fund, sell.

Hedging Your Bets

To counter currency risk, some global funds hedge their bets by buying less volatile currencies.

A fund manager purchasing German bonds, for example, would sell marks on the foreign exchange market and buy a currency that will not fall so much in value, such as the U.S. dollar. The result is a currency-hedged German bond position.

This type of fund is much less volatile than a non-hedged bond fund. However, because of the hedging, the potential profits are lower than with non-hedged funds.

The Risk Involved

Individual bonds carry only limited risk, if you hold them until they mature.

Bond funds, however, never mature. As soon as some of the fund's bonds mature or the fund sells them, they are replaced with other bonds.

If interest rates rise, the fund can actually lose money.

The Road to Riches

Foreign bond funds have a history of doing really well or really lousy, depending on foreign interest rates.

Beginning investors should stay away from non-hedged foreign bond funds and stick to hedged funds, such as the Global Strategy World Bond Fund.

You should limit your foreign bond investments to 5 to 10 percent of your portfolio.

The Least You Need to Know

➤ Bonds represent formal IOUs between the issuer and the lender. The issuer agrees to repay the lender, with interest, on a specified date in the future.

➤ Bondholders, unlike shareholders, do not participate in a company's profit growth.

➤ The bond price is usually set at $1000 per bond.

➤ Bond prices and interest rates move in opposite directions. When interest rates go up, bond prices go down. When interest rates go down, bond prices go up.

➤ The yield to maturity includes the annual interest gained or lost on the difference between the bond's purchase price and face value.

➤ Strip coupon bonds do not pay interest and are therefore sold at a discount to the bond's face value.

➤ The best time to buy bonds is when interest rates have reached a peak and are just beginning to fall.

➤ Never buy bonds unless interest rates are high.

➤ In general, funds that invest primarily in long-term bonds will be more volatile than funds that invest primarily in intermediate-term bonds.

eenie, meenie, miny, moe...

FUND A   FUND B   FUND C   FUND D

Chapter 16

Everything You Need to Know About Mutual Funds

In This Chapter

➤ What are mutual funds?

➤ Open-end vs. closed-end

➤ Why should I buy one?

➤ Types of funds

➤ How do I buy one?

➤ Buying on margin

Have you ever wished that you could hire a professional money manager to watch over your money, who

1. really knows the ins and outs of the investment world;

2. would make informed decisions about where to invest your money, and when;

3. could consistently earn for you 15- to 16-percent profit, year after year;

4. would, if your portfolio occasionally lost money, earn it back for you?

That's essentially what you get by investing in a mutual fund.

The Eggs-in-Many-Baskets Theory

One of the cardinal investment strategies for limiting stock market risk is known as *diversification*.

If you buy just one stock, such as IBM, and it goes down—or way down, as in IBM's case in the early 1990s—you'll lose money.

If you buy shares in 100 companies, there's a good chance that some of the stocks in the portfolio will lose money, while the others will make money. This is true even if you choose the companies in which to invest by sticking the newspaper's stock pages to the wall and throwing darts at them.

At the end of the day, week, month, quarter or year, a single stock may have gone up or down. But the diversified portfolio will usually make a profit. That's the power of diversification. And that's what you get with a mutual fund.

Mutual Diversity

As individuals, few of us can afford to buy even one share of 100 companies. But as investors in a mutual fund, we can reap the benefits of diversity while sharing the costs.

The mutual fund will take your money and pool it together with money from many other investors. Along with their money, the mutual fund manager can invest in a broad range of stocks, bonds or other instruments.

Voila! Instant diversity.

More About Funds

In Canada, mutual fund companies must register with the provincial securities commission. In the U.S., mutual fund companies must register with the Securities and Exchange Commission. In either case, they're well-regulated, and their managers are well-qualified to make investments on their funds' behalf.

Major banks sell their own mutual funds. But many trust companies, insurance companies and private companies sell mutual funds as well. In fact, more than 50 percent of Canadian mutual fund assets are controlled by hundreds of private companies. They have names such as Altamira, Trimark, Bolton Tremblay, AGF, Templeton, and 20/20.

When deciding where to purchase a mutual

Mutual funds are professionally managed investment portfolios funded by thousands of people like you and me. But by putting even $1000 in a mutual fund, we purchase the opportunity to participate in markets for stocks, bonds and precious metals in Canada and in foreign countries.

You cannot buy one of the private companies' mutual funds (Templeton, Trimark, etc.) at your local bank. Similarly, you cannot buy your favourite bank's mutual fund through a private company such as Templeton or Trimark. They're all competing for your money. So compare them and choose the one that suits you.

fund, most people automatically head to their friendly neighbourhood bank and purchase the first mutual fund that the teller recommends. Don't fall into the trap. Make sure you check out all the choices before committing your hard-earned money.

Don't Worry...Be Happy

Investments in a mutual fund are not insured. But that shouldn't worry you too much. Here's why.

First, the big picture: In the course of Canadian history, no investor has ever lost money as a result of a mutual fund company going out of business.

"Yeah, but there's always a first time," you say. "So I should choose a bank's mutual fund, right?"

Not necessarily. Mutual funds sold through banks are no safer than mutual funds purchased from independent companies.

In any case, no matter who operates the fund, you won't lose your money if a mutual fund company goes out of business. You lose your money only if *all* the companies in which the mutual fund has invested go out of business. And that's not very likely to happen.

Shares, Value, etc.

Mutual fund companies issue shares in return for your investment. The price of a mutual fund's shares varies from day to day. Some days it's a little higher, other days it's a little lower. Over the long term, however, the share price usually goes up. Some go up more than others.

A mutual fund's net asset value (NAV) is calculated dividing the fund's total net assets by the total number of shares outstanding. If you read the chapter on stocks, you know this already.

The resulting figure is the price that you have to pay for one share in the mutual fund.

Alternatively, you could just look for the figure in the business section of your newspaper, under Mutual Funds.

The NAV fluctuates daily. Some days it may be up 5 cents; other days it may be down 10 cents. That's called volatility.

Stock prices of individual companies fluctuate in relation to supply and demand. When there are more buyers than sellers, the share price rises. When there are more sellers than buyers, the share price falls.

Same with mutual funds. When the stocks that make up the mutual fund rise in price, so too will the mutual fund's share price. When the stock prices fall, so will the mutual fund's.

Open-End Funds

If you own shares in an open-end mutual fund, you'll almost never have trouble finding someone to buy your shares or sell you more shares at the current NAV. If investors don't want to deal with you, the fund itself will.

The most popular mutual funds today that are listed in the mutual fund section of your daily newspaper are open-ended—Altamira, AGF, Trimark, Royal Trust and so forth.

Closed-End Funds

Most mutual funds currently traded in Canada are open-ended. That's like saying most of the screws used in Canada are slot-headed. Then you find out that there are all those other screws with bigger slots and smaller slots, little square holes and big square holes, holes shaped like stars...

In keeping with the "screw" theory of life, there are also things called closed-end mutual funds. These funds issue a limited number of shares when they're first set up. Once they sell all the shares and there are none left to sell, the fund is closed. At that point, no new shares are issued, and the fund company will no longer redeem your shares.

That's where the stock exchange comes in. You can still buy and sell shares in a closed-end fund on the stock exchange. The price will fluctuate, just like shares in other companies. Sometimes the price per share will be higher than the NAV—selling at a premium. Sometimes it will be less—selling at a discount.

However, you should never buy shares in a closed-end fund when they're first issued. Instead, you should wait until they first start trading on the stock exchange.

The reason? It costs money to pay legal fees and other expenses involved in arranging a share issue. So when their shares first begin trading on the stock exchange, closed-end funds usually sell at a discount to their NAV. This means the shares sell for less than the price at which they were first issued.

A prudent strategy is to wait for the fund to sell at a 20- to 30-percent discount to its NAV before you buy. Once they begin selling at a premium to their NAV, you should then consider selling your shares.

A Typical Listing of a Closed-End Fund

Fund name	Stock exchange	NAV	Market price	Premium discount
Korea Fund	NY	$10.14	$13.50	+33.1%

Here's what it all means:

➤ Shares in the Korea Fund are traded on the New York Stock Exchange.

➤ The current net asset value is $10.14.

➤ If this were an open-end fund, you would pay just $10.14 a share. But this is a closed-end fund. So you'll have to pay the market price: $13.50.

➤ Shares in the Korea Fund currently sell at a premium of 33.1 percent to its NAV. In other words, its $13.50-per-share price tag is 33.1 percent more than the NAV of $10.14.

Like the shares of other corporate stocks, shares in closed-end mutual funds rise and fall according to supply and demand. When more people want to buy than to sell the closed-end fund, the market price will rise above the NAV, and vice versa.

A few financial wizards have discovered that instead of leaving your money in a mutual fund for years, you can make a higher return by moving your money every month into the previous month's 10 best-performing funds. They say that if you have the inclination to do this, and you're prepared to pay the fees involved, you can beat the market return over a long period.

Load: What Does It Mean?

Fund companies commonly charge a commission on the shares they sell. This commission is also called a *load*.

Contrary to popular opinion, they're not ripping you off by charging a commission. The commission simply compensates the fund company, financial planner and stockbroker for providing you with a service.

Front-End Load

If you choose a front-end load fund, you pay a commission ranging from 2 to 9 percent every time you buy shares.

Back-End Load

With a back-end load fund, your entire initial investment goes into the mutual fund. You pay no direct sales commission up front. But you have to leave your money in the fund for a minimum of five or six years. Otherwise you have to pay a commission when you remove it, called a back-end load.

The typical back-end load fund charges a 6-percent commission in the first year, based on the value of your portfolio when you sell your shares; 5 percent in the second year; 4 percent after three years, and so on.

Most people should keep their money in a fund for at least five years anyway, so the back-end load won't affect you.

All in the Family

When the same company sells a number of different mutual funds, they're called a family. In many cases, you can transfer your money once or twice from one fund to another within the same family without paying a fee.

Go for Broke

You may wonder how your financial planner gets paid if you keep your money in a fund for six years and don't pay any commissions. The answer is that there are other fees involved in a mutual fund that the investor never sees. For the most part, these are the fund's management fees, taken off the top of the fund as it accumulates. The financial planner is paid from these fees at the outset.

These fees are explained in the fund's annual report.

No-Load Funds

There may be no such thing as a free lunch. But no-load mutual funds come pretty close.

With no-load funds, you don't have to pay a commission to buy or sell your shares. That's the good news.

But before you take your wad of bills down to the mutual fund store, wait until you hear the bad news. All mutual funds, including no-loads, pay their investment advisory team an annual management fee of between 0.2 to 2 percent of the fund's assets. This compensates them for making all the fund's investment decisions. Mutual funds also have to pay operating expenses to cover accounting costs, office rent, pencils, stick-'em notes and postage stamps.

These additional charges are deducted from the assets in the fund's portfolio.

No-load mutual funds do not provide the same quality of service as you'll receive from a professional financial planner or stockbroker. For instance, no-load fund companies will not tell you when to switch your money out of one fund that's under-performing the market and into another that's outperforming the market.

Nor will they recommend a competitor's fund, no matter how well it's performing.

An independent financial planner looks out for your best interests. He will help you find the fund that's best suited to your current needs and goals.

As a general rule, fund companies that sell front- and back-end load funds do not sell no-load funds. Similarly, no-load fund companies do not usually sell mutual funds requiring a load.

All three types make money, providing you invest for the long term.

Beginning investors should think seriously about purchasing no-load funds only through an independent financial planner or stockbroker, rather than buying the shares directly from the fund company.

In any case, investors who avoid mutual funds because they charge a commission are only cheating themselves. Don't think about commissions at all. Focus on performance and service.

Even if you have to pay a 5- to 9-percent commission, the potential gains of a good mutual fund over five to 10 years will make the commission pale by comparison.

Types of Funds

All mutual fund families offer investors a number of different types of mutual funds from which to choose. These include the following:

1. equity funds

2. specialty funds

3. international funds

4. bond funds

5. income funds

6. balanced funds

7. money market funds.

1. Equity Funds

Equity funds invest in common stocks. They can be Canadian, American or foreign.

Equity funds aim for long-term capital appreciation. That means they want the stocks held by the fund to increase in value over time.

If you're trying to double your money by next year, forget about equity funds. If you're saving for retirement, then equity funds are your best bet.

Investors who can wait patiently for five years or more to let their money grow should put 60 to 70 percent of their investments in equity funds. Over the long term, equity funds have outperformed all other investment vehicles.

All equity funds invest in common stocks. But the similarities end there.

Some funds invest for value. They look for stocks that are priced cheaply relative to assets or earnings. Others invest for growth. They don't look for stocks that are priced cheaply but ones that are issued by companies that are growing. Other funds invest in a combination of the two.

There's more: Some equity funds invest strictly in smaller companies. Others stick with the big guys.

All About Small-Cap Stocks

If they grow at all, smaller companies tend to grow far more quickly than do larger ones. A small company can take off on the strength of a single new product or service. The same new product or service will usually have only a modest impact on a larger company.

Historically, the stocks of smaller companies have outperformed larger companies' stocks—but not always.

In 18 of the 23 years from 1960 to 1983, small-company stocks outperformed large-company stocks by a margin of almost six to one.

From 1984 to 1990, large-company stocks outperformed small-company stocks every year except 1988.

The past few years have favoured smaller company stocks.

More About Equity Funds

Many equity funds have established track records over the last one, five, and 10 years. Which one tells you more?

Conventional wisdom says you should look for a good long-term track record, and stay away from last year's hot funds. I have only one objection to that advice: It's wrong.

According to a study by the *Wall Street Journal,* last year's best-performing equity funds will still provide excellent returns this year. The funds with good five- or 10-year track records are usually not your best bet.

The study followed three investors:

➤ The first bought the top 25 percent of equity funds based on their performance over the past year.

➤ The second bought the top 25 percent of equity funds based on their performance over the past five years.

➤ The third bought the top 25 percent of equity funds based on their performance over the past 10 years.

And the winner is...

The top-performing equity funds over 10 years earned average five-year gains of... 82.6 percent.

The top-performing equity funds over five years earned average five-year gains of... 80.7 percent.

The top-performing equity funds over one year earned average five-year gains of... 95.6 percent.

173

Conclusion: When it comes to future five-year performance, the past year is more important than the previous five- or 10-year periods.

Here's why: Some equity funds invest in growth stocks. Some invest in value stocks. Some invest in a combination. Growth and value stocks both tend to go through long periods when they're in or out of favour, and their prices rise and fall accordingly.

If you buy a stock fund with the best five- or 10-year track record, there's a good chance that it's about to go out of favour. On the other hand, last year's top-performing fund may just be coming into favour, and could be popular for some time to come.

Every 3 or 4 years, you should weed out the diversified equity funds that under-perform the market, and reinvest some of your money in funds that outperform the market. That way, some of your money will always go into the top-performing funds of the previous year.

All investors should consider investing 10 to 20 percent of their portfolio in international equity mutual funds to diversify their risk and increase their gains.

2. Specialty Funds

Specialty funds invest in only one sector, such as gold funds, resource funds or energy funds.

Specialty funds do only as well as the sector they invest in. When they're hot, they sizzle. When they're not, they fizzle. In most cases, last year's hot specialty funds are often next year's big losers. Never buy last year's hot specialty funds just because they did well last year.

3. International Funds

Canada has the sixth-largest stock market in the world. But all the money that's invested on Canadian stock markets adds up to only 3 percent of the total amount available to companies throughout the world.

That means that if you limit your equity investments to Canada, you miss about 97 percent of the opportunities elsewhere in the world.

With this in mind, some mutual funds invest in stocks in Japan, Britain, Germany, France, Italy, Mexico and the Far East, to name a few.

Other countries often grow more quickly than does Canada. When they do, companies in those countries reap higher profits. With higher profits come higher stock prices. If you invest in them, you win.

4. Bond Funds

Rather than investing with the aim of increasing the value of their holdings, bond funds focus on income. They usually invest in government, corporate and strip coupon bonds. (For more on these weird and wonderful creatures, see Chapter 15 on bonds.)

Like individual bonds, bond mutual funds respond to interest rates. When interest rates rise, bond mutual funds fall in value. When interest rates fall, bond mutual funds rise in value.

The price fluctuations (volatility) of a particular bond fund are directly proportional to the average maturity of all the bonds held in the fund's portfolio.

The longer it takes for its bond holdings to mature, the more sensitive the bond fund will be to changes in interest rates.

In general, funds that invest primarily in long-term bonds (maturing in 20 to 25 years) will be more volatile than funds that invest primarily in intermediate-term bonds (maturing in five to 10 years).

A short-term bond fund that invests primarily in bonds maturing in one to three years will be the least volatile.

Foreign Bond Funds

The Canadian bond market represents only 4 percent of the world's government bond market. So if you're limiting your bond investments solely to Canada, you may be missing out (see Chapter 15).

5. Income Funds

Income funds aim to produce income. They do not aim for capital gains. That means they're not looking for their investments to increase substantially in value. They just want the investments to generate money in predictable amounts.

A large percentage of the money in such a fund is always invested in government and corporate bonds. These funds are appropriate for investors who want income, but very little risk. People on pensions like them.

6. Balanced Funds

Using a balanced investment approach, these funds invest in some stocks, some bonds, some gold and some real estate. All you have to do is sit back, relax and let the fund manager maintain the balance. Over the long term, these funds usually generate lower returns than do most equity funds.

These funds are for people who want to invest their money once, and never think about it again.

However, investing once and forgetting about your money is not a very good investment strategy.

7. Money Market Funds

Money market funds invest primarily in Treasury bills. You can't get much safer than that. These funds almost always pay a higher rate of interest than does a bank savings account, and all the interest earned will be converted into additional shares in your account.

As with all other mutual funds, your money is highly liquid. If you want to take your money back, you can usually have a cheque in your hands within 24 to 48 hours.

Money market funds offer an excellent place to store your money while you decide what to do with it over the long term.

What Are Treasury Bills?

The Canadian government regularly needs to borrow enormous amounts of money for short periods. Once a week, it sells Treasury bills in an auction to banks and other large financial institutions.

Treasury bills—or T-bills, as they're called—are very short-term bonds that mature in three months, six months or one year. These IOUs are backed by the Canadian government, and they're among the safest investments in the world. And there's a huge market for them, which makes them very easy to buy and sell.

Dividends

Like stocks, mutual funds pay dividends to their shareholders. They're paid on an annual, semiannual, or quarterly basis.

You can choose to collect the dividend yourself. Or you can tell the fund administrators to use your dividends to buy more shares in the fund.

By the way, these dividends are eligible for the dividend tax credit, which you can use to reduce your annual income taxes.

How to Buy a Mutual Fund

You can invest in a mutual fund directly. Or you can work with a financial planner. A financial planner matches your needs and goals to the appropriate fund.

If you're single, make a lot of money, have few expenses, want immediate gratification, and don't mind taking a few risks, the planner will suggest an appropriate strategy.

176

If you're married with three kids, unemployed, paying off a mortgage, looking forward to Aunt Beulah's arrival from Scotland to stay in your basement for the next 13 years, and would like to collect a pension income when she finally leaves, the planner will suggest another strategy.

With the name of each fund that the planner recommends, you should also receive the fund's prospectus.

The Lone Investor

If you go it alone, you should call a number of fund companies—the more the better—and ask each of them for a prospectus. This is a booklet full of figures and tables that will tell you how and where the fund invests its money, and with what success.

You should feel comfortable with the fund's past performance, future outlook, fees, rules and regulations before you commit any money.

Since you're making your own decisions, you will deal directly with the fund company or with a discount broker.

The mutual fund prospectus contains information about the fund: its investment strategy, its history, the fees it charges, rules for cashing in or moving your money, etc. It also contains an application form for prospective investors. It's put together by the fund company.

Discount Brokers

Discount brokers charge less than a full-service broker to perform the same tasks. But they don't offer advice, and they don't really care if you make investments appropriate to your situation.

You can keep track of the performance of mutual funds over the Internet. At www.globefund.com, for example, and at www.quicken.ca, you can find charts, graphs and information about fund characteristics and performance. Other good sources of information include the following:

Investorama	www.investorama.com
Thomson Information	www.marketedge.com
U.S. Information	www.wallstreetcity.com

Other discount brokers include CT Market Partners (www.ctsecurities.com), operated by Canada Trust, and Hongkong Bank's Discount Trading Service (www.hkbc.com).

For information on mutual funds, try the Canadian Mutual Fund Portfolio Pages (www.pal.com)

Two of the best are Green Line Investor Services Inc. (800-268-8166) and Priority Brokerage (888-597-9999). Others include CIBC Investors Edge (800-567-EDGE) and E*Trade (888-TRADE-88).

When filling out an application form, make sure that you request telephone redemption and switching privileges. That way, you can move your money from one fund to another, or remove your money completely, with just a telephone call.

Also consider setting up an automatic investment plan. That way, your money will be withdrawn automatically from your bank account each month and transferred directly into the mutual fund of your choice.

You should also consider having all dividends and capital gains reinvested back into the fund. This will put as much money as possible to work for you in the fund.

A Few Good Funds

Altamira Equity Fund   An excellent no-load diversified equity fund.

➤ Invests in small and large company stocks.

➤ Aims for value and growth, so it invests in companies whose stocks are priced cheaply and also looks for companies with large growth potential.

➤ Average annual gains between 1989 and 1993: over 30 percent.

➤ Phone: 416-413-5359.

➤ Write: Altamira Investment Services Inc., 250 Bloor St. East, Suite 200, Toronto, Ontario, M4W 1E6.

Templeton Growth Fund   An excellent load mutual fund.

➤ Buys bargains when nobody else wants them—straw hats in January.

➤ Average annual return since 1956: over 15 percent.

➤ Phone: 800-387-0830.

Trimark Fund   One of the best international equity funds.

➤ Average annual return since 1984: over 15 percent.

➤ Phone: 800-387-9823 (Ontario & Quebec) or 800-387-9841 (elsewhere in Canada).

U.S. No-Loads

In the U.S., there are more than 1000 no-load mutual funds, many of which have excellent long-term track records over 15 to 20 years.

To purchase one of these U.S. mutual funds, just write or telephone the fund company. Many have toll-free 800 numbers, accessible from Canada. Ask for a prospectus, plus a W-8 tax form. (This form tells the U.S. Internal Revenue Service that you're not a U.S. resident and should not be subject to withholding of capital gains.)

According to Revenue Canada, your foreign capital gains still qualify for the $100 000 capital gains exemption.

The U.S. government will withhold some of your dividends. But you can get them back when you file your Canadian tax return.

Some U.S. mutual fund companies will not send a prospectus to Canadian residents. Big deal. Just open an account with a U.S. discount broker. That way, you can buy and sell any U.S. funds with a single phone call.

One of the best U.S. discount brokers is Muriel Siebert & Company. Inc., 885 Third Avenue, Suite 1720, New York, NY 10022. (Phone: 212-644-2400.)

A Few Good U.S. Funds

No-load U.S. equity funds:

➤ **Twentieth Century's Ultra Fund**   Write: Twentieth Century Investors, Inc. P.O. Box 419200, Kansas City, Missouri 64141-6200; Phone: 816-531-5575.

➤ **The Berger 100 Fund**   Write: Berger Associates Inc., P.O. Box 5005, Denver, Colorado 80217; Phone: 800-551-5849 or 303-329-0200.

➤ **The Kaufman Fund**   Write: Kaufman Fund Inc., 17 Battery Place, Suite 2624, New York, New York 10004; Phone: 800-321-9043 or 212-344-2661.

Margin

Margin is money that you borrow from your broker to buy investments. If you purchase $5000 worth of a mutual fund or stocks through a brokerage firm, the firm will usually allow you to borrow another $5000. So you can now buy $10 000 worth of shares, even though you have only $5000.

The firm will insist that you maintain this 50-percent ratio of borrowed money to your own money.

Say you've bought $5000 (50 percent of $10 000) worth of a mutual fund trading at a price of $6 per share. If the share price falls below $6, your broker will call you and ask you to put up more cash to maintain your 50-percent minimum margin requirement.

If you don't have enough money, you'll have to sell some of your shares to make up the difference.

When the stock market is advancing, you can earn substantially higher profits by investing on margin. For instance, if you have $5000 to invest in a fund, and the fund goes up 25 percent, you make $1250. But if you borrowed an additional $5000 to buy $10 000 worth of the fund, you'd earn $2500, even though only $5000 of your original investment was yours.

You have to pay for the borrowed money, at a prevailing interest rate. But even then, you'd be ahead of the game.

Sometimes, however, the stock market declines. When it does, you'll lose even more if you invest on margin. For example, if your stock or mutual fund falls 25 percent in value, from $10 000 to $7500, you'll be down $2500. That's one-quarter of your total investment, but one-half of your original $5000. And you still have to pay interest on your $5000 loan.

The Least You Need to Know

➤ Mutual funds are professionally managed investment portfolios that allow individual investors to put as little as $100 per month into stocks, bonds, gold and real estate.

➤ Open-end mutual funds will always sell you more shares in the fund or buy back the shares you already own.

➤ Closed-end funds no longer issue new shares or redeem your shares, so you have to buy and sell them on the stock market.

➤ Front-end loads charge you a commission up front. Back-end loads charge you a commission only if you redeem your shares early. No-load funds don't charge any commission to buy or sell your shares.

➤ There are many different types of funds, including equity, specialty, international, bond, income, balanced and money market funds.

➤ When it comes to diversified equity funds, the past year's performance is more important than the previous five- or 10-year periods.

➤ Canadian investors can open up a U.S. account and purchase mutual funds that are sold only in the United States.

➤ Investors who purchase their mutual fund shares through a brokerage firm can double their purchasing power by borrowing money from their broker. This borrowed money is known as margin.

WHOOOOO!!!

Chapter 17

For Seniors: Counting on the Government

In This Chapter

➤ How secure is Old Age Security?

➤ When to apply for a Guaranteed Income Supplement

➤ Putting off receiving Canada Pension Plan or Quebec Pension Plan benefits

When you look forward—happily or otherwise—to your 65th birthday, you probably feel a vague sense of reassurance that no matter what happens, you can always rely on the government to keep a roof over your head and a can of beans on the table. With the Canada Pension Plan, Old Age Security and other programs, the government will provide you with the bare minimum that you need to get by.

Of course, we're not getting something for nothing. Most of us have paid for these programs throughout our working lives. And chances are that at least some of us will not live long enough to get back the full value of our contributions. But that's another story.

Where Do I Sign?

It's not enough to turn 65, sit back and wait for your first cheque. To collect payments from most of these programs, an individual has to fill out an application form. Hey, this is the government. What did you expect?

Application forms are available through federal Health Canada offices, listed in the *Blue Pages* of your telephone book. You'll have to prove your age (just as you did when you wanted to buy your first case of beer. Oh, to be young again!)

It's best to gather all the application forms a few months before you turn 65, so the government will have lots of time to lose the forms...so you can send another set...so you might collect a payment when you turn 65—if you're lucky!

Old Age Security

This program has been around since 1952. That's not very impressive. Most of us have been around even longer.

Initially, an individual over 70 years of age received $40 per month. Today, that payment amounts to more than $380, and you have to be 65 or older to qualify.

You can receive OAS whether or not you're still working, or even if you've never worked at all. But you must be a Canadian citizen or legal resident on the day before your application is approved, and you must have lived in Canada for 10 years before you apply. If you live outside Canada, you can still qualify if you've lived for three times as long in Canada as in another country. (Don't ask us. We don't make the rules.)

If you forget to apply, you can still receive up to five years' worth of back payments, but you don't receive interest.

It's Too Good to Be True

You're right. It is. If you earn more than $83 988 in taxable income, you'll have to pay back all the OAS benefits you receive. You'll still receive them—but when tax time comes, you'll have to pay them all back as taxes.

If you earn between $55 000 and $83 000, you'll have to pay back a portion of your OAS benefits proportionate to your income.

As the years pass, these amounts will increase because of inflation. If you won't turn 65 for another 20 years, you'll likely have to earn about $150 000 per year to forgo your entire OAS benefit.

To avoid paying back your entire OAS benefit, leave your RRSP intact for as long as you can, and move the funds into a Registered Retirement Investment Fund when you turn 69.

The Guaranteed Income Supplement

If your income is lower than $24 per year—that's right: $24!—you can fill out a form to receive a Guaranteed Income Supplement with a maximum value of $457.13. For every $24 that you earn, your

GIS diminishes by $1. This means that you can earn up to $10 992 and still get a GIS benefit. If you're married or live with a partner, you can earn a combined income of $14 304, and still get a GIS benefit.

You have to apply for it every year.

Couples and Other Strangers

If your partner is between the ages of 60 and 65, he or she may be eligible for a Spouse's Allowance. It's just like OAS and GIS, except that you get to collect it early.

Your mate can also collect a Widowed Spouse's Allowance after you teeter off this mortal coil, as long as you were collecting OAS and/or GIS while you were still alive and kicking.

Your partner can earn up to $15 048 per year and still collect a Widowed Spouse's Allowance benefit.

Details, Details

If you can't figure out what you qualify for, or if you can't live on the amount that you receive, check with your local Health Canada office. You might find that you qualify for another program that will add a bit of extra income to your monthly allowance.

Provincial Programs

In some provinces, residents who receive OAS and GIS also qualify for provincial payments. You should check with your provincial social services department to see if you're one of the lucky ones.

Canada and Quebec Pension Plans

These plans, which began in 1966, are similar but not exactly the same. One is distinct from the other; separate but equal... You get the idea.

These programs are financed by mandatory contributions deducted from your paycheque or through direct payments to Revenue Canada. The amount you receive depends on the amount you contribute.

If you're healthy, you can receive up to approximately $660 a month when you retire; if you're disabled, you can receive about $220 per month more.

Widows and orphans of CPP and QPP recipients, and children of disabled CPP and QPP recipients, also receive a benefit.

If you didn't earn enough to make a maximum contribution, or if you've only paid

You can start collecting CPP and QPP when you turn 60, but for every month of your age under 65, you lose 0.5 percent of your pension eligibility, up to a maximum of 30 percent.

Nor can you collect the pension if you *earn* more than you'd *receive* from the pension—about $8800 a year.

"If you take the early CPP or QPP, you'll receive the pension for more years, but you'll get less each month. If you take the pension later, you'll receive more each month but for fewer years."

—Robert Kerr, C.A.

The Only Retirement Guide You'll Ever Need

into the plan for a few years, you'll receive less than the maximum when you retire.

How Much Will I Get?

Your CPP and QPP benefits are determined by calculating the number of years you've contributed to the plan and your average earnings over those years.

But don't worry. The government makes this calculation for you and sends you a statement every year.

If you want more information, contact your local Income Security Program office or an office of the *Regies des Rentes du Quebec.*

Put It Off

You can wait for up to five years after you turn 65 to start collecting your CPP or QPP benefits and increase the total payment by up to 30 percent. But you'd better be sure you'll be around long enough to enjoy the extra benefits and compensate for the benefits that you gave up.

It's Not Over Until It's Over

The current government in Ottawa wants to replace the Old Age Security benefit and Guaranteed Income Supplement with something called the *Senior Benefit.* It would take effect in 2001 for people under 60 before January 1, 1996.

The new benefit would increase supplementary income for people earning less than $40 000 per year, and reduce it for people earning more.

Canadian Pensioners Concerned and other pension-related activists are storming the barricades over this one, and it may not take effect.

To CPP or Not to CPP

There have been dire warnings in recent years that there won't be enough money available for all of us to collect CPP benefits by the time baby boomers reach 65 and start devouring all the pension money.

These warnings are without foundation. There will be enough money—we just might have to pay more for it while we're still working.

Under a plan developed by a gang of actuaries in leather jackets, we could increase our contributions when interest rates are high. This would maximize the amount earned by our contributions. When interest rates are low, we'd keep paying the amount required to fund the plan on a pay-as-you-go basis. That means we'd pay enough to the plan to cover the amount owing to eligible pensioners.

Other actuaries, wearing red trunks, say we don't have to increase our contributions. By the time the government gets the economy back into shape (That's what they said. Honest!), the next generation will have more money to fund the CPP.

One side is right.

If you want more details, talk to an actuary.

The Least You Need to Know

➤ To collect payments from OAS, CPP and QPP, an individual has to fill out an application form.

➤ You can receive OAS whether or not you're still working, or even if you've never worked at all.

➤ Your CPP and QPP benefits are determined by calculating the number of years you've contributed to the plan and your average earnings over those years. The government will provide you with this calculation once a year.

➤ You can start collecting CPP and QPP when you turn 60, which will reduce your benefits, or you can wait until you reach 70 to maximize your benefits.

Investment Strategies: The Game Plan

The surest way to make money from investing is to buy low and sell high.

Unfortunately, many of us do the opposite. We buy high and sell low. Why do we act like such foolish ninnies?

Out of fear. We're afraid to get in. So we wait until the price of our selected investment has risen before we buy. And once we're in, we're afraid to get out. So we watch the price of our investment fall before we finally sell.

This is not a good way to make money.

Here are some investment strategies that will help you to buy low and sell high. Most of them involve equity investments and mutual funds.

Dollar-Cost Averaging: The Steady Eddy Theory

This sounds complicated. Most discussions about investments do. But it's actually one of the best strategies for an investor, and one of the easiest to understand.

Here's how it works: Instead of investing all your money in one shot, you invest a fixed amount at regular intervals. You decide when and how much to invest. You can invest $100 every two weeks, for example, or $500 a month for five months, or $1000 every three months for a year.

With each round, you buy only as many shares as your money will pay for. No more, no less. So you automatically buy more shares when their price is low and fewer shares when their price is high.

Steady Eddy in Action

For example, let's say you have $500 to invest in mutual funds. Instead of investing it all at once, you invest $100 each month for five months.

➤ In January the fund sells at $10 a share, so you pay $100 for 10 shares.

➤ In February, the fund trades at $5 a share. Your $100 investment now buys 20 shares.

➤ In March, the share price edges back to $7.50. You buy 13 1/3 shares for $100.

➤ In April, the share price is back up to $10. Once again you buy 10 shares.

➤ In May, things really pick up. Your fund's share price rises to $15. With $100, you can buy only 6 2/3 shares.

Investment managers disagree about the ideal investment strategy. Some say passive management—investing in index funds, for example—combines the best returns with the most peace of mind for an investor. Others say that active management—picking investments based on market trends, etc.—while apparently more risky, produces better returns. And it's more fun, too.

In our example, we applied our theory over five months. But to really maximize your gains, you should invest a consistent amount, on a monthly basis, over a much longer period. The point: Be consistent.

You now have a total of 60 shares. If you'd invested your entire $500 when your fund was selling at $10 a share, you'd have bought only 50 shares.

At $15 a share, they'd now be worth $750.

Instead, following the Steady Eddy theory of dollar-cost averaging, your 60 shares are worth a total of $900.

You're $150 ahead of the game.

This isn't magic. It results from investing a fixed amount of money at regular intervals,

Most studies show that it's better to buy and hold rather than trying to time the market. Investors who held their shares in Peter Lynch's Fidelity Magellan Fund, for example, over a 10-year period in the 1980s, earned an average 20-percent annual return. Investors who tried to time the market—who bought and sold units in the fund based on market timing instead of simply buying the units and holding them—lost on average 1 percent each year.

so you automatically buy more shares when the price is low, and fewer shares when the price is high.

You Have to Stick It Out!

To invest successfully using dollar-cost averaging, you have to commit yourself to investing for the long term. Once you start, you can't cash in your chips after a month or two because you want the money for a trip to Acapulco.

Nor can you cash in when the market starts to fall. You have to stick with it.

In fact, the lower prices fall, the more bargains you'll pick up, and the faster your portfolio will grow.

The Dow Doubler: Double the Fun

Here's another catchy theory. It's called the Dow Doubler, and it is based on the fact that in almost every decade since 1890, the Dow has doubled between the beginning and the end of the decade.

➤ On April 19, 1897, the Dow hit a low for the decade of 38.49.

➤ On September 5, 1899, it hit the high for the decade of 77.61, an increase of 101.6 percent.

➤ On January 13, 1950, the Dow hit a low for the following decade of 196.81. On December 31, 1959, the Dow reached 679.36, an increase of 242.2 percent.

➤ On August 12, 1982, the Dow hit a decade low of 776.92. On December 29, 1989, it reached 2753.20, up 254.4 percent.

On October 11, 1990, the Dow hit a low for the decade (so far) of 2365.10. If it at least doubles before the end of the decade, as it has in every decade but two since 1890, it will hit 4730.20 before the end of 1999. (In fact, the Dow has already exceeded this mark, and it's only 1997. It broke 7000 recently, and some market participants expect it to break 10 000 before the decade's over.)

More Nifty Stats

In seven of the nine decades since 1900, the stock market hit its lowest point within the first three years of the decade. Between 1910 and 1919, the decade's low point did not occur until 1915.

In the 1970s, the low point of the decade occurred in 1974, because of the OPEC crisis.

If our theory is correct, then the stock market reached its lowest point of the 1990s on October 11, 1990.

Take Me Higher

The stock market's high points in each decade have always occurred in the later years: in 1899, for example, 1907, 1919, 1929, 1937, 1946, 1959, 1966, 1979 and 1989. Therefore, we should expect to see this decade's high point occur in either 1997 or 1999.

In 1997, the markets reached their highest point so far this decade. Some people expect them to go much higher.

The Year of the Stock

Are some years better to invest in than others?Apparently so.

Financial gurus have conducted an exhaustive analysis of changes in the Dow Jones average in each year since 1891. Some years of a decade appear to be better than others for investments. In fact, judging by the last nine decades, the fifth year of a decade brings a consistent improvement in the Dow.

In fact, a down year has never occurred in the fifth year of a decade.

This theory held in1995. Markets began their steady rise in that year, which was a good one for investments. In the seventh (7th) and tenth (10th) years of a decade, however, the Dow performs poorly. Once again, this trend seems to prevail in the 90s. In October 1997, the markets began to fluctuate, losing up to 10 percent of their value in a brief period before regaining it again.

The Magic Number: 19.4 Percent

When the S&P 500 Index declines by 19.4 percent, it provides a good opportunity for investors to buy. Over the following year, there's a better-than-average chance that the market will rise significantly.

➤ On February 18, 1993, for example, the S&P 500 declined by 19.4 percent. A year later, the S&P 500 had risen by 87 percent.

➤ On May 28, 1962, the S&P 500 fell by 19.4 percent. A year later, it had risen again by 26 percent.

  It doesn't always happen. On November 26, 1973, the S&P 500 fell by 19.4 percent. A year later, it had fallen by 28 percent.

But out of 19 occasions since 1932 when the S&P 500 has declined by 19.4 percent, it has risen during the following year 14 times. And in 11 of those years, it has risen by double-digit figures!

189

The Presidential Theory

In every term of a U.S. president, there occur some good years for investors and some bad years. Taken altogether, these constitute the presidential cycle.

Each presidential cycle lasts 4 years.

First Year   The first year in the cycle is the post-election year. In that year, the president bumbles along, getting used to the office. He also has to pay for all the stupid promises that his predecessor made in the hope of getting elected. (Sometimes he's his own predecessor, and he has to pay for his own stupid promises.) People tend to forgive him. The markets perform poorly.

Second Year   This is the mid-term year. People aren't so forgiving, because the president's still not doing much and he's been around for a year already. The markets perform poorly.

Third Year   This year is called the pre-election year. Now things start to pick up. The president still doesn't know what he's doing. But he knows how to make himself look good. And he wants to get reelected. What's the best way to get reelected? Try to make everybody rich, and let them think you did it. Stock markets perform almost four times better in this year of the cycle than in the previous two years.

Fourth Year   The last year in the cycle is the election year. The president pulls out all the stops. You want money, he's got money. You want a highway, he'll build you a highway. You want a dog, here's a dog. The market goes gangbusters again.

Over the past 27 U.S. presidential administrations, the stock market gained a total of 148 percent during the post-election and mid-term years. In the pre-election and election years—the last two years—of each administration, the stock market has gained a total of 474 percent.

More Proof

Throughout every four-year cycle since 1916, the low point in the stock market has occurred either in the post-election or mid-term years, except during Herbert Hoover's administration. (In those four years, as a result of the Depression, the low point occurred during the election year of 1932. Hoover lost. Who'd vote for a guy who led the country into a depression?)

Since 1961, the low point in every bear market has occurred during the post-election or mid-term years (1962, 1966, 1970, 1974, 1978, 1982 and 1990).

Some Months Are Better than Others

The best six-month period to invest in the stock market: November through April.

The worst six-month period to invest in the stock market: May through October.

Here's an amazing example, based on real data.

Two investors start with $10 000.

Moe invests only from May until October, the worst months. In the other six months she keeps her money in cash.

Curly invests only from November to April, the best months, and keeps his money in cash for the rest of the year.

They both do this for 44 years, from 1949 to 1992.

At the end of 44 years, Moe, who invested in the bad months, had gained $5083.11.

Curly, who invested in the good months, had gained $185 234.62.

January: Start the Year Off with a Bang

When it comes to the stock market, January is a very special month. That's because the performance of the stock market in January indicates its performance over the following 11 months.

Between 1947 and 1996, the S&P 500 index increased in each of 29 years by more than 1 percent in January. In each of those years, the stock market's annual return was positive. And in 23 of those years, the return from February through December exceeded the January return.

The one exception was 1987. That year, as a result of the market crash in October, the return for the entire year was only 5.7 percent, compared to an increase of 13.2 percent in January.

Small Is Beautiful

During the month of January, the stocks of small companies out-perform the stocks of big companies.

In Canada and the U.S. alike, this has occurred in all but three of the last 50 years. (Those years were 1969, 1973 and 1990, when small-company stocks took a drubbing.)

Whenever small-company stocks get hammered badly during a year, then the following January is usually a good time to invest in them.

The ones that perform best are the smaller companies whose stocks are included in mutual funds such as the Altamira Select American Fund, and the Everest Special Equity Fund.

9-to-5, Monday-to-Friday

The *best day* on which to buy stocks: Friday.

The *worst day* on which to buy stocks: Monday.

The *best 60 minutes* during which to buy stocks: the last hour in each trading day.

The last trading day of each month and the first four trading days of each new month generate more profits than all the rest of the days in the month combined.

If, between 1987 and 1991, you'd purchased equity mutual funds on the day preceding the last trading day of each month and then sold your shares at the close of the fourth trading day of the new month, you would have beaten a buy-and-hold strategy. (That's nothing fancy. You buy. You hold. That's it.)

A $10 000 nest egg invested in repeated five-day patterns, beginning in 1987, would have grown to $18 292 by 1991. Using a buy-and-hold strategy, it would have grown to only $17 217.

This five-day switching strategy gets even better if you invest on the two trading days before the U.S markets close for a holiday. These holidays are as follows:

New Year's Day

Presidents' Day

Memorial Day

Independence Day

Labour Day

Thanksgiving

Christmas

How to Do It

You will be investing only five days per month, and you will be switching frequently between stock funds and money market funds. (Money market funds are basically cash funds.)

With all this switching, you should invest only in no-load funds to avoid commission costs.

In addition, you'll be investing in stock funds only a quarter of the time. So your risk is very limited. You should seriously consider using 50-percent margin (that means borrow more money, equivalent to 50 percent of your initial investment) to increase your profits.

This strategy works equally well for U.S. and Canadian funds.

Unfortunately, most mutual funds will not allow you to buy and sell so frequently. In any case, over the long term, a simple strategy of dollar-cost averaging will generate better results.

Another Trading Strategy

According to financial writer Christopher Byron, you can beat the markets by investing equally in units of the top 10 no-load, all-equity mutual funds every month. Over a 20-year period beginning in 1976, according to his computer calculations, a $10 000 investment moved month by month into the top 10 funds would have averaged an annual return of 18 percent, compared to the Dow's average return of 13 percent.

You Can't Beat General Motors

By looking at a single stock—General Motors—you can figure out how the entire market will move. That's because what's good for General Motors is good for the rest of the economy.

The reverse is also true: What's bad for General Motors is bad for the economy.

Although far from perfect, GM frequently leads the rest of the market at important tops and bottoms.

If GM is hitting new highs, it's unlikely that a bear market will occur. If GM is wallowing in red ink, it's not likely that you'll see a bull market.

Two Steps Forward, One Step Back

Almost every time the Dow gains at least 10 percent per year in two consecutive years, the stock market then takes a nose-dive.

In fact, between 1897 and 1993, the Dow Jones Industrial Average has recorded double-digit gains during two consecutive years on 18 occasions. It did it again between 1995 and 1997. Following 18 of these 19 rises, the stock market declined.

It probably happens because the market needs to cool down. But it's worth remembering, so you can get out while the getting's good.

The Least You Need to Know

➤ At regular intervals—once a month, say—you should invest a fixed amount of money into mutual funds, no matter how your investments are performing. This strategy automatically separates your emotions from your investments.

➤ The best years to invest are the fifth (1995) and eighth (1998) years of a decade. The worst years are usually the tenth (2000) and the seventh (1997) years.

➤ Excellent buying opportunities usually occur after the S&P 500 Index has fallen by 19.4 percent.

➤ The cycle of presidential elections influences the stock market and the economy.

➤ The best six months to invest in the stock market are November through April. The worst six months are May through October.

➤ If the stock market is up in January, then there's a good chance that the rest of the year will show positive results.

➤ The best days to invest are the last trading day of each month and the first four trading days of the new month.

➤ After two consecutive years of double-digit increases in performance, the Dow usually declines.

Part 5
Money Issues You Don't Have to Deal with Every Day

Because most of us work for a living—whether we're bricklayers, accountants, mothers of two, or the prime minister—we all have financial responsibilities: rent or a mortgage, car payments, clothing expenses, groceries... you name it. The list seems endless.

Many of us get so caught up in the day-to-day grind of work that we often overlook another responsibility: protecting ourselves and our families financially. Financial responsibility goes beyond making sure the telephone bill gets paid each month. It requires you to think a bit harder about how you can help you and your family in the event of a financial emergency, take advantage of your employee benefits at work, protect your health and wealth through insurance, and tackle taxes. You're going to learn all about those very issues in the next few chapters.

Chapter 19

Money on the Job

In This Chapter

➤ The best perk you'll ever receive from your boss

➤ Dipping into your RRSP? Watch your fingers!

➤ How to squeeze more out of your paycheque

➤ An emergency plan if you're fired

You have the world at your feet. Two different prospective employers you interviewed with last week offer you positions in their company. Here's the lowdown.

Job Offer #1: You have your own office with a view that faces the Pacific Ocean. Your boss doesn't expect you to clock worktime hours more than 9 to 5. You have two executive assistants, a company car, $65 000 in income, and weekends off. You're allowed 10 sick days a year, two weeks' vacation. They offer you a reimbursement feature for your health-care costs, and there's no retirement savings program.

Job Offer #2: Your office faces a billboard—no window. You have a secretary, a parking space (no company car), $64 000 a year in income, two sick days a year, and one week's vacation for the first year (which increases to two weeks after 12 months). You have access to a major medical plan, a group retirement savings plan, an employee-stock-purchase plan and a pension.

Which do you choose? The lake view? No way. You get the gold star if you chose Job Offer #2. Why? Because of the opportunity to earn 50 to 100 percent on your money. This chapter will explain all the opportunities that you can receive working 9-to-5.

Working 9-to-5—It IS a Way to Make a Living!

You have access to one of the most convenient and important investment resources—right at your employer's doorstep. It's your employer's retirement plan, which is one of the most important asset-building tools available to consumers. Once you participate in your employer's retirement savings program, you avoid one of the biggest mistakes too many people are making: doing nothing.

The younger you start, the better—the more time your money has to grow, and the less you might have to save overall. Look at a couple of examples:

Sylvia gets her first job at age 21. Over the next eight years, she accumulates a bit more than $10 000. Eight years later, she gets married, has two children, and decides to put her career on hold. She stops investing and lets her money ride, earning around 8 percent (compounded monthly) on her $10 000 until she retires at age 65. She has accumulated $176 448.

Myron doesn't invest a penny until he's about 29 years old. On his 29th birthday, he decides to stash $70 a month into a retirement account that earns the same amount as Sylvia's: 8 percent. He does that for 36 years, all the way to age 65, contributing a total of $30 240. His total accumulation? $174 771.

Who's better off? They both have about the same amount of money by age 65. But Sylvia's initial wad of dough was only $10 000. Myron contributed three times that amount—$30 240. Why is this? *Because Sylvia started earlier and had more time for her money to grow.*

Even though Canadians have socked away billions of dollars into some type of company-sponsored retirement program, there is solid evidence that young Canadians are not saving enough.

Why the problem? Many people are living moment to moment and can't think about the future. Others don't want money taken out of their cheque because they "need it NOW." Ya know what? These people who can't afford the deduction now, won't be able to afford retirement. Still others do not contribute because they just don't understand how the dang thing works.

Another culprit is that many people are savers, and a company retirement program sends chills down the spines of Canadians who couldn't stand the thought of losing money by investing. Saving is something you used to do when you were a kid, often dropping coins into a piggy bank. Sure, you can save today. A prime example is the emergency fund you should save in a SAFE place (such as a money market fund), that will cover three to six months' worth of living expenses.

Contributing to a retirement plan practises the strategy of tax-deferred investing. Stocks, bonds and mutual funds are purchased within a qualified retirement savings plan. (We'll learn more about RRSPs in Chapter 23). Then, by deferring your income taxes, you can increase your investment returns.

Investing is a different story: you create goals and work toward those goals. True, whenever you invest in a product, there is a potential of risk. If you look at the facts, however, you can see how investing in your company's profit-sharing program can be one of the best investment deals you'll make. Presumably, your company will continue to grow, especially if you continue to work as hard as you do. Shouldn't you share in the rewards that your hard work earns for the company?

If you have at least 10 years until you retire, invest your RRSP for growth instead of stockpiling your money in a money market fund or cash account.

The Fabulous RRSP

RRSP stands for Registered Retirement Savings Plan. Money invested in an RRSP brings two basic benefits, one immediate, the other deferred. The first benefit comes in the form of a deduction from your taxable income equal to the amount you invest in an RRSP. The second comes as your RRSP investment grows, tax-free, until you withdraw it—preferably after you retire.

You can move your money, within an RRSP, into all sorts of investments, from guaranteed investment certificates to mutual funds to stocks and bonds.

Dip into Your RRSP? Sure, but Watch Your Fingers

If you cash in all or part of your RRSP, then the amount you withdraw will be added to your income for that year and will be taxed as ordinary income.

Meanwhile, the financial institution that administers your RRSP will withhold a percentage of the money you withdraw and send it to Revenue Canada. This withheld money is simply a prepaid tax. The size of the withholding tax depends on the amount you withdraw.

➤ up to $5000, you pay 10 percent withholding tax;

➤ $5001 to $15 000, you pay 20 percent;

➤ over $15 000, you pay 30 percent.

For this reason, you're better off withdrawing $5000 or less at a time. This allows you to keep more cash until you file your next tax return. The best strategy, however, is to withdraw nothing at all from your RRSP until you retire.

Take Advantage of Other Company Plans

Most large companies offer traditional pension plans, known as a defined benefit plan, but about 30 percent fewer companies are offering such plans to employees these days. Instead, they're shifting the burden of saving for retirement onto you, the employee, through defined contribution plans. Make sure you understand all the benefits you are garnering under your company's plan. Most large companies have an employee benefits officer who should be able to explain to you in plain language how their plan works.

A *defined benefit plan* guarantees that you receive a fixed monthly sum at retirement and for the rest of your life. That's why it's called *defined*; the benefit you'll receive at retirement is defined in advance. Typically, it is based on the average of the last five years' salary, the number of years of employment, and your age at retirement. You don't make any contributions—the employer makes them each year so that when you reach retirement age there will be enough money in the plan to pay your lifetime benefits.

If your company offers a *defined contribution plan*, you'll have more flexibility than with a traditional defined benefit plan. There are two types of defined contribution plans: a money purchase plan and a profit-sharing plan.

So how does a *money purchase plan* work? You must usually work at your job for at least one year to participate. The reason it's called a money purchase plan is that the retirement benefits amount to whatever the assets in the account will purchase at the time you retire. The only employer obligation is to make a defined contribution for each worker each year regardless of profits. These plans are different from defined benefit plans in that there are no guaranteed benefits at the time you retire.

A *profit-sharing plan*, on the other hand, obligates the company to contribute part of its profits each year, if any, into each worker's account. However, the company can change the rate of contributions, based on profits, or eliminate them in any year. Monthly benefits are whatever the money you have in your account will buy when you retire.

Your contributions are made with pre-tax dollars to defined contribution plans, and the money grows tax-deferred, which is a great advantage.

No matter what type of plan is available to you, make sure you ask your employee benefits officer the following questions:

1. How are my retirement benefits computed?

2. How long will it take until I'm *vested*? (That's how long it will take for plan contributions made by the company to be owned by you.)

Squeezing More Out of Your Paycheque

No time to trek down to your local bank to buy Canada Savings Bonds (CSBs)? Look no farther than your paycheque. Most major companies offer you a chance to purchase CSBs through automatic payroll deductions. You don't get any tax breaks, but these deductions are a great way of breaking the "see-it-buy-it" mentality, because the money is deducted automatically from your cheque. Plus, you can use the program to build your stash of "safe" money—money that you can't afford to lose.

Here's one more tip for getting the most out of your paycheque: Have your cheque deposited directly into your bank account. This sounds simple, but many consumers don't do it. They should take advantage of this paperless transaction. No bank lines or traffic to wait in. Plus, direct deposit guarantees immediate access to your cash.

Besides the added convenience, you can make a little extra money off direct deposit with this little strategy: Have your paycheque directly deposited into a high-interest savings account to earn the better rate of interest than a conventional chequing account. You'll earn interest on payday since your cheque was directly deposited. When you need money, write a cheque to yourself and deposit it in your non-interest-bearing chequing account to pay the bills.

You're F-I-R-E-D

Before the pink slip arrives, make sure you have an emergency fund. About three to six months' worth of living expenses is the rule. Keep this money in a money market fund that has a cheque-writing feature. This way, as you're adding to your emergency fund, you can take advantage of the higher rates. Do not keep this money in a chequing account.

Unless you live under a rock, you're probably aware of all the layoffs that have taken place in Corporate Canada in the past decade. Whether it's because of technology or companies tightening their belts isn't the point. The point is what you should do if it happens to you. You have an overwhelming number of decisions to make. This section will help answer some questions about what to do with all the financial issues you face.

Does your company provide continued medical benefits in the event you leave voluntarily or involuntarily? Many companies offer you an option to continue health insurance coverage at the same rate that the company pays, for a maximum of 18 months. After that, you're on your own.

What will happen to your pension? You may have to take all your contributions in a *lump sum distribution*. Then you can roll it over into an RRSP *deposited directly from your employer* and keep up the tax-deferred savings you've established. By doing so, you won't get hit by Ottawa's tax penalty.

You will have to meet with your employee benefits department to determine what is allowed according to their plan. During this meeting, find out how much of your benefits you own. This is known as being vested. You may have to leave it with the company until you retire. Get the specifics from the benefits department.

Do you have access to outplacement counselors through your company? If so, take them up on it!

Finally, are you going to receive any type of severance? Two weeks is pretty standard, and employers can pay you in a lump sum or over a period of a few weeks. You can take the lump sum, but know that you'll face a bigger tax bill next April if you receive the money at the end of the year. The decision is up to you. If you are going to receive a severance, why not lobby for more? The worst thing that could happen is that they say no.

The Least You Need to Know

➤ Take advantage of your employer's retirement plan. It's one of the best investments you can make. If you're not sure how it works, sit down with your company's benefits specialist and get her to explain it to you.

➤ If your company offers it, take the payroll deduction to invest in Canada Savings Bonds. You'll thank yourself later.

➤ Have your paycheque directly deposited into your bank account. You'll save yourself some time and earn an extra day's worth of interest if you have it deposited in an interest-earning account.

➤ If the worst happens and you're fired or laid off, make sure you find out whether you can continue your health insurance, what happens with your pension, and whether you'll get any severance pay.

Chapter 20

Covering Your Assets: Insurance and You

Many folks believe that paying a lot of money on insurance premiums is like flushing your money down the toilet—that is, until tragedy strikes. Then those expensive insurance premiums seem like the best thing since the invention of the paper clip.

You need to insure your health and protect your wealth. And the more you have to protect, the more you'll spend on insurance. Typical insurance policies include homeowner's insurance to protect your home, automobile insurance to help in case of an accident (whether or not it's your fault!), life insurance to help your loved ones financially when you die, and disability insurance to cover you if you can't perform your current job.

This chapter defines which types of insurance you need. In addition, it will help you get the best buy for your insurance dollars and show you how to shield yourself from unexpected disasters.

Making Sense of Insurance Mumbo-Jumbo

Your insurance needs are determined by the categories you fall under: single, married couple with no kids, married couple with kids, or married couple with adult children (empty nesters). The following sections explain the insurance needs for each category.

Single

You can skip the life insurance, but you'll need auto insurance (make sure you get comprehensive coverage if you have an outstanding car loan) and renter's insurance (unless you own your home). Disability insurance is also a good idea; you can usually get this through your employer.

Married without Children

Look into term life insurance, particularly if one spouse does not work or you own a home. Auto insurance is a must, unless you don't own a car, as is homeowner's or renter's insurance.

Get disability insurance through your employer, but look into a supplemental policy if your employer's coverage is not enough.

Married with Children

When children enter the picture, the necessity for insurance coverage increases. For one thing, you definitely need life insurance. Term life insurance is the best bet if you're in this age range. As you get older, the premiums may rise, so you'll need to reevaluate your situation and perhaps choose another policy. Your car insurance coverage may remain the same, with one addition. If you have children who can drive, see how much a multi-car discount policy would be. You may be able to save as much as 25 percent on your total premiums.

Disability insurance is more important when you have children. Choose a policy that's guaranteed renewable, and lock into a guaranteed annual premium that can't be increased and is noncancelable until you turn 65. Add a cost-of-living adjustment clause to your policy for an extra premium. This will raise your disability payments based on an index tied to the Consumer Price Index (CPI).

Finally, get complete coverage on your homeowner's insurance. Make sure you know what your policy does and does not cover, and purchase additional coverage if necessary.

Empty Nesters

The kids are gone and you have the house back to yourselves—Hallelujah! All previous insurance needs remain the same, although you may need insurance to cover any debts—such as death/funeral expenses, which are usually cared for by a good life insurance policy. Keep in mind the following exceptions:

➤ **Automobile insurance**   Senior citizens may get 20-percent discounts on auto insurance. Remember to get rid of your multi-car discount now that the children are on their own.

➤ **Homeowner's insurance**   Reevaluate your existing policy and what it covers. If you've sold the house and moved into a smaller place, you'll need less coverage—which means lower annual premium costs.

➤ **Long-term care insurance**   People with substantial resources don't need this type of coverage. Average annual premium costs are $1100 a year. Make sure that there's an inflation-protection rider, that the policy is renewable for life, and that there's a short elimination period, such as 20 to 60 days.

➤ **Life insurance**   Purchase a cash value life insurance policy to pay your estate taxes in the event of your death. Why? Keeping term insurance becomes too expensive as you get older. Plus, in a cash value insurance policy, the cash inside the policy builds up and may be used in the future to pay premiums or help pay estate taxes. This isn't true of term insurance.

The rest of this chapter explains the ins and outs of the different types of insurance.

Insuring Home Sweet Home

No matter where you live or whether you rent or own, you need some sort of insurance to cover your belongings. The following paragraphs explain what kind of insurance you need depending on your living arrangements.

If you rent your home, you need to have an insurance policy that covers the contents of your home. You can pay monthly, semiannually or yearly for your coverage. The amount you pay is known as a *premium*, and the amount of your premium depends on where you live. Do you live in a good neighbourhood or a bad one? Is there a 24-hour doorman? Is the apartment unoccupied for more than two hours per day? Another factor is whether you've taken out other insurance policies (such as car insurance) with the insurance agent. If you haven't, your premium will be higher. Typical premiums average $150 per year.

If you are a condo or co-op owner, you will need a policy that covers risks and damage to your personal property. Building property is covered for 10 percent of contents (such as cabinets and wall fixtures). Make sure you check with your insurance agent about anything that's not covered.

If you own your home, you should already have homeowner's insurance. Mortgage lenders require that you have property insurance before you buy a new home. If you're in the market for a new home and are getting homeowner's insurance for the first time, you should understand the basic forms of homeowner's coverage.

205

If you are looking at property that can possibly be subjected to natural disasters, such as floods, hurricanes and earthquakes, and you can't get additional coverage on these, don't buy the house.

Types of Coverage

If you want to get the right type of coverage for your home, compare the following types of homeowner's insurance. The items that are listed as types of coverage are known as perils, as in "all the things that could go wrong." In the industry, it is known as a *standard peril policy*. The more coverage you acquire, the higher your insurance premiums will be. It is up to you to decide if you want to pay more in insurance premiums and have more coverage. However, if you try to cut corners on your homeowner's insurance policy to save a few bucks, and tragedy strikes, you'll be sorry.

The most basic homeowner's policy covers the most common perils such as glass breakage, fire or lightning, smoke damage, explosion, riots, damage caused by vehicles, damage caused by aircraft, theft, property loss and vandalism. Other policies cover such events as roof collapse from snow, heavy sleet or ice; damage from hot or frozen water pipes; heat or air conditioning explosion; damage caused by falling objects; damage caused by electrical surges to appliances (except televisions); and collapse of any part of your home.

For perils not covered by your policy, such as flood damage, you can purchase separate insurance.

Saving Money on Homeowner's Insurance

There's no escaping it—you must have homeowner's insurance to buy a house. What you *can* escape are the extra costs that most folks end up paying because they haven't done their homework. Here are a few financial secrets that will help trim the fat:

➤ **Raise your deductible amounts**   If you're willing to accept a $1000 deductible, you can save almost 15 percent on your premiums.

➤ **Take protective measures**   Installing a burglar alarm, dead bolts or a smoke detector, purchasing a hand-held fire extinguisher and having a nonsmoking household protects your home and lowers your premiums.

➤ **Get replacement cost insurance**   Most insurance policies plan to give you the actual cash value of your personal property in the event of loss or damage. Folks, it's not worth it. If you buy a $3500 leather couch today, five years from now it will be worth only $1500 (because it's used). If you have a fire when that couch is five years old, the insurance company will pay you $1500. Just try to find the same type of couch for $1500. It's not likely. However, if you have replacement cost insurance, the insurance company is required to pay you whatever it costs to purchase a new replacement item.

➤ **Purchase your homeowner's insurance from the same insurance company that insures your automobile** Purchasing both policies from the same agent or company may qualify you for a discount.

➤ **Pay your homeowner's insurance annually** Although most insurance policies have annual, semiannual and monthly terms, you'll save a few dollars if you pay it on an annual basis. For example, a renter's insurance policy with a $160-per-year annual premium may cost you $87 on a semiannual basis. This works out to be an extra $14 out of your pocket.

➤ **Make a home video of your property and all its contents** By doing so, you ensure—and insure—that your claims will be paid.

➤ **Familiarize yourself with the additional coverages and exceptions noted on your policy** For example, if your policy allows you to have additional coverage on credit card losses, don't take it. Why? Because most standard credit card companies limit you to a $50 loss per card. That's just wasting money. Read the fine print!

Car Coverage

The liability involved when you're in a car accident is phenomenal, which is why automobile insurance costs so much. You need to know what's required in your province and what's worth paying for. Comparing the differences between the two can save you a few dollars. The following sections cover what types of coverage are available and give you some money saving strategies.

Types of Coverage

Personal liability coverage is required in Canada and is split into two parts: bodily injury liability and property damage liability. Personal liability provides insurance against lawsuits. If you want to protect your assets in the event of a lawsuit, you'll need as much as $300 000 worth of coverage. Property damage liability covers damage done by your car to other people's cars and property. The standard minimum for this is $10 000.

If you're a victim of a hit-and-run accident, you'll need uninsured motorist coverage. Uninsured motorist coverage allows you to collect lost wages and payments for any medical expenses that result from an accident with an uninsured motorist. Do not skip over this type of insurance, especially since an increasingly high number of drivers have dropped their in-

Uninsured motorist coverage should not be confused with *underinsured* motorist coverage, which is the part of your policy that pays after the other driver's coverage has been used up.

As your car gets older, consider dropping your collision coverage. Why? Because the cost of collision coverage may be more than what your car is actually worth. By doing so, you can save almost one-third of your insurance costs.

surance coverage because of high premiums. And you should especially include this if you don't already have a comprehensive medical plan and long-term disability insurance.

You must also have comprehensive coverage if you have an outstanding car loan (which many of us do). Comprehensive coverage covers theft and damage to the car from riots, fire, flood, falling trees and theft.

Collision coverage, which pays for damage to your car if you're in an accident or replaces a vehicle that's a total loss, is optional unless you have a loan on your car. If you do have a loan, this type of coverage is usually required by the lender.

Medical payments coverage and personal injury protection (PIP) cover medical, hospital and funeral bills that result from an automobile accident—no matter who is at fault. PIP goes one step further and covers any lost wages. If you have a good medical plan or disability insurance policy, you may want to pass on these types of coverages, since they can be expensive.

Saving Some Moolah

When you apply for automobile insurance, you always want to look for the best rate possible, but that's not always easy. Insurers take into account certain considerations when they give you quotes on auto insurance. Keep these financial tidbits in mind to help cut costs on auto insurance:

➤ **Comparison shop**   You don't always have to go to your friendly insurance agent down the street. In fact, if you do your homework, you'll find that the price of similar auto coverage can vary as much as 80 percent from insurer to insurer. Check with the largest national insurers, including bank subsidiaries, which could potentially save you a few bucks if you buy directly from them.

➤ **Drive safely and defensively**   This tip is just common sense, but the fewer traffic violations and accidents you have under your belt, the lower your premiums will be. Maintain a good driving record!

➤ **Don't buy the latest "fad" or "hot" car**   In 1994, the vehicle stolen most often was the 1994 Chevy Blazer, which is why the average annual premium to insure this automobile is higher than the average premium for a not-so-trendy car.

➤ **Buy a car that will handle well if you are ever in an accident**   Ask the car sales rep how much of the car is damaged during an accident and whether or not it holds up well in an accident. For example, if you buy a car that falls apart in a fender bender, your insurance premiums will be much higher than if you buy a car that's a bit more resilient in an accident. In addition, find out how expensive any repairs may be. The more expensive it is to repair, the higher your premiums will be.

➤ **Raise your deductible and pay premiums annually**   Carrying a higher deductible will decrease your insurance premiums. For example, say you're a 30-year-old single female living in Toronto, driving a 1995 Pontiac Grand Am, and carrying full coverage on your car. You could pay $634 in semiannual (every six months) premiums with a $250 deductible, or you could pay $584 in semiannual premiums with a $500 deductible. You can reduce your premiums even further by paying annually.

REALLY?

If you are married, it's better to purchase a second-to-die insurance policy. This covers you and your spouse, but pays off in the death of the second person. This strategy saves you money in two ways. First, instead of purchasing two independent insurance policies and paying two premiums, the insured people pay only one lower premium on both of their lives. The total cost of a $1-million, second-to-die policy can save you more than 66 percent over the cost of purchasing two separate $500 000 policies.

The DOs and DON'Ts of Buying Life Insurance

Life insurance is a bugaboo in Canada because not many people understand it. It's really quite simple, though. Most folks buy life insurance to provide benefits for their survivors in case they die before "their time."

As you do for car insurance, you pay premiums when you buy life insurance. Your annual premiums are based on your age, your health, how much money your insurance company can earn by investing the money you give them (your premiums) until you die, and the expenses the insurance company incurs for mailings and commissions for its agents. Whew!

What makes life insurance a difficult concept to grasp is the many kinds suited to personal needs. The most common reason to purchase life insurance is to support your family members who depend on your income in the event that you die prematurely. Life insurance can also prove helpful by providing immediate cash when you die to repay business loans, for example, if you own a business.

Although life insurance can be confusing, figuring out the differences in insurance policies doesn't require a secret decoder ring. You just need to find out whether you need life insurance and, if so, how much you need.

Do you need life insurance? The rule of thumb is that if you're young and single and have no one else depending on your income, you don't need it. Even if you're married, if both of you are working, you probably don't need life insurance. But if family members depend upon your income, you definitely do.

209

How much insurance you need depends on how old you are and how well your family can live without your income. To determine this, consider the following three factors:

1. Your family would need immediate cash to cover death-related expenses. This would cover uninsured medical costs, funeral expenses, debts, taxes and estate-settlement fees.

2. Tack on six to 12 months' of your family's lost net income because of your death (to take immediate economic pressure off your family).

3. Calculate your family's expenses on an annual basis (you learned out how to do this on a monthly basis in Chapter 2). What percentage of these expenses is covered by your income? The mortgage still has to be paid, and Junior's university tuition bill is still due. Also, how much will these expenses grow over the next five to eight years?

Without any mind-bending calculations, here's a basic rule of thumb for purchasing life insurance. After the death of its principal income producer, a family requires 75 percent of its former after-tax income to maintain its standard of living. It must have at least 60 percent to get along at all. If you want to figure out your after-tax income without the help of an accountant, simply multiply your gross income by 60 percent if you earn a high income, 70 percent if you earn a moderate living, and 80 percent if you have a low income. Otherwise, if you want to simply figure out a rough estimate, just make it five to eight times your current wages.

Finally, you need to decide what kind of life insurance you need. Yuck! Because this could be a Canadian's most-despised question, we're going to make it easy on you and help you save a few bucks along the way. There are two basic types of life insurance coverage: term insurance and cash value insurance. Term insurance is usually the best bet for all but the very wealthy.

REALLY?

Check out the Web sites operated by several Canadian insurance companies to compare rates. Since specific details about a person's life and lifestyle influence the cost of insurance, rates are difficult to pin down. But you'll at least have fun.

Try www.accuquote.com, or www.islandnet.com/~insurance.

You can also find information on life insurance at www.luac.com, operated by the Life Underwriters Association of Canada. And, for information on disability insurance, try Aetna Canada's site at www.aetna.ca.

Term Insurance 101

Term insurance is usually the least expensive form of insurance coverage and is very affordable when you're young. As you get older, your risk of dying increases, so the cost of term insurance goes up. This risk is known as the *mortality rate*.

As with most other insurance coverage, you pay premiums for term insurance annually, semiannually or quarterly. For this premium, you receive a predetermined amount of life insurance protection. If you are the insured spouse and you die during the term you're insured, your beneficiaries will collect. If not, all of the premiums are gone since there is no cash build-up in the policy, as there is in other types of life insurance policies that promote savings features (and hefty commissions). You'll probably be required to take a physical examination to qualify for term insurance.

Term insurance is very inexpensive, which is why it's a popular life insurance policy. However, it only provides for death protection—there's no build-up of the money you pay in premiums.

When you buy term insurance, you can buy it with level (same) premiums for one year, called *annual renewable term* (ART), and renewable until age 90. Other term policies and specified periods are typically five, 10, 15 or 20 years. At the end of these periods, the term insurance is renewable at sharply higher premium levels because you're older and statistically more likely to die during the next period.

Young women who are nonsmokers tend to pay the lowest premiums for term insurance. Because the cost of term insurance does not depend solely on age (where the younger you are, the lower your premiums are), and women live longer than men, women will pay less— especially if they don't light up.

Some people refer to term insurance as "renting coverage" because the only way your insurance policy pays out is if you die during this period. The payouts are offered to your beneficiaries in a lump sum payment or a steady stream of payments.

Make sure your policy offers a *guaranteed renewability feature*, so you don't have to take a medical test to continue coverage for another term, especially as you get older. Also, if you have an annual renewable term policy, you can convert it to a whole-life policy—without a medical exam. This is called *guaranteed conversion*, and allows you to convert from rising-premium term insurance to a fixed-premium whole-life (cash value policy, which you'll learn about later in this chapter) policy. Here's a tip: If you think you may do this sometime down the road, make sure your term insurance policy is convertible into a whole-life policy without another medical examination. There's an additional cost for this provision, but as you get older you'll end up saving more in premiums by doing so and avoiding the medical examination.

Here are some things to keep in mind when looking at a term insurance policy:

➤ **Make sure the illustrations that your insurance agent gives you illustrate the rates you will pay and show the maximum guaranteed rate they can require you to pay** Remember, policy illustrations are not guarantees—even if they're in black and white. Term premiums are subject to change based on mortality and the insurance company finances.

➤ **Compare a level *premium term policy* to an annual renewable term**

You know that premiums on ordinary ART policies increase every year, right? Well, some companies offer a form of level premium term, in which they project that the annual premium will remain the same for five, 10 or 20 years. At the end of the specified period, your policy may kick back into a policy that has increasing premiums every year, or remain level for five years and then kick back into increasing premiums. Ask your agent if the premiums are projected or guaranteed. Insurance companies are not obligated to meet projected premiums—even if they are in the illustrations they give you.

➤ **Don't always settle for a short-term level term policy**   Why? Because the premiums may skyrocket after the short term is over. Again, because this is the life insurance industry, it depends on the policy. Make sure the agent explains all details in simple language.

➤ **Choose a guaranteed annual renewable term to avoid medical exams**   This ensures that you don't have to have a new medical exam every year to renew your term policy. Avoid such policies, which have what are known as *reentry terms*.

Cash Value Insurance

Sometimes known as *permanent insurance*, cash value insurance generally covers longer-term needs because term insurance becomes too expensive as you get older. But beware: Cash value insurance only makes sense for a few people and generates a lot of commissions for the insurance agent…unless you buy low-load or no-load insurance.

Cash value insurance combines life insurance plus a savings account. Most of the money you pay in premiums goes toward life insurance, and a few bucks are deposited into this account that is supposed to grow in value over time. Sound like a winner?

Wrong. The biggest hit your account takes in the early years you're building it is the commission that your insurance agent earns, which is shown to you in the illustration he shows you. What most folks don't know is that the commission is built right into the premium you pay for the insurance. It may take years until the true return (what the insurance company promised you) on your account is equal to what it's supposed to be. To find out how much and what portion of your premium is going into your account, ask your insurance agent to show you the *surrender value* on the piece of paper (usually a ledger) he has. If the amount in the first few years is ZILCH, that's what your little account is getting.

Interestingly enough, both term and cash value policies come in two varieties: participating and nonparticipating. Why all this gobbledygook? It seems confusing, but pay attention and you'll know more than anyone you know about how to make life insurance *work for you*!

Participating insurance entitles you to receive dividends (kind of like stock dividends) from the policy. These dividends are considered a refund of the portion of the premium that the insurance company did not pay in death benefits or administrative expenses over the previous year. This means that if the insurance company is collecting all these premiums, and no one died or administrative costs for the year were low, all the policy holders would get a "refund" in the form of dividends.

So what do you do with these dividends? You can take them as cash—and, of course, pay taxes, because the dividends are considered income. You can reinvest your dividends and *reduce* the future premiums you have to pay. Or you can buy additional "paid-up" (more) insurance. The choice is yours.

Nonparticipating policies pay no dividends, so there's nothing to reinvest. Instead, your premiums are fixed when you buy a policy at a set amount. True, these premiums on a nonparticipating policy will be less than those on a participating policy, but non-participating policies do not offer the perks of reinvesting your dividends for future growth…or whatever your choice.

Be careful. Some insurance company illustrations show that dividends from a paid-up policy can cover the premiums for a new policy—and they don't. Instead, the new policies will really borrow against the death benefit (like a loan) in order to pay the premiums. Read the fine print!

Because cash value insurance policies are not straightforward (it would make life too easy if they were), here's a rundown of the terms you can expect to hear about from an insurance agent.

Whole Life   Your premium stays the same every year, and your death benefit is fixed. Since the amount of the premium is much more than what you would need to pay death benefits in the early years, the extra money is "deposited" into your "account" (inside the policy), which earns interest and grows tax-deferred. You can choose from two types of whole-life policies. In the first, you pay the same level premiums into your old age—where you can borrow against the policy to get some extra cash in your retirement years. In the second, you pay premiums for a fixed number of years only; after that, the cash value in your "account" pays for the premiums. This is known as vanishing premiums. But be careful. If you don't have enough cash value built up to pay for those future premiums, your policy will be the thing that vanishes! And then you're stuck with kicking in more money. Whole-life premiums are often invested in long-term bonds and mortgages.

Universal Life   Unlike a standard whole-life insurance policy, universal life offers you flexibility because it allows you to decide to change the premium payments or the amount of the death benefit, as long as certain minimums are met. You decide how to design your policy. Universal life premiums are invested in and reflect the current short-term rates available in the money market.

Variable Life   Even though the annual premiums are fixed, the cash value of your

If you plan to keep this variable life policy for a long time, invest the cash value portion of your policy in a growth stock mutual fund to take advantage of long-term market performance.

Some disability factoids:

One year of disability can wipe out 10 years' worth of savings.

Some 43 percent of all foreclosures result from a disability in the family.

Less than 50 percent of the labour force is covered by disability insurance.

If you are paying part of the premium on disability insurance and your employer is paying the remainder, the benefits you receive are taxable equal to the amount of the premium your employer pays. For example, let's say your annual premium on your disability insurance policy is $1200. You pay a third of your annual premium ($400), and your employer pays the other two-thirds ($800). If you were to become disabled and start collecting benefits, the portion of the premium that your employer paid would be considered taxable income. You would owe ordinary income taxes on your monthly benefits cheque.

account doesn't earn a fixed rate of return. The growth of your account in the policy depends on what investment choices you make. Generally, the investment choices are mutual funds managed by the insurance company. You have the option of shifting your money around. Note that the death benefit also rises and falls based on the performance, but it will never drop below the original amount of insurance coverage you specified on your contract.

Insure Your Paycheque!

Have you ever thought about what would happen if you were suddenly unable to perform the work that provides your income? You should. If you're between the ages of 35 and 65, your chances of dying are equal to your chances of being unable to work for three months or more because of a disability through illness or injury. It is stressful enough trying to deal with an injury or illness; you don't want to have to worry about whether you're going to receive your salary while you're off work.

Your earning power is the most valuable asset that you will ever own—not your home, your car, or even your antique furniture. If you own your home, you probably have homeowner's insurance in case of loss or damage, and automobile insurance protects you and your family in case of a car accident. So why not insure your paycheque, too?

If you're like most folks, you probably have some type of access to a company-sponsored disability plan. Most companies extend a form of paid sick leave or actual disability payments in case you're unable to work for a long period under the plan. According to these plans, in order for you to receive benefits, you must be totally disabled. Other companies have both short-term and long-term disability plans.

Ask your employer what provisions the company provides for both short- and long-term disability. The industry standard is 26 weeks for short-term disability, and you must qualify for most long-term disability plans. On average, an employer will pay the premiums for its employees' short-term disability insurance policy. For a long-term disability policy, it is standard for the employer and the employee to split the cost of the premium.

Make sure that you find out as much as you can about your company's disability plan. One woman we know did her homework before she went in for surgery. She was able to take a short-term disability leave for eight weeks and received 60 percent of her salary while recuperating at home. Many folks who don't do their homework go back to work a lot sooner without recovering fully, and risk injuring themselves further.

If your company does not sponsor a plan, you can purchase your own individual policy. However, you have to have a job to receive disability insurance—no ifs, ands or buts. But only you can determine which type of disability policy is best. Your goal should be to maximize your coverage without paying for any unnecessary benefits.

Annual individual policy premiums range anywhere from $800 to $1800—sometimes a lot more—depending on the bells and whistles you add to the policy. You will need enough coverage to provide between 60 and 70 percent of your gross earned income. Sit down and figure out what your living expenses would be if you were disabled for three to six months or more. Keep in mind that you'll have to cover the mortgage or rent, automobile expenses, food, clothing and utilities. Plus, you will incur additional expenses: medicine, doctor visits, and possibly nursing care.

Check your company's terms carefully. One clause to watch out for concerns *residual benefits*. If your company does not offer residual benefits, it will not pay you the difference between the income you are able to earn after your disability and the original amount of your guaranteed monthly payments.

If you are not eligible for disability insurance, start doing your own self-insure program. You still need to protect yourself, especially if you are in a risky occupation. Start your own nest egg by putting your own monthly premiums aside into safe investments.

Keep these other factors in mind if you're considering buying disability insurance:

➤ **If you have a risky job, you will pay a higher premium for disability insurance** The cost of disability insurance is determined by your job and the amount of income you want. If you are in a hazardous occupation class (for example, if you are a firefighter, carpenter or construction worker), you might not be able to receive long-term disability at any cost, unless it's through a company or a union.

➤ **Stay in good health and maintain a good credit report** You will be re-

215

quired to take a medical exam to qualify for disability insurance. Plus, the insurance company looks into your credit history. If you have a poor credit history or have recently filed for bankruptcy, an insurance company might not cover you.

➤ **Start your policy as soon as you can**   Why? The younger you are, the less your annual premiums will be.

➤ **Set a long elimination period**   This is the period of time before the benefits start. What you can do is match your emergency fund to this time period. Your premiums may be reduced by nearly 10 percent.

➤ **Avoid policies that pay only if you are totally disabled**   Instead, look for a policy that covers the "own occupation." This guarantees that you will receive the full guaranteed disability payment, no matter what other work you do, as long as you are not able to return to your original occupation.

➤ **Make sure your policy is noncancelable as long as you keep paying the premiums**   Also make sure it has a guaranteed annual premium that can never be increased. Also crucial is a *waiver of premiums clause*, which states that you don't have to pay any more premiums once you become disabled.

➤ **Shop around**   Want the best price? Get quotes from three different insurance agents.

Insurance Products You DON'T Need

You want to cover your life, health and wealth, right? That's why you're reading this chapter: to protect yourself and your loved ones. Unfortunately, many companies are jumping on the insurance bandwagon to take advantage of consumers, making them think they need these superfluous policies. Not so. Here's a list of what to avoid.

Credit life and credit disability policies   Sold by credit card companies, such as VISA and MasterCard, these policies will pay a small monthly income in case of liability or a small benefit in case you die with an outstanding loan. Skip this coverage and purchase disability insurance instead.

Extended warranties   Never purchase an extended warranty on anything—a television, VCR, or even an automobile. If something breaks down, it's likely that it would cost less to pay for it out of your own pocket.

Flight insurance   This type of insurance is based on fears and misconceptions. Instead of protecting yourself with flight insurance in case you die while flying, choose a good life insurance policy that protects you wherever you are—even if you're at 31 000 feet.

Dental insurance   Many employers offer this type of coverage through company-sponsored health insurance plans. Take advantage of it. If your employer does not offer this, the routine cleanings cost much less than your annual premiums would.

Life insurance for your children   Touted on late-night television, this form of insurance boasts inexpensive monthly premiums to provide coverage for your children. It's not necessary at all, and it can be quite expensive. Besides, what parents would spend the benefits from a life insurance policy on their children if something terrible happened?

The Least You Need to Know

➤ Contents insurance is inexpensive and can help you replace your belongings in case of fire, theft or other disaster.

➤ Homeowner's insurance is required by mortgage lenders. It's usually best to get as much coverage as you can afford. You can save money on premiums by raising your deductible, paying your premium annually, and using the same insurance company for your home and car.

➤ Car insurance is required by law. You can save money on your premiums by being a safe driver, driving a reliable car, and shopping around.

➤ There are two types of life insurance: term and cash value. Term insurance is a better deal unless you're older or wealthy.

➤ Long-term disabilities that leave you unable to work can result in financial disaster. Take advantage of any disability insurance available through your employer, and consider buying supplemental insurance if necessary.

Part 6
Getting Ready for the Year 2000

The year 2000 seems so far away. But it's not. Less than three years from now, we will be in a new century. There will be new rules, new hair styles, and new types of investment products. One thing won't change, however, no matter what century it is: how you plan for the future. You can create your future tomorrows through what you do today.

In this part, you'll learn how to manage your money online (and you don't need to be a computer nerd!), how to start saving for your child's university education, and how to plan for your golden years. Start planning today—the future will be here before you know it.

Chapter 21

Tackling Taxes

In This Chapter

➤ Avoiding common tax mistakes

➤ Strategies to keep tax liabilities to a (legal) minimum

➤ Finding a good tax pro

Tax planning doesn't just concern the wealthy. The money you save in taxes creates more investment dollars that can be put to work for you and your family if you start your tax planning now. Plus, prepping for April's tax season ahead of the typical last-minute schedule will help you get your records in order for when you really need them.

Being smart about your taxes is more than just correctly using a black pen instead of a pencil on your tax return. Your investment strategies impact on your tax situation—and vice versa. How? You'll see how in this chapter, and you'll find out how to avoid common problems people make when it comes to tax planning. Because tax planning isn't always the easiest task to complete on your own, this chapter also reviews the best ways to find a competent tax professional who can help you.

The Ten Most Common Tax Mistakes

Mistake 1: Failing to keep good records

Getting organized is imperative. At some point, most people have the motivation to sort out their tax records, but they seem to drop the ball several months later. If you are one of those consumers whose sock drawer is stuffed with unopened envelopes holding your mutual fund statements and past tax returns, kick the habit. It's time to clean house.

You have several options for maintaining good records, including tax software programs for your computer and your basic file folder for file statements. Tax preparation software packages for your computer can save you time and money. You just have to answer a few questions, and the software program plugs the information into the appropriate tax form. In addition, most tax software packages print and file your returns automatically. Such software programs include Cantax personal income tax software; Dr. Tax, professional Canadian tax preparation and e-file software in both English and French; GriffTax; HomeTax; Icicle Computers, Canadian personal income tax returns run in Excel for Mac or Windows and ClarisWorks; and QuickTax, Canadian personal income tax and professional tax software (English and French) from Intuit Canada.

Mistake 2: Not withholding the right amount of taxes

People who underpay their taxes are assessed heavy penalties by Revenue Canada. On the other hand, if you're anticipating a tax refund, all that means is that you've overpaid the government. You could have put that "extra" money to work for you in an investment instead of lending it to Ottawa.

If you make estimated tax payments (as do many self-employed individuals or people who earn a whopping taxable income from investments outside a tax-deferred account), you should constantly monitor your tax-paying situation. Your goal should be to not overpay but not underpay: try to get as close to the mark as possible.

Mistake 3: Getting help when it's too late

This mistake is so common that it's not even funny. It's like trying to prevent a cavity that has already made its way into your molar—impossible. Because many of your personal finance and investment decisions will affect your tax plan, get preventative help before it's too late.

Once you assess your personal financial picture and investment game plan, you'll need to consistently monitor it, especially as you build your wealth and accumulate a higher net worth.

Mistake 4: Not contributing to a tax-deferred investment program

Up to certain limits, retirement savings plans allow you to reduce your taxable income by the amount of your contribution and take advantage of the power of tax-deferred compounding.

Here's the magic of tax-deferred compounding at work. If for 30 years you invest $2000 a year in a mutual fund in your RRSP instead of in a taxable account, assuming a 9-percent annual return, you will accumulate almost $300 000. In contrast, you would have accumulated only $184 000 in a taxable account in the same period. The capital gains and dividend distributions made would be tax-deferred for the entire 30 years. So just do it!

Mistake 5: Not paying down your mortgage when you can

You pay your mortgage in after-tax dollars. That means that for every $1 you pay to your mortgage lender, you have to earn up to $2 before tax. The sooner you pay off the mortgage, the more money you'll have to spend on other things, or to invest for a rainy day.

Mistake 6: Forgetting to check last year's income tax return

For example, if you have $10 000 worth of gains in one tax year and $10 000 worth of losses, you can net the losses against the gains, and not have any taxable income from your investments. The mistake people make is forgetting to carry forward the remaining loss amount on next year's return.

Mistake 7: Not taking a profit for fear of a capital gain

When you buy low and sell high, you earn a profit, which is a capital gain. And depending on your income tax bracket, you are subject to paying capital gains. Of course, you should review the tax implications that a capital gain will have on your investment portfolio—and tax return—with your tax professional, but don't shy away from taking a gain. After all, why are you investing in the first place? To lose money? We hope not.

Capital gains are profit, expressed as the difference between purchase price and selling price, when the difference is positive.

Mistake 8: Not taking advantage of spousal income-splitting

By taking advantage of spousal RRSPs, income-splitting opportunities and other perfectly legal but effective manoeuvres, couples can reduce their total taxable

223

income, even if one person pays more and the other person less than usual.

Mistake 9: Anticipating a large refund

If you regularly look forward to receiving a huge income tax refund, know this: You're having too much in taxes withheld from your paycheque and, in effect, giving an interest-free loan to Ottawa. Talk to your employer's human resources office about reducing the amount withheld on your paycheque for income tax.

Mistake 10: Forgetting to attach the right copy to your tax return

Sounds silly, but it happens. Attach all your T4s, medical and charitable-donation receipts, and other documents to your return in order to avoid future correspondence with Revenue Canada. And, above all, make copies of all your returns and correspondence...just in case!

Investments and Taxes

Whenever you invest your moolah, you have tax consequences to consider. For example, when you buy low and sell high, you earn a profit, which is a capital gain. And depending on your income tax bracket, if it's a sizeable gain, it can really make a difference to your bottom-line return figures.

How can you determine if you should invest your money in an investment vehicle that stresses capital gains or income (usually in the form of interest payments or dividends that are taxed at your income tax rate)? The decision depends on your investment ob-jective, but different decisions will create different tax consequences.

Here's an example. Let's say you are in a higher tax bracket and invest more of your money in taxable bond funds. You get a pretty steady income stream through interest payments (remember, bonds pay interest). These interest payments are taxed at your income tax rate. If you are taking out any cash distributions, that is a taxable event and subject to tax in your tax bracket.

On the other hand, if you are investing in an investment that stresses capital gains (profit), it's a different story. For example, if you are investing in growth funds (no divi-dend income, rather long-term appreciation), any capital gains you realize are taxed at a maximum rate much lower than taxable income brackets for high-income individuals.

The rule of thumb is this: Don't necessarily base your investment decisions solely on tax implications. If they did, many investors would never sell their investments! Your investment strategy is more important than a tax strategy. If you think market prices are dropping, you should take your profits and pay your taxes. A capital gain is always better than a capital loss!

Two of the Biggest Tax Blunders Ever

When folks hear "tax-free" or "tax-exempt," they jump for joy. The allure of tax-free investing is appealing, but it's not for everybody.

Often investors put their money in tax-exempt investments, such as labour-sponsored mutual funds, for the wrong reasons. Investors jump at the chance to boast of receiving tax-free income. But many of these funds tend to have lower yields than comparable taxable mutual funds for investors in lower tax brackets.

Folks commit another blunder when they forget to swap or exchange investments to take a tax loss and offset any other capital gains. If you sell an investment for a profit, you must pay captain gains tax on that profit.

If you sell an investment at a loss, you can get a tax benefit, too. For example, if you have exchange privileges with your mutual fund family, consider using it in the event that you are going to take a loss. Why? First, if you exchange shares of one mutual fund for shares of another mutual fund, it is considered a sale and a new purchase. If the sale of the first mutual fund constitutes a loss, you can use that amount to offset any other capital gains you have realized. This is considered a tax swap. Although your investment position is the same, you've saved on taxes. You must wait at least a month before repurchasing the shares to take the tax loss on the initial sale. If you don't wait, it is known as a "wash sale," and you don't get to claim the loss.

Fourteen Tax Tips

Here are a few general tax tips that may or may not be applicable in your personal situation, based on suggestions from Blair Goates, a certified management accountant in Lethbridge, Alberta (www.lis.ab/goates/index.html).

1. Maintain appropriate records. Although Revenue Canada may not require certain receipts and other documentation when you file your return, you may be requested to submit them at a later date. If you cannot support your claim or deduction, it will be disallowed.

2. BE HONEST! Although you may think you can get away with not claiming cash income or alimony receipts, this is tax evasion, which is illegal and has strong penalties.

3. Contribute to an RRSP if funds are available. This is the most widely used tax shelter in Canada. It may be beneficial to take out a short-term loan to contribute to an RRSP to increase your tax refund, and then to use the refund to pay off your loan. The loan interest to borrow for RRSPs is not deductible.

4. If you make charitable donations, have the spouse with the higher taxable income claim the credit.

5. If your children attend a school lunch program, keep the receipts and claim the expense as a child-care deduction.

6. If you are self-employed, pay your wife and children a consulting fee or salary for work performed related to your business. Have the children clean your office, handle your mail, answer the telephone, take messages, do typing, and other tasks that will justify their remuneration.

7. If you operate a home business, keep your receipts and claim an appropriate part of your rent, utilities, mortgage interest, property taxes, insurance, telephone, maintenance and repairs, and depreciation on office equipment and furniture.

8. Keep a mileage log for business use of your automobile. This area can get complicated, and it may be worth your while to seek professional tax advice if you use your vehicle for business purposes.

9. E-file your return if you are expecting a tax refund. Stay away from tax refund discounters. The interest or fee you pay is usually outrageous.

10. Seek professional advice if the following apply to you:

    a) You're planning your estate

    b) You inherit or obtain a windfall of assets or cash

    c) You have U.S taxable income

    d) You own a business

    e) You're planning retirement

    f) You're considering an investment

    g) You're planning on separation or divorce

    h) You have capital gains.

11. Recent changes to the *Income Tax Act* allow a taxpayer who has borrowed money for investment purposes and since sold the investment at a loss to continue to deduct interest costs incurred while continuing to repay the loan. Exceptions to this provision include real estate holdings and depreciable property.

12. The recognition of a capital gain can be partly deferred by the use of a reserve to shelter any proceeds that have yet to be received from the sale.

13. The proceeds from an RRSP can be brought into income in any year prior to retirement, as long as you are willing to pay the additional tax costs involved. In years of reduced income, the income tax liability may be minimal.

14. Upon death, all assets of the taxpayer are deemed to have been disposed of at fair market value. In the absence of the tax-free rollover to your spouse, such valuations may necessitate large amounts of cash to settle the taxes that will be owing on the deceased's final income tax return. To avoid the forced liquidation of assets, it is a good idea to consider the purchase of a life insurance policy to provide the funds that may be needed.

Finding a Tax Pro

If you don't understand the tax system, you probably pay more in taxes than is necessary. A good tax professional will cut through the muck and identify tax-reduction strategies that will help reduce your tax bill, possibly increase your deductions, and decrease the likelihood of an audit (which can be triggered by any mistakes you make).

Hiring a professional isn't cheap, but you can save a few bucks if you know what to look for. Keep the following tips in mind before you hire anybody:

➤ **Don't hire the first tax adviser you find** You don't buy the first house you look at, so apply the same theory here. You will be telling this person the most intimate financial details of your life. Make sure you interview at least five tax professionals face-to-face before you make your final decision. If the person is a true professional, she should spend quality time with you, ask a lot of questions and, above all, listen to you.

➤ **Ask the tax adviser about credentials** Most tax advisers have accounting credentials from the Canadian Institute of Chartered Accountants (CA), the Certified General Accountants (CGA) or the Society of Management Accountants (CMA).

➤ **Understand how the adviser gets paid** There are flat fees, hourly fees, and fees based on a percentage of your return. The method of compensation is important because it can sway an adviser to recommend one course of action over another. By knowing the adviser's motivation, you can guard against any self-serving advice.

You do not want to be troubled by a nagging concern that your CFP is recommending products because of the commissions those products generate rather than for their appropriateness to your situation. Make sure you get a written estimate of any fees you must pay.

You will need a CA, CGA or CMA if your tax situation is complex. For example, if you are self-employed, run a small business, or have a high salary and claim many deductions, one of these professionals can not only help you prepare your return but help you plan your taxes throughout the year. She looks at your entire financial picture and how each of your financial decisions (whether it's unloading a poorly performing stock or buying real estate for income) will affect your tax situation over the long haul. In addition, she can save you thousands of dollars in taxes by helping you conduct your financial affairs in a way that minimizes the government's tax bite.

Follow these guidelines when using a tax professional:

➤ **Get a letter of engagement**   This will list in detail what the accountant will do for you and what he will charge. Since a CA usually charges more than any other tax preparer, the letter should state whether you are charged on an hourly basis or by a flat fee per return. You should also get an estimate of the time the accountant will spend on your return. If he works on an hourly basis, ask him to guess how long it will take to do your tax preparations and complete your returns. However, if he charges you a flat fee, see what other types of services are included in this fee, such as tax planning advice or attendance at an audit.

➤ **Don't simply dump your box of receipts**   And don't tell the accountant, "It's up to you to figure this all out." One way to minimize their fees is to provide accurate records. You'll end up paying bucks deluxe if you're disorganized.

➤ **Find out how many tax returns the accountant works on each year**   If it's fewer than 300, consider him a candidate. If he prepares any more than that, he's probably sacrificing quality. Also, see what percentage of your accountant's clients had to file past the deadline last year. If it's more than 20 percent, the accountant is probably swimming in (and behind on) paperwork.

Certified Financial Planner: A Jack-of-All-Trades

Imagine someone who knows your entire financial picture and can prepare your tax return. Sound like a financial dream come true? A certified financial planner (CFP) can create a budget for you, help you build an investment portfolio, and assist you with retirement and estate planning, and tax preparation. Since CFPs must be licensed by the International Board of Standards and Practices for Certified Financial Planners (IBCFP), look for their accreditation. There are a lot of financial planners out there masquerading as professionals; unless they have the acronym, don't deal with them.

CFPs do *not* have the same credentials as an accountant. People who choose CFPs to help with their tax preparation often do so because they know their whole financial picture.

CFPs are compensated in one of three ways: on a commission-only, fee-only, or commission-and-fee basis. The least expensive of the three for you (if you plan to maintain a working relationship with this person) is fee only. For tax preparation, the most common form of payment will be fee only. Fee-only planners do not get a dime for any type of investment recommendations they make, which is one of the reasons this condition works out best for most folks. When you find a fee-only planner, she should give you a no-cost, no-frills initial consultation to assess your financial condition. Based on this information, the CFP will give you an estimated fee that is set in advance. Typical rates average $75 an hour, depending on the complexities involved.

To find a qualified CFP in your area, contact the Canadian Association of Financial

Planners (CAFP) at 416-593-6592, or check the CAFP's Web site (www.cafp.org).

H&R Block, and the Like

Places such as H&R Block process millions of tax returns each year and file electronically, which speeds up your refund if you are expecting one. In addition, some chains offer an instant refund, which is actually a loan that is paid back when your refund arrives from Revenue Canada.

Fees for instant refunds are costly because they're based on an interest rate on this short-term loan that can run as high as 20 to 30 percent on an annual basis.

If you don't have a complicated tax situation, check out a national tax preparation chain. They are convenient, and they help you on a first-come, first-served basis. However, keep in mind that you probably won't establish a long-term relationship with your tax preparer as you would with other tax professionals, and your tax preparer may not file as thorough and accurate a return as a better-trained professional. The best way to find a national chain near you is to look in the *Yellow Pages*.

Going It Alone

Even if you have a CA do your taxes, you should know every single detail that goes into your income tax return! If you prepare your own tax return, you know the ins and outs, and can monitor your tax situation. Just make sure you keep up with any major changes in federal tax laws.

If you do go it alone, Revenue Canada can actually help you. Although the government won't fill out your return, it will help you do so free of charge. Revenue Canada offices distribute tax preparation and other publications and answer tax questions over the phone—check your government phone listings for the Revenue Canada office 800 number in your area—and via the ministry's Web site (www.rc.gc.ca).

The Least You Need to Know

➤ The key to having a less stressful tax time is to keep your tax-related documents organized. Tax-preparation software can help you do this.

➤ Investing in an RRSP is a great way to reduce your tax liability.

➤ Before you invest in stocks, bonds or mutual funds, make sure you assess what effect those investments will have on your tax situation. However, don't base your decision solely on the tax consequences.

➤ Accountants are necessary only if your tax situation is complex. Less expensive sources of help include certified financial planners and tax preparation chains such as H & R Block.

➤ The cheapest way to handle your taxes is to do it yourself. Revenue Canada can help; it provides tax booklets and over-the-phone advice.

THANKS, DAD.

Chapter 22

Getting the Kids Through School

> ## In This Chapter
>
> ➤ How to teach your children about money—even at an early age
>
> ➤ Getting a ballpark figure for what Junior's university education is going to cost
>
> ➤ How you can afford to send your kids to school
>
> ➤ RESPs offer parents a break

A university education is one of the best investments you can make. Studies show that the earning power of a university-educated individual is $500 000 dollars more than that of a person who has a high school degree. Statistics Canada forecasts that by the year 2000, 65 percent of new jobs will require a post-secondary education.

However, a post-secondary education is also one of the largest investments you will ever make. As of 1997, the average cost of one year of education at a Canadian university was about $7000—and that's just for tuition, fees, and room and board! Government cutbacks and inflation continue to affect the cost of post-secondary education. The cost of attending university (in residence) is projected to reach $20 637 per year by the year 2006, according to the USC Education Savings Plans' 1996/97 Cost Index. Advance planning for your child's education has never been more important.

That's why you need to arm yourself with enough information as soon as possible. Why? The more time you have on your side, the better off you'll be—the younger the child, the less you need to save each month. This chapter shows you how to teach your

You can teach your kids at any age about saving by using the "penny jar" concept. Keep a large, clear jar in their room and whenever they get any change, have them put it in a container. It's financial planning at its easiest; they get to see what happens when the money grows.

children important lessons in financial planning and help you plan specific financial strategies for getting your kids through school.

Children and Money—They Go Hand in Hand

Before you tackle the problem of learning different money strategies to finance your child's university or college education, it's time for a little homework for your kids: Money 101.

Start talking to your children about money: how to save it and how to invest it. The earlier you begin, the better off your children will be in the future. People who don't learn about handling money at a young age often don't know how to handle it as an adult. The following are some strategies for teaching your child about this important topic:

➤ **Tailor your lessons according to your children's ages**   For example, if you have a four-year-old and a ten-year-old, speak with them separately. Why? Because the ten-year-old already knows how to add, subtract, multiply and divide (if our fifth-grade education serves us correctly!) and your youngest does not. However, your four-year-old can understand the importance of "how much." Older children can handle more financial responsibility and grasp more difficult financial subjects, such as comparison shopping and the value of a dollar.

➤ **Teach your children that they can't have everything they want** (Some adults need this lesson, too; remember the '80s, when the motto was "Greed Is Good"?) A good way to start is to let them know that the next time they're wailing for the latest toy fads, they should make a decision to have one or the other—but not both. An example: If you're shopping and your five-year-old wants a Power Rangers megablaster survival kit or a Barney and Baby Bop sleeping bag, have your child make a decision between the two. Child psychologists advocate that this is the first—and most crucial—concept to convey to kids in basic financial planning: decision-making.

➤ **Teach your younger children about the differences between coins** Explain that all coins are different in value: Show them how a quarter is worth more than a dime, a dime is worth more than a nickel, and so on. Studies show that the earlier you begin, the better. Plus, it gives your child the opportunity to recognize different types of coins and to become comfortable with numbers. Children between the ages of five and seven often handle this concept well.

➤ **Explain how you get money** Many youngsters think ATMs are magical: press a few numbers and—*poof!*—instant cash. We grownups wish it were that easy. If your children frequently visit the bank machine with you, make sure they understand that in order to take money out of the machine, you have to put money in. Explain that you get your money from your job. If you have the opportunity, take your children to work with you to help them learn why mom or dad is gone all day. It will teach them that people have to work to pay bills, such as for the house, food and clothing. Explain that you receive a paycheque that you deposit into your bank account and that's why you can take money out of the ATM.

➤ **Give them an allowance**   Children who receive an allowance tend to develop better money-management skills and will feel more in control of their own finances later on in life. It is up to you whether you tie the allowance to household chores, but if your children do more than their fair share of household chores, you can reward them—with a "bonus."

Child psychologists indicate that six- to seven-year-old children are capable of handling an allowance. The rule of thumb is to give your child a specified amount of money at regular intervals, typically on a weekly basis. And never skip a payment! (You wouldn't want your boss to accidentally forget to pay you, would you?) Tell them it's their "paycheque," just like mom and dad receive a weekly/monthly paycheque from their employers. Make sure you regularly increase the amount, too, such as every six months or on their birthdays.

Teach them how to plan and save with the allowance. How should allowance money be spent? It is really up to the child. If Junior wants to spend all five bucks on candy as soon as he receives his allowance, let him. But let him know that once all the money is spent, he has to wait until next week for his next allowance payment. Missing out on other opportunities later in the week will give Junior a good indication of why he should save his money.

➤ **Have your child keep a money diary**   Every time she receives an allowance or even a gift, have your child write the date, the amount, and the total received. Usually, by the time children turn seven, this is a good habit for them to practise. If your child takes out any money, it should be recorded, too. It's a great way to have your children learn the answer to that perennial question: "Where does all the money go?"

➤ **Open savings accounts for your children**   One of the best ways to teach your children about the interest that they can earn from a savings account is to take them to the bank with you when you open up their account. Tell your child that in exchange for letting the bank "hold

If you give your children an allowance, make sure you give them more than just the right amount to cover school lunches or transportation. The extra money you give them should allow them to learn about saving and investing.

233

Make sure you open up a no-fee account for your child. Why? Because the amount of money that will be deposited probably won't meet typical minimum-balance requirements. No need to have Junior get nicked by fees and charges at a tender young age.

Make sure you know what your child's bank's policy is on service fees and charges. Explain to the bank representative that this is a child's account to see if there can be a reduction in fees and charges, or if they could waive the service charges that could wipe out all the interest on Junior's account.

onto" his money, the bank will give him a bonus by paying interest on that money. (You don't need to explain to them the mathematical equations or whether the account should have its interest compounded annually or quarterly. But *you* should know the difference!) Many banks and financial institutions have developed programs specifically for young children to teach them about money. Industry standards stipulate that one parent has to co-sign on the account and on any subsequent deposits and withdrawals.

➤ **Make sure they understand the basic elements of borrowing** Not that your child is going to be applying for a mortgage loan, but he should understand what it means to borrow money. If your child knows the basics about earning interest on a savings account, then he can understand this lesson: If they come to you to borrow a few dollars, tell them that you are going to charge them interest. And then duck. Really, folks, children need to understand that they have to pay the money back—and at a price. You don't have to charge them 10 percent—1 percent will do. And then have them figure out the amount.

These lessons in financial planning are imperative for you and your children. Once you have these tasks accomplished, you can involve your children in planning for their financial future.

RESPs: A Plan for Your Children's Future

Most financial planners today recommend a registered education savings plan (RESP) as a vehicle for saving money for your child's education.

With an RESP, you can contribute up to $4000 a year, and no more than $42 000 over the life of the plan, for each child, grandchild, great-grandchild, etc. (Just how old are you, anyway?)

Unlike an RRSP, an RESP doesn't enable you to deduct your contributions from your taxable income. However, the income generated inside the plan can compound tax-free for up to 25 years.

For every dollar (up to $2000 per year) that you deposit into your RESP from January 1, 1998, on, the federal government will put 20 cents into a government account for your nominee as a Canada education savings grant (CESG). This means a government account building at up to $400 per year (until the year your child turns 17) or a maximum of $400 x 18 years = $7200.

You can either contribute to a group RESP or set up a self-directed RESP through a financial planner.

"I Won't Grow Up. I Don't Wanna Go to School"

If the RESP's beneficiary refuses to go to school, you can transfer the funds to another beneficiary. But the new beneficiary has to be a full-time student attending a post-secondary institution.

If no beneficiary uses the RESP funds to attend a post-secondary institution, you can take back all the money that you contributed to the plan and transfer up to $50 000 of income (including interest on the RESP) into your RRSP, provided you have contribution room and meet the other requirements. If you don't have sufficient RRSP contribution room, you can take the interest as income and pay tax at your marginal tax rate plus 20 percent (plus an additional 10 percent in Quebec). But you lose all the tax-free compounding.

In general, if you decide to get one of these plans, you better make sure somebody attends a post-secondary institution, or else you'll lose the opportunity to make money on your investments elsewhere.

An Alternative: Mutual Funds

A more prudent approach is to open a mutual fund in your child's name. You can either use the child's monthly tax credit cheque or use your own money to invest in the child's name.

If you choose to invest the child's tax credit cheque, any money that the child earns should not be attributed back to the parents.

If you choose to give your child the money to invest, the rules are a little different.

Make sure you keep your children involved in the money that you invest for their university education. The more informed they are at a younger age, the better equipped they will be to handle financial responsibilities in the future.

➤ For children under age 18, capital gains earned from money given to the child are not attributed back to the parents. Since most of a stock mutual fund's appreciation comes from capital gains, the majority of the gains will stay in the child's name and not be attributed back to you. However, interest and dividend income is attributed back to the contributing parent.

➤ If you invest $1000 each year into a good quality equity mutual fund, the 10- to 15-percent annual return your child will receive will turn that $1000 annual contribution into $50 000 to $60 000 over a 15-year period. Over a 20-year period, it could easily turn into more than $100 000. That buys a lot of textbooks.

When you **diversify** your investment portfolio, you practise the art of not putting all your eggs in one basket. By doing this, you spread the risk around, and, therefore, if one of your securities takes a tumble, all the others are still intact.

When you invest in an **equity mutual fund**, your money is invested in a mutual fund that invests solely in equities, synonymous with stocks.

When you invest in a **no-load mutual fund**, you don't pay any sales charges or commissions. However, keep in mind that there are fund expenses, such as management fees and administrative costs.

Investment Tailoring for Tots

Mutual funds represent a pool of money managed by professional money managers and invested in a group of securities, like different types of stocks and bonds. They offer a great way to diversify your investment portfolio because you spread your risk among the different types of securities.

There is a mutual fund for everybody—even for kids. The biggest pieces of advice to keep in mind? Start early, and don't be too conservative. You can choose other types of mutual funds—especially those that invest in growth stocks, which will outperform all other financial securities over the long haul.

Keep the following tips in mind when searching for the right mutual fund in which to stash your cash. (You can find mutual funds that will fit your investment objective from some of the newsletters listed here.)

➤ Find a mutual fund company that will waive the minimum investment requirement, which is typically $1000 to $2500.

➤ Make sure your mutual fund family offers you telephone switching privileges. Why? Because as you get closer to sending your children off to university, you are going to have to alter your investment strategies.

For parents of young children, the earlier you begin, the better off you'll be. Use the following guidelines when you start charting your course:

From ages 1 to 10   Pick a no-load mutual fund with a good, solid track record. Although past performance is not an indicator of future performance, it will give you an idea of how a fund performed during different phases of the economic cycle and during financial market changes. The idea is to focus on stock funds that traditionally deliver a better return over the long haul, and that meet your investment objective of long-term growth. Plus, because you have more time on your side until the kids start university, you don't have to be as conservative in your investment strategy.

From age 11 to the first day of university   Because you are working within a smaller time frame—a maximum of seven years—you'll need lower volatility. Time to start shifting a portion of your investment out of stocks and into fixed-income investments, such as conservative bond funds or money market funds. The closer you draw to the first day of university, the more you allocate to the money market fund. Why? Because of the safety of principal. By the time your children reach 15 or 16, you should begin shifting out of stocks entirely.

From the first day of university and beyond   Most folks make the mistake of working hard to meet those educational expenses on the first day...and then quitting. Wrong! You need to work constantly at your investment strategy throughout Junior's university years. The bottom line is to maintain your principal, so a money market fund with cheque-writing features fits the bill here.

University Bonds for the University Bound

If you don't get the tax break on savings bonds, zero-coupon bonds can be just the ticket to help with Junior's university costs—as long as you either hold onto them until maturity, or buy them low and sell them high.

Here's how they work. You purchase them at a discount from their face value, and the interest you earn each year allows the bond to increase in value. You collect the principal plus the accrued interest at maturity. (Although you don't receive an interest cheque, you are required by Revenue Canada to report the interest as income.) Once the bond reaches maturity, the bond is worth its full face value. The longer until the maturity of the bond, the lower the price you'll initially pay. Why? Because there's more time for the interest to build up the value of the bond. That's why these bonds are so popular for long-term investors: they allow you to match up future liabilities, such as your children's hefty tuition bills.

If you are close to the income limits, and you stand to gain a profit from the bonds when you cash them in, only cash in a small amount for each tuition year.

All bonds react intensely to the direction of interest rates. So if you bought a 10-year zero-coupon bond at a discount, and plan on selling it within the next six years instead of waiting until maturity, you have no idea what interest rates and bond prices will be. You may get lucky and the value of the bond will rise, so you can sell it and get

When you buy a zero-coupon bond, make sure you pay no more than the bond's accrued value, which is the purchase price plus the interest that's built up so far. It should be stated on the confirmation trade notice that you receive from your broker or discount broker.

The best time to begin looking for financial aid is one year prior to when you will actually need the funds.

a profit. If bond prices fall, however, you're better off waiting until maturity to get the full face value of the bond. You can purchase zero-coupon bonds in maturities from six months to 30 years with as little as $1000.

Zero-coupon bonds sound like an intimidating investment, but slap the title "university savings bonds" on them, and parents think they're the next best thing since sliced bread. Just keep in mind that you have to pay taxes on the accrued interest!

Loans for Full-Time Students

A full-time student can apply for a Canada student loan through his educational institution or a provincial or territorial student assistance office. Depending on the province or territory, the student may be asked to submit an application directly to either the school or the student assistance office.

Financial aid offices at most colleges and universities, as well as admissions offices at private vocational schools, also have information materials and application forms for the Canada Student Loans Program.

To be eligible, the student must meet the following requirements:

➤ Be a Canadian citizen or permanent resident of Canada;

➤ Be a resident of a province or territory that participates in the Canada Student Loans Program. The province of Quebec and the Northwest Territories operate their own student assistance plans. (Generally, the student's province or territory of residence is where she has most recently lived for at least 12 consecutive months, excluding full-time attendance at a post-secondary institution);

➤ Satisfy the appropriate provincial or territorial student assistance office that financial resources available to the student are not enough to cover her education costs, by completing an application form;

➤ Enrol, or be qualified to enrol, in at least 60 percent of a full-time course load at a designated post-secondary educational institution. Students with permanent disabilities are required to enrol in at least 40 percent of a full-time course load;

and

➤ Enrol, or be qualified to enrol, in a program leading to a degree, diploma or certificate. The program must be at least 12 weeks in length within a period of 15 consecutive weeks.

To continue to be eligible for full-time Canada student loans in subsequent years students must meet these additional requirements:

➤ The student must successfully complete at least 60 percent of a full-time post-secondary course load for which she has received a Canada student loan. This means, for example, passing three out of five courses. A student can't receive assistance for more than 520 weeks of study (if the student received his first student loan before August 1, 1995, under the Canada Student Loans Act), or for more than 340 weeks of study (if the student received his first student loan on or after August 1, 1995, under the *Canada Student Financial Assistance Act*), except students enroled in doctoral programs who are eligible for up to 400 weeks of assistance.

➤ The student must complete the program within the number of periods of study normally specified by the school for completion of that program, plus one additional period. For example, for a program that normally takes four years to complete, loans may be available for the first four years of the program, plus one extra year.

➤ The student can't have been denied further assistance for reasons such as failing to make payments on his Canada student loan for 60 days or more, or because his previous Canada student loan was included in bankruptcy proceedings.

The amount of money a student receives depends on his assessed need, calculated using the following formula:

Assessed Costs – Assessed Resources = Assessed Need

Repaying a Loan

It is the student's responsibility to contact his lender to arrange for repayment of his loans. Within six months of ceasing to be a full-time student, he must sign a consolidation agreement with the lender. A consolidation agreement establishes the terms and conditions of his repayment schedule.

Failure to make these repayment arrangements on time may result in disqualification from further student assistance and affect the individual's credit rating. A poor credit rating could make it difficult for a person to borrow for a house, a car or a business, or to obtain a credit card.

For loans negotiated before August 1, 1993, interest is charged to students beginning six months after completion of studies. For loans taken out after August 1, 1993, students become responsible for interest on the first day of the month following completion of studies.

As is the case with any other loan, the payments that the student makes are applied first to the interest and then to the principal. An individual may pay down or pay off his student loan at any time without penalty.

The Least You Need to Know

➤ Teaching your kids about money while they're young will help them handle it better when they're older. An allowance can be a useful tool in helping them understand basic financial planning.

➤ Start saving and investing early. Don't worry about being too aggressive in your approach in the beginning; for example, investing in growth stock mutual funds could be an option. As time passes, however, you'll want to switch your assets into more conservative investments, such as a money market fund.

➤ Consider an RESP (registered education savings plan), which provides tax-free growth of money within the plan and a contribution by the federal government. Alternatively, a program of consistent mutual fund investing can achieve the same results, and you retain all the accumulated interest—minus taxes—if your children don't go to university.

➤ The Canada Student Loans program helps university and community college students meet their expenses.

Chapter 23

You're Never Too Young to Think About Retiring

> ## In This Chapter
>
> ➤ What's an RRSP?
>
> ➤ Do I need one?
>
> ➤ How much can I contribute?
>
> ➤ What are self-directed RRSPs? Spousal RRSPs?
>
> ➤ Consider RRIFs, annuities

For most Canadians, Registered Retirement Savings Plans (RRSPs) are the first investment they'll ever make, and the last investment they'll ever need.

Most people think they're too young to think about retirement. That's a big mistake. If you're fortunate enough to start one of these things when you're young, you'll never have to worry when you're old.

Unfortunately, most of us spend our time and money when we're young on everything *but* an RRSP. And even our parents don't tell us not to. Too bad.

If RRSPs were developed by anybody but the government, they might be more popular. Because they're associated with the government, some people think they're just another trick devised to separate us from our hard-earned money.

REALLY?

You get a tax deduction when you first contribute to an RRSP. And all the interest, dividends and capital gains compound themselves tax-free, as long they remain in the RRSP.

How RRSPs Work

Even people who have RRSPs, however, don't really know how they work. They don't realize, for example, that they can move their money, within an RRSP, into all sorts of investments, from guaranteed investment certificates to mutual funds to stocks and bonds. Often they just give their money to the bank and say, "This is for my RRSP." That's like handing a cab driver a $100 bill and saying, "Take me for a ride."

Think of an RRSP as a briefcase. The briefcase keeps its contents protected from elements outside. In the case of an RRSP, the briefcase protects your money from the sticky tentacles of the government. On money held in an RRSP, you pay no taxes. And when you first put the money into an RRSP, when calculating your income tax, you can deduct the RRSP contributions from your total annual income for that year.

That means you pay less tax. And your money grows tax-free.

Once the money's in an RRSP, you shouldn't just forget about it. It's like any other investment. It can grow quickly, it can grow slowly, sometimes it grows not at all, and sometimes it even loses value. The big difference between money invested in an RRSP and money invested in Uncle Hughie's Bean Farm is that your RRSP investment grows tax-free.

Outside an RRSP, your money may earn $100, and you'd pay, say, $25 in tax, leaving you with $75. Inside an RRSP, your money may make $100, and you'd pay no tax. So you still have $100 left to reinvest.

Why You Should Have an RRSP

There are two reasons why everyone under the age of 69 should own an RRSP, and they both involve reducing taxes: once when you invest and again as your investment grows.

If you earn $40 000 this year and don't invest a penny in an RRSP, you'll pay tax on the entire $40 000.

However, if you invest $5000 of that $40 000 into an RRSP, then Revenue Canada will tax only the remaining $35 000 of your $40 000 salary.

If you invest that $5000 in a good mutual fund, you should be able to earn 10 percent to 15 percent per year, on average. At 15 percent a year, that $5000 will become $20 250 in just 10 years.

You may earn $40 000 from your job. But you may also run a business or own rental property that makes money. The money you make is added to your earned income. So is alimony, if you're collecting it and you don't choose to let your spouse pay the tax instead.

If you pay alimony, or own a business or a rental property that loses money, you deduct the losses from the income you get from your job to calculate your total earned income.

All these details and more are available in booklets from Revenue Canada.

What's **earned income**? For most Canadians, it's their gross salary from their job, before any deductions such as income tax or UIC. If you make $40 000 a year from your job and have no other income, your earned income is $40 000.

The Sky—or 18 Percent—Is the Limit

You can contribute up to 18 percent of your earned income from the previous year, to a maximum of $13 500. This limit is frozen until the year 2003. Then it rises to $14 500 in 2004 and to $15 500 in 2005. In the following year, the limit will be indexed. (This could all change again in future years, if the government decides it needs the money.) For those of us who may still have time to contribute to our RRSPs before 2006, this comes as good news.

The contribution limit applies to all our contributions to a registered pension fund, whether we make them ourselves or they're made on our behalf (with our money, don't forget) by our employer. Most of us work full time for an employer, who deposits a portion of our earnings into a company pension plan. That means we have to subtract our pension contributions (PA) from our total maximum RRSP contribution—18 percent of last year's earned income—to determine the amount that we can contribute ourselves.

A Calculation

If you earned $40 000 in 1997 and paid $1500 into your company's pension plan, you could contribute up to $5700 to your 1998 RRSP. Here's the calculation:

1. Multiply $40 000 by 18 percent to determine your maximum contribution.

2. Subtract the $1500 that you paid into your company plan.

3. If you came up with $5700, give yourself a kiss.

Fortunately, your employer will do most of this number-crunching for you. You'll find your annual pension contribution (called a pension adjustment) on your T4 slip each year.

And you don't have to do the rest of this calculation to find your maximum RRSP contribution limit, because Revenue Canada does it for you and sends you a computerized statement each year that shows your contribution limit.

Tax Insights

Your marginal tax rate determines the amount of tax that you'll save by investing in an RRSP. For most of us, our marginal tax rate is the amount of tax we pay on every dollar we earn in annual salary. The more we earn, the more we pay.

These were the marginal tax rates for the average Canadian last year. (They vary a bit depending on your province of residence.)

Taxable Income	Marginal Rate
Up to $29 590	27%
$29 590 to $59 180	42%
Above $59 180	52%

If you earn $40 000 a year, your marginal tax rate will be about 42 percent. So if you contribute $5000 to an RRSP, you will save yourself $2100 in taxes. (Multiply $5000 x 42%.)

If you hadn't invested $5000 in an RRSP, you'd pay that tax—$2100—to the government.

For someone earning $65 000 a year, who pays 62 percent of his earned income in taxes, a $5000 contribution would save $2600. (Multiply $5000 by 52 percent. That comes to $2600.)

If this fellow hadn't invested $5000 in an RRSP, he'd pay $2600 to the government.

Doesn't it make more sense to put the money into an RRSP?

The Ins and Outs of RRSPs

1. **You don't have to take your tax deduction in the same year as you make your contribution. You can claim it in any future year.**

   This can come in handy. If your income goes up in a couple of years, you'll pay tax at a higher rate. The more you make, the more the government takes.

   If you're taxed at a higher rate, then your contribution is worth more in terms of the money you'll save in taxes.

   On the other hand, unless your taxable income now falls within the lowest federal tax bracket, and your salary increase would raise it to the middle or top tax bracket, you might as well take your refund now.

2. **On money held within an RRSP, the interest, dividends and capital gains can grow at a compound rate, tax-free. You don't pay tax on the money until you withdraw it from the plan.**

Because they have to pay tax on the money when they remove it from an RRSP, many people wonder why they should bother investing in an RRSP at all.

Here's why: Even after you pay the tax when you remove your money from an RRSP, you still end up with substantially more than you'd have if you'd invested it outside an RRSP.

Here's an example:

> *Ms. A* invests $5000 inside an RRSP.
>
> *Mr. B* invests $5000 outside an RRSP.
>
> Each pays tax at a rate of 52 percent and earns 12 percent a year on the invested money.
>
> Who has more 20 years down the road?
>
> *Ms. A* has more than $70 000.
>
> *Mr. B* has less than $34 000.

Why? The money invested in the RRSP earned interest on top of interest. Outside an RRSP, money earns interest, and then you pay tax on the interest, which cuts your earnings in half.

3. **You can keep almost any type of investment in your RRSP, from the "soup" of equities to the "nuts" of bonds. In general, the following investments qualify:**

➤ Guaranteed investment certificates (GICs) and term deposits

➤ Money deposited in Canadian funds in a bank, trust company or credit union

➤ Mutual funds registered with Revenue Canada

➤ Certain bonds (including Canada Savings Bonds), debentures, and similar obligations guaranteed by the Government of Canada, a province, a municipality or a Crown corporation

➤ Shares, rights, warrants and call options listed on stock exchanges in Montreal, Toronto, Winnipeg, Alberta or Vancouver

➤ Shares of unlisted Canadian public corporations

➤ Shares listed on prescribed foreign stock exchanges, including Paris, London, New York, American, Mexican, National, Pacific Coast, Boston, Philadelphia-Baltimore, Chicago Board of Trade, Washington, Cincinnati, Pittsburgh, Detroit, Salt Lake, Mid West, Spokane, The American Exchange, and the NASDAQ (National Association of Securities Dealers Automated Quotation system)

➤ A bond, debenture, note or similar obligation issued by a public corporation

➤ A mortgage secured by real property located in Canada, as long as certain conditions are met

➤ Mortgage-backed securities

➤ Qualifying retirement annuities

➤ Shares of small business corporations, subject to stringent requirements

Unfortunately, most people put all their RRSP money in a savings account or GIC, instead of in higher-yielding investments.

Values and Other Terms

Book value: The book value of your RRSP is simply the amount of money that you've contributed to the plan.

Market value: The market value of your RRSP is the amount that all your RRSP investments would fetch if you sold them all today.

If you contribute $1000 to your RRSP, buying 100 shares of a mutual fund trading at $10 per share, your RRSP's book value will be $1000.

If the share price rises to $15, your RRSP's market value will increase to $1500. But its book value remains at $1000.

As you'll see, there's a reason for explaining this distinction.

Foreign Content

As of 1994, you could invest up to 20 percent of your RRSP's book value outside Canada. The money you invest in your RRSP outside Canada is called its *foreign content.*

Foreign content includes mutual funds that invest primarily outside Canada or individual stocks of companies that have incorporated outside Canada.

Almost all shares traded on the New York, American or NASDAQ stock exchanges are considered to be foreign content.

If a foreign mutual fund rises substantially in value, it won't throw your RRSP's foreign-content ratio out of whack. (Book value is the amount you invest, remember?)

However, dividends from stocks in your RRSP that are automatically reinvested can add to the RRSP's book value. If your RRSP's foreign content exceeds the limit, the government will charge you 1 percent per month of the excess.

The financial institution that holds your RRSP will calculate the percentage of foreign exposure and let you know if you exceed the limit

We should all try to maximize the foreign content in our RRSPs. Here's why: All the money that's invested in Canada adds up to only 3 percent of all the money in the world. That means 97 percent of the action goes on somewhere else.

Currency rates are another reason to invest outside Canada. In 1991, the Canadian dollar was worth US 89 cents. Three years later, it was worth US 72 cents. If you held a U.S. investment, and all it did was break even, you would have made money, because your U.S. dollars would be worth more than they were when you made the investment. (If you think I'm going to discuss the complexities of foreign exchange, you're crazy.)

Make Yours Maximum

If you don't make your maximum contribution this year, you can add the remaining eligible amount to your contribution next year, or the year after that, for up to seven years.

For example, say your 1993 maximum RRSP contribution was $5700 and you contributed only $3700. You're still eligible to contribute $2000, and you can make this contribution any time over the next seven years, in addition to your maximum annual contribution for that year.

Do It Today

As your piano teacher says, don't put off until tomorrow what you can do today. You should always try to make your maximum contribution each year. First, the money in your RRSP starts to grow as soon as you invest it. If you wait to invest, your money won't grow.

Second, being only human, you'll probably be tempted to spend the money elsewhere. And then you'll never make the remaining RRSP contribution at all.

You're allowed to over-contribute to an RRSP to a maximum of $8000 over the course of your lifetime. If you over-contribute by more than $8000, the government will charge you a penalty of 1 percent per month on the over-contribution. So if you have an extra $8000 lying around, you might want to over-contribute on purpose.

You won't be able to deduct it from your total taxable income. But it will earn interest, tax-free, inside the plan. If you can earn 15 percent on your money, you'll make about $1200 each year on your additional $8000 contribution.

If you made the over-contribution in January 1998, Revenue Canada won't tell you to remove it until you file your tax return the following year. Then you still have the rest of the year plus another full calendar year to remove the $8000. You've already paid tax on it, so you don't have to pay tax on it again when you remove it.

In the meantime, the money earned on your $8000 over-contribution during those three years of tax-free compounding stays inside the plan. If you earned 15 percent a year, you've accumulated about $3500.

If you can double that $3500 every four years, you'll have $28 000 in 12 years. In 20 years you'll have $112 000. And in 32 years, you'll have $996 000. All for making an $8000 mistake.

In fact, you don't have to remove the $8000 at all. Instead, when the time comes, you can just use it as your RRSP contribution for that year.

How Do You Set Up an RRSP?

You can set up an RRSP at any bank or trust company, or through a financial planner, stock broker or life insurance agent.

You fill out a form and sign it. A few weeks later, you get an official tax receipt in the mail.

How Many RRSPs Do You Need?

Some people buy an RRSP here and an RRSP there. Pretty soon they have an RRSP for every day of the week.

All you really need is one: a self-directed RRSP.

With a self-directed RRSP, you can include different investments within the same plan. Do you want a Canada Trust GIC? That's fine. Do you want a Royal Bank term deposit? That's fine, too. How about stocks, bonds, mutual funds, mortgage-backed securities, strip coupon bonds, or Canada Savings Bonds? They're all fine.

The point is, you can hold all your RRSP investments within the same self-directed plan. This gives you the flexibility to change your investment mix at any time.

If one financial institution offers a better deal than the others, you can switch. And you no longer have to worry about deposit insurance, because you can put $60 000 in CIBC GICs, $60 000 in TD Bank term deposits. (Strip coupon bonds, mortgage-backed securities and Treasury bills have no limit.)

Most financial institutions handle self-administered RRSPs and charge an administration fee of about $100 to $150 for the service. You can deduct these administration fees from your taxable income. However, you can't deduct brokerage fees charged for the purchase or sale of securities within an RRSP.

The flexibility you get from a self-directed RRSP is worth the fee.

Spousal Plans

If you're legally married, you can contribute a portion or all of your allowable contribution to your spouse's RRSP. Why would you do such a thing? Taxes, what else?

If your spouse earns less than you do and pays tax at a lower rate, then you both save on income tax. First, you claim the tax deduction, even though you contribute to your spouse's RRSP. Then, when your spouse withdraws the money from the spousal plan, your spouse reports the income and pays the taxes, presumably at a lower rate.

You have to leave the money in the plan for two years or more. Otherwise, the contributing spouse gets taxed.

If your spouse has no earned income, you can still contribute on your spouse's behalf to an RRSP. It doesn't matter if your spouse has any earned income or not. Nor does it matter if your spouse has already made the maximum contribution to an RRSP. What matters is your own contribution.

However, your combined contribution to your own and your spouse's RRSP cannot exceed your personal contribution limit.

And to get really ridiculous, you can contribute to your spouse's RRSP even if you're over age 69, providing you still have earned income and your spouse is not over the age of 69.

Home Sweet Home

Introduced in the 1992 federal budget, the Home Buyers' Plan allows individuals to withdraw funds tax-free from their RRSPs and use the money to purchase a home from someone else.

Then they have to pay the money back to their RRSP.

The home can take the form of a house, mobile home, apartment, condominium or co-operative.

You can withdraw up to $20 000 tax-free. That means a couple can withdraw up to $40 000.

Here's the catch: You have to pay the money back over 15 equal annual installments. These payments are not tax-deductible. If you miss a payment or make only a partial payment, then your taxable income will be increased by the amount of the shortfall.

If you borrow $15 000 from your RRSP, then you'll have to repay it in annual installments of $1000 apiece over the next 15 years.

If you pay only $600 one year, you'll have to pay tax on the remaining $400 of the annual installment.

The first installment must be made by the end of the second year following the year of the withdrawal. If you removed the money in 1994, the first installment payment would not be due until the end of 1996.

Read the Fine Print

Before you can remove the money from your RRSP, you must have a written agreement to acquire a qualifying home that will be used as your primary residence within one year of purchase. The home must be located in Canada, and it must be your main year-round residence.

It doesn't matter whether the home is new, used or under construction. Nor does it matter whether this is the first home you've ever bought. However, you cannot use the plan to pay for a home that you've already purchased.

Participants in the plan can make RRSP contributions in the same year in which they make the withdrawal. But you have to make the contribution at least 91 days before you withdraw the money.

Some Good Points and Bad Points

Good point: The Home Buyers' Plan enables young people to make a down payment on a home they couldn't otherwise afford.

Bad point: Since you've removed the money from your RRSP, your tax-sheltered retirement fund can no longer grow at a compound rate. Once you remove the money, it's a lot harder than you think to catch up.

For example, at age 31, you withdraw $10 000 from your RRSP and use it as a down payment on a house. Then you pay back the money in 15 annual installments. At age 69, you'll have about $85 000 in your RRSP, assuming a 7-percent annual return.

If you'd left the money in your RRSP to compound tax-free, assuming that same 7-percent yield, you'd have about $150 000 in the plan at age 69.

(On the other hand, your house might increase in value too. But that's not a sure thing. Compound growth within an RRSP is.)

Who Goes There?

The best investments to hold inside your RRSP are mutual funds. In fact, whether you hold them inside or outside your RRSP, mutual funds should make up the majority of your portfolio.

Investment advisers used to recommend keeping interest-bearing investments inside your RRSP, and investments that accumulate dividends and capital gains outside your RRSP. That's because you pay tax on unprotected interest income; you don't pay tax on your first $100 000 in capital gains.

But today, with interest rates so low, that doesn't make sense. Instead, your goal should be maximum yield through long-term growth

You can obtain maximum yield through long-term growth from a diversified portfolio of mutual funds.

Cases in Point: Sylvia and Willy

Compare two investors: .

Sylvia invests $2000 a year in an RRSP composed of GICs earning 6 percent annually.

Willy makes the same $2000 RRSP contribution, except that his RRSP is composed of good-quality equity mutual funds earning 16 percent a year.

Poor Sylvia. In 30 years, she'll have $167 603. Willy will have more than $1.2 million. Who's better off?

Another Example

You don't have to keep all your money in mutual funds. But you should invest at least some of it there. Even if they return just 1 percent more than your other investments, they can still make a huge difference down the road.

For example, Sylvia makes a $2000 annual contribution to her RRSP and earns 13 percent on her money. In 30 years she'll have $662 630.

Willy's investments earn just 1 percent more. At 14 percent, he has $813 474 after 30 years.

That extra 1-percent yield was worth an additional $150 844.

A Solid Portfolio

A solid, conservative RRSP portfolio might consist of Canadian and foreign equity funds, income and bond funds, some GICs, CSBs, money market funds, and gold.

➤ The equity fund provides the maximum long-term growth.

➤ The income and bond funds provide the steady stream of income, year after year.

➤ The cash component of the portfolio is the slush fund, providing both safety and available capital to scoop up bargains as prices fall in other areas.

➤ The gold fund provides potential for growth while maintaining purchasing power.

Invest Now, Profit Later

Many people follow a ritual when they make their annual RRSP contribution. They stand outside a trust company in the freezing cold, stamping their feet and blowing on their fingers, talking to the same people they met last year at the same time, in the same place.

You have to stop meeting this way.

First of all, you're making your contribution at the very last minute, at the end of the year. That means you've lost an entire year of tax-free compound interest.

The sooner you make your contribution, the sooner your money starts compounding tax-free. Believe it or not, this can really make a difference.

For example, Sylvia makes her RRSP contribution at the beginning of the year. Willy makes his RRSP contribution at the end of the year. Each invests $3500 and earns 12 percent annually.

In 30 years, Sylvia will have $946 000. Willy will have only $845 000. That's a difference of a hundred grand! (In fact, the higher the return on your investment, the bigger the difference.)

Your Ultimate Goal

If you want as much as you can accumulate when you retire, always make your maximum RRSP contribution.

Many people think that because they have $100 000 saved up for retirement, they'll never have to worry about money again. The trouble is, retirement comes a lot sooner than anyone expects, and is a lot more expensive than most people anticipate.

If you have $100 000 earning 4 percent in the bank, and you want to remove $15 000 a year to cover your living expenses, how many years will it take to run out of money?

The answer: seven years.

At 10 percent, you could remove $15 000 for 10 years before your $100 000 ran out.

If you invest the money instead, in some good-quality mutual funds, you can earn 10 to 15 percent per year. At those rates, you can take out $15 000 a year for a long, long time

Withdrawals

When the time comes to withdraw money from your RRSP, you have three basic choices:

➤ lump-sum withdrawals

➤ annuities

➤ RRIFs

You must choose at least one of these options by the end of the year in which you turn age 69.

The Lump Sum

If you cash in all or part of your RRSP, then the amount you withdraw will be added to your income for that year and will be taxed as ordinary income.

Meanwhile, the financial institution that administers your RRSP will withhold a percentage of the money you withdraw and send it to Revenue Canada. This withheld money is simply a prepaid tax. The size of the withholding tax depends on the amount you withdraw.

Up to $5000	you pay 10 percent in withholding tax
$5001 to $15 000	you pay 20 percent
Over $15 000	you pay 30 percent

For this reason, you're better off withdrawing $5000 or less at a time. This allows you to keep more cash until you file your next tax return.

The Annuity

The purchaser of an annuity is called the *Annuitant*. The company that sells the annuity is called the *Issuer*. The annuitant gives the issuer money in return for monthly income payments for life.

When you transfer your money from an RRSP to the issuer of an annuity, you don't have to pay tax on it. You pay tax only on the monthly payments you receive from the issuer.

There are basically three types of annuities: term certain, single life, and joint and last survivor.

➤ **Term certain annuities**   You receive payments for a fixed term. If you die (possibly of boredom from reading this stuff) before the term is up, your estate receives the payments.

➤ **Single life annuities**   This is the simplest type. You receive monthly payments for as long as you live.

➤ **Joint and last survivor life annuities**   Both you and your spouse continue to receive payments as long as either of you remains alive. The monthly payments are lower than they would be from a single life.

You can also choose an index—or escalating rate—annuity. This gives you monthly payments that never decrease, but may increase based on an interest-rate indicator. Your monthly payments will be lower than those of a straight life annuity during the early years, but the payments will eventually increase if and when interest rates rise.

Annuity Variations

With most annuities, you're locked in for life at the prevailing interest rate when you sign the contract. Insurance salesmen will tell you that people with annuities live longer than people without annuities. But if you buy one of these things when interest rates are low, you'll feel like killing yourself when inflation and interest rates start rising.

For example, say your fixed yearly payment is $10 000, and inflation rises to 5 percent a year. In 20 years, you'll need over $25 000 to maintain the purchasing power of today's $10 000. But since your payments are fixed, your purchasing power will fall.

Since RRIFs now last for life, they offer the best opportunity for deferring your taxes for the longest possible time.

More than 47 percent of Canadians over the age of 69 who were surveyed by Scotiabank in 1997 said they depend on their RRIF as a steady source of income for living expenses. About one-third felt concerned that they might outlive their savings.

Canadians live longer than ever these days. In fact, about 25 percent of men and 39 percent of woman who reach age 69 will live past 90. Each of them needs money to live. So will you.

To address this problem, some insurance companies, such as Sun Life, sell cashable or retractable annuities. You can cash these annuities early, and then renegotiate your annuity once interest rates rise.

Go for the RRIF

Better still, forget about an annuity and go for an RRIF. An RRIF is a Registered Retirement Income Fund. For most people turning 69, an RRIF is the best choice.

At age 69, or sooner if you wish, you simply transfer your RRSP into an RRIF. You can own as many RRIFs as you like. In most cases, the institution holding your RRSP can set up an RRIF for you.

You can keep the same investments in your RRIF that you held in your RRSP. You can also continue to buy and sell investments within an RRIF.

The main difference is that with the RRIF, you must withdraw a minimum amount of money each year, except during the year in which you set it up. The money you withdraw from the RRIF will be taxed as income.

How to Calculate Your Minimum RRIF Withdrawal

If you're under 69, take the number 90, subtract your age, and divide the amount of the RRIF by the resulting number.

For instance: You're 65 years old. You've got $100 000 in your RRIF. To find out how much you have to withdraw per year, subtract 65 from 90, which leaves you with 25. Now divide $100 000 by 25: That comes to $4000. That means you have to withdraw $4000 in the first year of your RRIF.

In each subsequent year, you use the same calculation (90 minus your age, divided into the total market value of the RRIF).

When you reach age 69, you have to use a different calculation to determine the minimum withdrawal. Since RRIF payments are now received for life, a specific factor is used in calculating the minimum withdrawal.

Plan Beneficiaries

You should designate your spouse or a financially dependent child as the beneficiary of your RRSP or RRIF. Then, if you die, your spouse can put the money tax-free into his or her RRSP or RRIF.

If there's no surviving spouse and the RRSP/RRIF funds are left to a financially dependent child or grandchild, the funds will be taxed at the child's marginal tax rate or used to purchase an annuity until the child turns 18.

If there's no surviving spouse and no children under age 18, the money goes to your estate and is reported as income on your final tax return. (That's right. First you die. Then you pay more taxes.)

Should You Borrow the Money to Invest?

People who don't have enough cash on hand to maximize their RRSP contributions should consider borrowing the money.

Remember that when we borrow money to invest outside our RRSP, the interest on the loan is tax deductible. Interest on money borrowed for RRSPs, however, is not deductible.

But it can still be worth borrowing, as long as you can pay back the loan within a year. The longer it takes to pay back the money, the less benefit you'll receive.

Most financial institutions will lend you the money at the prime interest rate, providing you purchase your RRSP through that institution.

Let's say your maximum RRSP contribution is $8000, and you have only $5000 to invest. If you borrow the other $3000 from the bank and pay 7-percent interest on the loan, and you earn 7 percent on your RRSP investment, it really doesn't make much difference whether you borrowed to invest or not. You pay 7 percent; and you earn 7 percent.

However, once you pay off the loan, your investment continues to compound tax-free.

The clincher, though, is the tax rebate. If you're in the 42-percent marginal tax bracket, that $3000 contribution will provide you with a rebate of $1260.

Now you're way ahead of the game. You can use that money to help pay down the loan, buy a new stereo, take a trip to Florida, or buy copies of this book for all your friends.

The Least You Need to Know

> ➤ Everyone age 69 or younger should own an RRSP.

> ➤ Try to make the maximum annual contribution to your RRSP.

➤ Try to contribute as early as you can in the year. Don't wait until the last minute.

➤ If your spouse earns less than you do, and you expect your spouse's income will be less than yours when you retire, consider a spousal RRSP.

➤ If you withdraw the funds before you retire, try to withdraw them when you're earning less income than usual, so you pay less tax.

➤ If you don't have cash to pay for your RRSP contribution, consider borrowing the money.

➤ Consider saving for your child's education by contributing to a mutual fund in your child's name.

➤ When you turn 69, don't buy an annuity unless interest rates are high. Otherwise, invest in an RRIF.

Chapter 24

Wills and Estate Planning

In This Chapter

➤ Do I really need one?

➤ What is a will?

➤ The two main types of wills

➤ Executors, trustees, and powers of attorney

As far as anyone knows, we can enjoy our money only while we're alive. And none of us knows how long that might be. You might live to be 97. Some people do. You might also die tomorrow. Some people do that, too.

No one can predict with any certainty the length of time that each of us has to grope and stumble around the planet. And as we learned early in this book, uncertainty is the bane of all investors.

A will gives us another chance to eliminate uncertainty from our financial lives. We may not know exactly when we'll bog off. But we can know exactly where our money goes when we do. And we can rest assured that the government won't take it all, as long as we have a will.

Over our lifetimes, we can all build a small fortune. At the end of the day, do you want your small fortune to go to your loved ones, or to the provincial government? Do you

Make an Objectives Sheet, listing your instructions in detail so that in the event you become disabled or die, your instructions are carried out the way you intended. Also, once you review your plan with a lawyer, make sure you implement strategies that will shelter as much as possible from taxation.

That's where your will comes in.

want to force your family into a courtroom to battle it out with a bunch of lawyers to see who gets what?

If you don't, it's your responsibility to make a will. The little time it takes now can save your family thousands of dollars in expensive litigation later.

Accidents Happen, but Not to Your Money

What would happen to your money if you were accidentally killed in a car crash tomorrow? Would your assets be dispersed in an orderly fashion? Would your family know exactly what assets you own? How about those shares in Acme Buggy Whips that you bought last year from weird Uncle Harry? What about those gold bars you keep locked in the safety deposit box? Do you have a record of your entire estate? Do you know how much you are currently worth or how much you'll be worth later?

What Is a Will?

A will is your plan for how you want your assets to be dispersed after your death. It's basically a list of the individuals or institutions who will get your assets when you die.

The Two Main Types

There are two types of will: outright disposition and trust.

1. An *outright disposition will* names the beneficiaries who will receive your assets. The disposition of the assets usually occurs as soon as possible after your death.

2. A *trust will* places the assets inside a trust for the beneficiary. The trust contains two basic parts:

   ➤ The capital portion: the assets that are held inside the trust until the trust is dissolved.

   ➤ The income portion: the assets that will provide a regular income to the beneficiary.

   When the trust is dissolved, the ultimate beneficiary receives all the assets. Trust wills are frequently left for children who, upon reaching a certain age, receive all the assets within the trust to spend as they please.

All I Own Is in My Suitcase

Let's start big and work our way down: Do you own a house? How about a car? What about life insurance? A watch? Okay, how about those boots from Mexico?

The point is, you may be worth more than you think.

It's Your Choice

You wouldn't want the government to manage your money for you now. Nor would you want the government to manage your money after you die. But it will, unless you designate a person to act as the executor and/or trustee of your estate.

Without a will, the court will designate an executor for you. And the government-appointed executor may or may not be the best person to do the job. As a result, your assets may not be distributed to your family and friends as you had planned.

What Does the Executor Do?

The executor makes sure that the provisions of your will are carried out. For example, the executor has to prove to the courts that the will is valid. This is known as probating the will. The executor is also responsible for the following:

➤ burying or disposing of your remains;

➤ collecting any money owed to the estate;

➤ paying all the debts owed by the estate (including income and estate taxes);

➤ providing a list of the deceased's assets; and

➤ distributing the assets to the beneficiaries in accordance with the will.

Who Should I Select as the Executor?

You can name one or more individuals as executors. The person (or people) you select should be honest, intelligent, and preferably *younger* than you.

Does the Executor Receive a Fee?

The standard fee for the administrative services of the executor is approximately 4 percent of the value of the estate, providing that the assets are quickly distributable. However, if the assets are held inside a trust, then the trustee receives a care-and-management fee of approximately 1/4 percent each year, based on the average market value of the estate. In addition, the trustee is usually allowed 5 percent per year of any income earned inside the trust.

These fees can sometimes be substantial. So depending on the value of your estate, it makes sense to select someone who you'd like to see receive the money.

Should I Choose My Bank as Executor of My Estate?

Most banks have trust departments that will act as executor for your estate, and many people choose to go this route. However, if your will is not complex, then you should consider having a close friend or relative act as executor.

If the executor is already familiar with your assets and beneficiaries, then so much the better. What you want to avoid is an executor with a conflict of interest.

Providing your children are over age 18, you should seriously consider giving them a role in the process. Not only will it be good experience for them in handling the assets, it will also save administrative fees.

Lawyers vs. Accountants

One of the most popular choices for an executor is your lawyer. However, it is important to note that while lawyers may have superior knowledge of the administrative processes involved, they have little if any professional training when it comes to investing the funds.

On the other side of the coin, your accountant has professional training in taxes and estate planning, but lacks the administrative know-how of a lawyer.

If your will requires trusts to be set up and administered, then you should consider a trust company to act as trustee.

What Does the Trustee Do?

The trustee is responsible for administering a trust as long as it remains in force.

In your will, give your beneficiary the right to change trustees on the basis of certain circumstances, so your will is not locked into a bank trust department that it can never get out of.

Trust companies are qualified to administer and invest the funds in a competent manner. On the other hand, they are notoriously conservative money managers. In addition, beneficiaries often feel uncomfortable with the impersonal service that they receive from a trust company.

What Should My Will Contain?

Here are the contents of a basic will:

> ➤ Your name, address and occupation;

➤ An explanation of how you want your assets to be distributed;

➤ Your signature and the date on which you signed the will;

➤ A note stating that you are revoking all your previous wills;

➤ The name of the person (or persons) who you would like to act as executor(s) of the estate. You should also select a contingency person, just in case the first person(s) selected can't do the job.

➤ If you have any special requests, such as leaving money to your favourite charity or donating your eyes to science, then you should indicate them in your will.

➤ A contingency clause to cover the distribution of your assets in the event that the primary beneficiary dies at the same time as you do.

Those of you who are still young don't have to decide how much you are going to leave your beneficiaries now, because you don't know what the value of your future estate will be. Instead, designate a percentage of your assets. And for those of you who designate financial assets, such as shares of stock or bond certificates, if you sell them before you die—but forget to remove them from your will—your estate will have to go out and repurchase them to give to your heirs. Be careful!

➤ The signatures of two witnesses (who are not beneficiaries) and their initials on each page of the will and on any changes made to the will.

Should I Ever Change My Will?

Absolutely! Over time, your circumstances change. You may get married, divorced or have children, in which case you have to assign new beneficiaries. So it's prudent to review your will on a regular basis (at least every five years).

If you plan on getting married, you should note that in most cases, marriage automatically revokes any previous wills made by the two partners. But separation or divorce does not revoke a will unless a clause in the will specifically says that it should.

Death-tax provisions may change, which could affect the distribution of your assets.

If you decide to revise your will, you do not have to consult any of the previously named beneficiaries.

Where Should I Keep My Will?

The best place to keep your will is with your lawyer. That way, in the event of your death, it can be easily retrieved.

You should also keep an unsigned copy of the will in your files at home.

Making a will *is not* a do-it-yourself financial planning strategy. Handwritten wills are invalid unless proper procedures are followed. Videotape wills don't really count, either, unless they're used to "back up" your state of mind when creating the will. That's why you need to make sure you get yourself a qualified lawyer who specializes in estate planning.

Should A Husband and Wife Have Separate Wills?

Yes. Even if one partner does not have a career or very many assets in his or her own name, the person should still have a will.

For example, if the husband alone has a will, then his wife will receive all of his assets upon his death. However, if she then passed away before she had time to make a will, the government decides what to do with the assets. Presumably, you didn't elect a government to meddle in your personal affairs.

Do It Yourself—or Not?

If you broke your leg, would you try to set it yourself? Probably not. You'd seek out a qualified physician. The same reasoning applies to your will.

Writing your own will is usually a mistake. For one thing, beneficiaries usually end up paying a lot of money to lawyers as they try to sort out all the technicalities.

When Does a Will Become Effective?

If you have a will, it becomes effective as soon as you die. This can be a big advantage to your heirs, who otherwise wouldn't receive any assets for a long period.

If you don't have a will, all the assets will be temporarily tied up—for months or even for years. Meanwhile, bills may need to be paid and your estate managed. But there will be nobody to do it, because you didn't take the time to prepare your will.

In addition, it usually costs more to administer an estate without a will.

If You and Your Spouse Both Die, Who Looks After the Children?

Have you decided on a guardian to look after your children in case you and your spouse both die?

Most people select the child's grandparents for the job. In fact, this isn't your best choice. That's because the grandparents are older. If they receive guardianship of your children and then pass away shortly afterward, the children suffer.

A better choice is to find a younger couple you trust. But make sure that they're up for the job.

Creative Financial Strategies that Will Help You Now—and Then

You might want to consider one of the following financial plans. No matter what creative strategy you use, you must consult with your tax adviser and your lawyer to find out which plan will work best in your situation.

Give All Your Money to Your Spouse

A creative estate planning strategy—and probably the simplest to do—is to title most of your assets in *joint tenancy with rights of survivorship*. This means that everything you own automatically transfers to the survivor (usually a spouse, although it can be another person you designate). Make sure you review this with your lawyer because this may not be a good option for you, depending upon the value of your assets.

An Irrevocable Trust

Concerned about giving money to children or grandchildren who might spend it foolishly? Set up an *irrevocable trust*. In fact, you can set up as many of these as you want, depending on the number of beneficiaries you name. Each year you make a gift to each trust. The trust will dictate when your heirs can receive the income or assets from the trust.

The Family Limited Partnership

Considered a thorn in the government's side, this *family limited partnership* is still making its way through the legal system. It's a simple idea in which a legal family limited partnership holds assets outside the taxable estate. One of the spouses, acting as general partner, holds 10 percent of the assets of the partnership. The remaining 90 percent of the assets are divided among the limited partners, who initially are husband and wife.

After the partnership has been set up, each year the parents give a small partnership interest to their kids. Over a period of years, the children will own 90 percent limited-partner shares in the entire family limited partnership. The advantage is that the remaining 10 percent controls the 90 percent owned by the limited partners—the children. This controlling interest decides how the money is to be managed. Once this spouse dies, the surviving spouse receives controlling interest.

What Is a Living Will?

It's not unusual for a loved one to require care to survive. But how much care is enough?

Do you want to be kept alive by artificial means? Do you want to be resuscitated after you've stopped breathing? Do you want to be kept alive even though you're in a coma and unlikely ever to regain full consciousness?

With a living will, you can relieve your family of these agonizing decisions. A living will simply describes the level of care you want if you become terminally ill. Your lawyer can help you draft it.

Power of Attorney: More than a Loud Voice

If you couldn't manage your own finances, who could manage them for you? The person you select gets power of attorney over your finances.

If you're mentally incapable of administering your own affairs, the person to whom you've given power of attorney can take complete control of your financial affairs. He can sign cheques, allocate dividend payments to your bank accounts, and make other financial decisions on your behalf.

Once again, a lawyer can handle the paperwork when you designate someone to hold power of attorney.

The Least You Need to Know

➤ Everybody 18 years of age and older should have a will.

➤ If you don't have a will, then the government will decide what happens to your assets.

➤ Always hire a competent lawyer to prepare your will for you.

➤ Make sure that your family knows where all your important documents are located.

➤ Think carefully before deciding on an executor of your estate. It is not a decision to be taken lightly.

➤ Make sure you review your will at least every five years.

➤ Everyone should consider granting power of attorney to a spouse or friend in the event that you become incapacitated and can't manage your finances.

➤ Don't put it off. Make an appointment with your financial planner and lawyer today.

Appendix A

The following are more useful tips on credit cards from the U.S. National Association of Consumer Agency Administrators. The list is continued from Chapter 8, p. 73.

1. Verify that your credit card has a "grace period" before interest is charged. The issuer is required to mail your bill at least 14 days before payment is due. Some credit cards charge interest immediately; no grace period exists.

2. When charging on a credit card, draw lines through the empty spaces on charge slips above the total. Verify the amount on receipts with the amount on charge slips.

3. Keep a list of your credit card numbers separate from the cards. Report lost cards immediately. You aren't liable for charges if the loss is reported before the card is used. If the credit card is used before you report it missing, liability can't exceed $50.

4. Your card issuer must credit your account with your payment on the day payment is received.

5. To report credit card problems, contact your provincial consumer affairs office, or the federal consumer affairs ministry.

6. When completing a credit card application, if you're uncomfortable giving out some personal information, you may want to exclude it. Explain your reasons to the card issuer.

7. Don't let salespeople write phone numbers and addresses on charge slips, or credit card numbers on cheques. These numbers don't assist merchants in any way and increase the risk of fraud.

8. Never sign a blank credit card receipt. Someone can fill it in with a false, incorrect amount.

9. If a salesperson makes a mistake on your credit card slip, ask for the slip and make sure it is destroyed. If the salesperson must keep it for accounting purposes, get a copy.

10. Never write your credit card number on envelopes or postcards where anyone could easily see it. People can make charges to your account. The actual card is not needed to make purchases.

11. When questioning a credit card charge on your bill:

    ➤ Always write a letter disputing the charge

    ➤ Request proof the charge is correct

    ➤ Keep copies of all correspondence

    ➤ Do not send the letter with your payment

    ➤ Send only to address specified for billing problems.

12. When questioning credit card charges, the issuer must provide proof that the charge is correct if you ask for verification in your letter.

13. Every time you apply for credit, it appears on your credit report. Too many applications may give the impression that you need credit badly or are being denied as a poor risk.

14. You can review your credit history and make corrections to outdated or inaccurate information. You don't need a company to do it for you (see Chapter 9).

15. Beware of companies promising to "clear" your credit and avoid paying them up front for the service.

16. If a credit repair company tells you how to "hide" bad credit or how to establish a new credit history, the plan may be illegal and you may face severe fines or a prison term.

17. Sometimes credit repair companies have "900" or similar pay-per-call telephone numbers. You will be charged for these calls at a cost of $50 or more.

18. Do not provide your chequing account number over the phone to anyone claiming to need your number for "verification" purposes. The number can be fraudulently magnetically encoded on cheques.

19. Credit can't be denied due to advancing age. Creditors must consider income such as Social Security, pensions and other retirement benefits.

20. If married, enquire whether credit accounts are held jointly. This helps to establish credit in your own name if you become divorced or widowed.

Index

More Great Canadian Complete Idiot's Guides!

If you liked this *Complete Idiot's Guide*, check out these other titles!

The Complete Idiot's Guide to Making Money with Mutual Funds for Canadians

by Alan Lavine, Gail Liberman, and Stephen Nelson

Mutual funds are attracting more investors than ever before and this informative, easy-to-understand guide shows investors how to create a portfolio that will help them achieve their personal financial goals. Packed with Canadian information, this entertaining volume includes the authors' best mutual fund picks as well as an analysis of many popular funds.

272 pages $21.95
ISBN 0-13-082536-0

The Complete Idiot's Guide to Making Money in the Canadian Stock Market

by Christy Heady and Stephen Nelson

The Complete Idiot's Guide to Making Money in the Canadian Stock Market helps you make sense of the complicated world of finance. You will discover the best financial strategies, feel confident about investing your money and build your wealth with the help of this exciting new guide.

368 pages $24.95
ISBN 0-13-779134-8

The Complete Idiot's Guide to Personal Finance for Canadians—New Edition

by Bruce McDougall

Packed with information on investment strategies, tax changes, stock market trends, and RRSPs, plus all the essential money basics, *The Complete Idiot's Guide to Personal Finance for Canadians* is an updated version of a Canadian bestseller. This informative book is the ultimate guide for those who want to invest and save with confidence.

272 pages $19.95
ISBN 0-13-080126-7

272